Logic

Logic 306

D1c

Logic
An Introductory Course

W. H. Newton-Smith
Balliol College, Oxford

Routledge & Kegan Paul
London, Melbourne and Henley

For
Raine Kelly Newton-Smith

First published in 1985
by Routledge & Kegan Paul plc

14 Leicester Square, London WC2H 7PH, England

464 St Kilda Road, Melbourne,
Victoria 3004, Australia and

Broadway House, Newtown Road,
Henley-on-Thames, Oxon RG9 1EN, England

Photoset in Times New Roman, 10 on 12 pt
by Kelly Typesetting Ltd, Bradford-on-Avon, Wiltshire
Made and printed in Great Britain by the
Guernsey Press Co. Ltd., Guernsey, Channel Islands.

British Library Cataloguing in Publication Data

Newton-Smith, W. H.
Logic: an introductory course.
1. Logic
I. Title
160

ISBN 0-7100-9777-8

Contents

Preface

This is an introduction to logic. It is designed for the level of first year university students with no background in mathematics. My intention is to convey some sense of the utility of formal systems in the representation and analyses of deductive arguments. In addition attention is given to some of the philosophical problems which arise in the course of this and to some of the philosophical benefits which result.

The formal system used is based on Gentzen's rules for natural deduction and influenced by E. J. Lemmon's *Beginning Logic* (London: Nelson, 1982). The most difficult part of the book is section 4 of Chapter 4 which can be omitted without affecting what follows. In that section a completeness proof for the propositional calculus is given in a form that generalizes to the predicate calculus. Easier proofs are available. However, in my experience only students with a serious interest in logic bother to work through completeness proofs and they can master the more difficult version. Much or all of Chapter 8 on the semantics for the predicate calculus could be omitted from the first reading or first course. This material has been included for the sake of students who will be going on to read contemporary literature in the philosophy of language.

A computer teaching programme is available to supplement the text. This provides a further source from which the student can learn much of the material contained in the text. In particular it enables him or her to test his or her understanding without needing to wait until an instructor can mark exercises. At the moment it is available on cassette and on disc for the BBC Micro from Routledge & Kegan Paul (Broadway House, Newtown Road, Henley-on-Thames, Oxon RG9 1EN) or Oxcom Ltd (92 Lonsdale Road, Oxford, OX2 7ER). A manual for the programme is included as an appendix to this book.

There is a distinction of particular importance to logic between using an expression and mentioning an expression. In the last sentence of the previous paragraph the expression 'this book' was used to refer to a particular thing; namely, the book you are now reading. In this last sentence (the one you have just read) the expression in quotations was not used to refer to this book. The presence of the quotation marks gives us a device for talking about the expression itself. We said that the expression was used to refer to a particular thing. We might also have said that the expression consisted of two words or eight letters. In such assertions we are mentioning not using the expression 'this book'. If we are *using* it it takes our attention to the book. If we are *mentioning* it, the quotation marks take our attention to the expression itself. If I say that Reagan is in Hollywood I am referring to a particular person using a particular word. If I say that 'Reagan' has six letters I am not talking about that person but mentioning the word for the sake of talking about it. If this distinction is not grasped and respected nonsense and/or paradox can arise. In this work quotation marks are used to direct our attention to expressions themselves. However, on occasion we will not bother to include the quotation marks if it is clear from the context that we are mentioning the expression for the sake of talking about it in rather than using it to say something. For example, if I were to use the sentence 'O has a nice shape' you would take me (correctly) to be talking about the expression and not about something called 'O'. If there were any doubt I could have used the sentence ' "O" has a nice shape.' Similarly, in this work quotation marks are used explicitly if there is any doubts as to what is intended.

This text was first written in the autumn of 1981 when I was a Commonwealth Visiting Professor at Trent University, Ontario. I am particularly grateful to the then Master and Fellows of Champlain College for providing such a pleasant and stimulating ambience within which to work. Then, as in the winter of 1984 when the final work on the text was done, I was on sabbatical leave from Balliol College, Oxford. I thank the Master and Fellows for this. Andrew Boucher and Martin Dale provided detailed comments on the manuscript at an early stage and their help has been invaluable. I thank, too, Mary Bugge, research secretary at Balliol College, for her patience and skill in typing a difficult manuscript. For the preparation of the index and help with the proofs I am indebted to Daniel Cohen and Ian Rumfitt. Andrew Boucher and Peter Gibbins, respectively Head of Programming and Director, of Oxcom Ltd produced the computer programme referred to above. For this and their friendship I offer a special thanks.

CHAPTER 1
Logic and language

1 WHAT IS LOGIC?

Logic, it is often said, is the study of valid arguments. It is a systematic attempt to distinguish valid arguments from invalid arguments. At this stage that characterization suffers from the fault of explaining the obscure in terms of the equally obscure. For what after all is validity? Or, for that matter, what is an argument? Beginning with the latter easier notion we can say that an argument has one or more premises and a conclusion. In advancing an argument one purports that the premise or premises support the conclusion. This relation of support is usually signalled by the use of such terms as 'therefore', 'thus', 'consequently', 'so, you see'. Consider that old and boring example of an argument:

> Socrates is a man.
> All men are mortal.
> Therefore, Socrates is mortal.

The premises are 'Socrates is a man' and 'All men are mortal'. 'Therefore' is the sign of an argument and the conclusion is 'Socrates is mortal'.

Real life is never so straightforward and clear-cut as it would be if everyone talked the way they would if they had read too many logic textbooks at an impressionable age. For example, we often advance arguments without stating all our premises.

> Icabod has failed his preliminary examinations twice.
> So, he will be sent down.

Implicit in the above argument is what we will call a *suppressed premise*; namely, that all students who fail their preliminary examinations twice are sent down. It may be so obvious in the context what premise is being assumed that it is just too tedious to spell it out. Spelling out premises which are part of a common background of shared beliefs is a form of pedantry. However, we have to bear in mind that any actual argument may have a suppressed premise which needs to be made explicit for the rigorous analysis of that argument. For the sake of complete rigour we will in this study practise a certain amount of pedantry.

We will return to further questions about the nature of arguments after a first characterization of the notion of validity. To this end consider the following simple little arguments:

I

The sky is blue and the grass is green.
Therefore, the sky is blue.

All Balliol students are clever.
Icabod is a Balliol student.
Therefore, Icabod is clever.

II

The sky is blue or the grass is orange.
Therefore, the grass is orange.

Icabod is clever.
Icabod is a Balliol student.
Therefore, all Balliol students are clever.

There is something unhappy about the arguments listed in II above. We can imagine contexts in which the premises would be true and the conclusion false. The arguments in I above have true conclusions whenever they have true premises. We will say that they are *valid*. That means that they have the following property: In any case in which the premise (premises) is (are) true, the conclusion must be true. Clearly the arguments in I do have this property. How could it ever be that the sky was blue and the grass green without the sky being blue? There is just no way that Icabod could be a Balliol student and all Balliol students be clever without Icabod being clever. The arguments in II lack the property of validity. The actual circumstances in the world make the premise of the first argument in II true but the conclusion is false. And in the case of the second argument in II we can imagine circumstances in which it is true that Icabod is clever and a Balliol student but in which there are (unfortunately) other non-clever Balliol students whose dullness makes the conclusion false. Logic is the systematic study of valid arguments. This means that we will be developing rigorous techniques for determining whether arguments are valid.

EXERCISES

1 Identify the premises and conclusions of the following arguments making explicit any suppressed premises:

   (a) Oysters are not fossils. For no fossil can be crossed in love and an oyster may be crossed in love.

   (b) No ducks waltz. No officers ever decline to waltz. Therefore, my poultry are not officers. *(All my poultry are ducks (Carroll))*

   (c) Icabod was a scoundrel. Whenever things went badly he blamed someone else.

2 TRUTH AND VALIDITY

An argument is valid if it has the property that if the premises were true the conclusion would have to be true. Why should we be especially interested in validity? It turns out that validity is a particularly nice property for an argument to have. For if you reason validly (that is, if your reasoning can be represented by a valid argument) and if you start with true premises you will never be led into error. And if you can get someone else to accept your premises as true, he has to accept as true anything which follows validly from those premises. Philosophers are very keen on valid arguments. They try and get you to agree to some innocent little premises and then offer what purport to be valid arguments having all manner of surprising and powerful conclusions. In Descartes' *Meditations* he starts with the innocuous premise: I think – and reaches the conclusion: God exists. Of course we are apt to feel that has implicitly relied on some extra suppressed premises with which we may disagree or that he has made a mistake in his argument. But if the premises were true and if the reasoning were valid then his conclusion that God exists would be true. And if we accepted his premises and his argument we would be bound to accept his conclusion. For a less contentious attempt at producing valid arguments one might think of Euclid's *Elements*. Euclid begins with his axioms from which he argues to such conclusions as, for instance, that the square on the hypotenuse of a right-angled triangle is equal to the sum of the squares on the other two sides. If his premises are true and his arguments valid, the conclusion must also be true. We express this by saying that valid arguments are *truth-preserving*. If you start with truths and reason validly what you end up with is truth. The fact that valid arguments preserve truth makes them attractive.

We can see from our definition of validity that whether the premises of an argument are in fact true has nothing to do with the question of the validity of the argument. We can have valid arguments with true premises and valid arguments with false premises. Consider the argument:

> The sky is green and the sea is pink.
> Therefore, the sea is pink.

That argument is valid. For if the premise were true the conclusion would have to be true. In fact, the conclusion is false but it would have been true if the premise had been true. Consider the following argument:

> Icabod is rich.
> All rich men are happy.
> Therefore Icabod is happy.

Are the premises true or false? I have no idea whether Icabod is rich. I do not know enough about rich men to know whether money brings happiness. But I can see that any circumstances that made both premises true would be bound to make the conclusion true. In assessing an argument for validity we do not need to assess the premises and conclusion for truth. We need only ask the hypothetical question: are the premises such that if they were to be true the conclusion would be bound to be true? To take one final example consider the argument:

> The sky is blue or the grass is green.
> Therefore the grass is green.

In this case both the premise and the conclusion are true but the argument is not valid. For we can imagine circumstances which would make the premise true but the conclusion false. For example, suppose red not green had been God's favourite colour and that He or She made the grass red while making the sky blue. In which case the premise would be true and the conclusion false. Thus the argument is invalid.

At an initial stage in learning logic the point being laboured is often a source of confusion. There is a tendency to consider only the actual truth-value of each premise and of the conclusion. This term '*truth-value*' is one that will play an important role in developing our logic. A premise or a conclusion can be either true or false and when we talk of its truth-value we are referring to whichever of these values, truth or falsity, it has. The assumption that there are no other possibilities is one which we will examine later. See in this regard Chapter 9, section 6. In the actual circumstances of the world the truth-value of the conclusion above that the grass is green is truth. In the possible circumstance we imagined (where God liked red better than green), its truth-value would be false. When we consider the question of the validity of an argument we must, with one exception, be interested in the truth-value of the conclusion in any possible circumstance in which the truth-value of each premise is truth. The exception is that if there is one circumstance in which the premises are true and the conclusion false the argument is invalid and we need not consider any other circumstances. If in the actual world we have *either* premises all false, conclusion false; *or*, premises all false, conclusion true; *or* some premises true, some false, conclusion true; *or*, some premises true, some false, conclusion false; *or*, premises true, conclusion true, we must consider any possible circumstances in which the premises are all true and ask if the conclusion is true in just those circumstances.

EXERCISES

1 Give an example of a valid argument in which both the premises and the conclusion are false and an example in which both are true.

2 Give an example of an invalid argument in which both premises and conclusion are false and an example in which both are true.

3 Give an alternative but equivalent definition of validity using the notion of falsehood rather than truth.

3 VALIDITY AND FORM

Consider the following arguments:

> I
>
> The grass is green and the sky is blue.
> Therefore, the grass is green.
>
> Money is time and time is money.
> Therefore, money is time.
>
> Fermions have spin $+\frac{1}{2}$ and pions have spin $-\frac{1}{2}$.
> Therefore, fermions have spin $+\frac{1}{2}$.
>
> II
>
> All persons are mortal.
> Socrates is a person.
> Therefore, Socrates is mortal.
>
> All students are rich.
> The president of the *NUS* is a student.
> Therefore, the president of the *NUS* is rich.
>
> All zemindars are powerful.
> Icabod is a zemindar.
> Therefore, Icabod is powerful.

We recognize that each of the arguments in list I and in list II is valid. Even those who have no idea what it is to have spin $+\frac{1}{2}$ or what it is to be a zemindar can recognize this. For we make this recognition in virtue of the *form* of the arguments. The form in the case of list I is easily described. Each argument is of the form: blank and blankety-blank therefore blank. The form of those in II is not so easily describable but it is easily recognizable. That aspect of the form of the arguments that is relevant to the question of their validity is called *logical structure* or *logical form*.

The specific content of the premise and the conclusion is not relevant to the determination of the validity of the arguments. Not only do you not need to know the actual truth-value of the premises and conclusions of an argument to determine its validity you do not even need to know what they mean. In fact a zemindar is a revenue-farmer in the Mogul empire. Just what it is for a fermion to have spin $+\frac{1}{2}$ is less easily explained. Of course you have to know that they are in fact sentences of English. And, as we have seen, you do have to know the meaning of certain key words such as 'an' and 'all'. To see the importance of these key words which we will call *logical constants*, replace 'and' by 'or' in list I and 'all' by 'some' in list II and examine the resulting arguments for validity.

It is because validity is a property dependent on form and not on content that we can aspire to develop a systematic study of valid arguments. We can describe the form of a given valid argument and show that all arguments of that form (there will be an indefinitely large number of such arguments) are valid. And it is this fact, the fact that validity depends on form and not content, that licenses us to introduce symbols into our logic. For instance, we can represent the form of the arguments in list I as: *A* and *B*. Therefore, *A*. We can recognize that any argument produced by replacing *A* and *B* by indicative sentences of English is going to be valid.

The stress that has been placed on validity may suggest that no argument that is not valid has merit. Consider the following two arguments:

> Almost everyone who smokes eighty cigarettes a day for more than twenty years gets cancer.
> Jones smoked eighty cigarettes a day for more than twenty years.
> Therefore, Jones will get cancer.

> Icabod got drunk on Monday on soda water and whisky.
> Icabod got drunk on Tuesday on soda water and brandy.
> Icabod got drunk on Wednesday on soda water and rye.
> Therefore, Icabod gets drunk on soda water.

Neither argument is valid. In both cases the premises could be true and the conclusion false. None the less we would hold that the premises in the first argument would, if true, support the conclusion. If the premises are true, there is no guarantee (as there is in the case of a valid argument) that the conclusion is true but it is reasonable to assume that it is true. We might say that it is probably true. We do not think that the premises in the second argument if true give a good reason for thinking that the conclusion is true. Arguments that are not valid will include those in which the premises support the conclusion in the sense of rendering it probable and those that do not. Our concern in this book is with the question of validity. Arguments that are valid will be said to be *deductive* arguments. In addition we count as deductive, arguments that have been or might be purported to be valid. Arguments of which it is claimed that the premises support the conclusion (render it probable) without guaranteeing its truth are called *inductive* arguments. Inductive arguments are sometimes good and sometimes not. The study of what makes such arguments good is a messy business and indeed some philosophers have even doubted whether any systematic study of what makes a good inductive argument good is possible. In any event in this text attention is restricted to deductive arguments.

EXERCISES

1 Give an example of an inductive argument in which you think the premises support the conclusion. Show that it is not a valid argument. Give an example of an inductive argument in which you think the premises do not support the conclusion.

2 Give an example of a valid argument. Give another argument of the same form. Give an example of a valid argument of a different form.

4 PROPOSITIONS

Logic studies the relation between premises and conclusion. But just what are premises and conclusions? Sentences have been used to specify the premises and the conclusions in the sample arguments but the premises and conclusions are not sentences.

The reason is that we can take one of our sample arguments and translate it into Serbo-Croat and have the *same* argument expressed in different languages. Since the argument is the same while the sentences used to express the premise and conclusion are different, the premises and conclusion cannot be sentences. They are rather what is expressed by the sentences. We will use the notion of a *proposition* to express what the English sentence and its translation into another language have in common: we will say that the sentences express the same proposition. This notion of a proposition applies within a language as well. For instance, we recognize that 'Caesar stabbed Brutus' and 'Brutus was stabbed by Caesar' have the same meaning and we can convey this by saying that they express the same proposition.

Propositions are vehicles for stating how things are or might be. Thus only indicative sentences which it makes sense to think of as being true or as being false are capable of expressing propositions. Interrogative sentences do not state how things might be but ask how things are and as such do not express propositions; nor do imperative sentences which command that things be a certain way.

Indicative sentences may be ambiguous. Consider the sentence: Cows do not like grass. That sentence might be used to express the falsehood that cows do not like the stuff growing in fields. Or, it might be used to express the truth that cows do not like marihuana. We will describe the kind of ambiguity that arises because a word in the sentence has more than one meaning as *semantical ambiguity*. A sentence which is semantically ambiguous can be used to express more than one proposition. Which proposition is being expressed when such a sentence is used will often be clear from the context. For the purpose of rigorously investigating arguments we will want to use a sentence which is not ambiguous to express what the speaker meant when using the ambiguous sentence.

Consider the sentence: Everyone loves a sailor. No word in that sentence is ambiguous yet the sentence is ambiguous. It could be used to state that each person loves at least one sailor (not necessarily the same one) or that everyone loves every sailor. Ambiguities of this sort will be called *syntactical ambiguity.* In general they can be resolved by re-writing the ambiguous sentence to give two sentences differing in word order, and possibly also in punctuation and/or in the actual words used. The above example can be disambiguated as follows:

> Everyone loves some sailor or other.
> Any sailor is loved by everyone.

We have introduced propositions as being what is expressed by sentences and we have seen that in the case of ambiguous sentences we cannot tell from the sentence itself what is being expressed. We have to look at the context to determine what a speaker meant. If a sentence contains demonstratives ('this', 'that', etc.), personal pronouns ('I', 'he', 'she', etc.), or words like 'here', 'now', we will have to look at the context to determine what is expressed. For instance, if you use the sentence 'I am in pain' and I use that same sentence we do not express the same thing. You say that one particular person, namely you, is in pain and I say that another different person, namely me, is in pain. Grasping the proposition expressed by a sentence requires not only grasping the meanings of the words used but also what is referred to by such words as 'I'. We will return later to the question of how one determines the proposition expressed by a sentence. For the moment I am only guarding against the possible misunderstanding that grasping a proposition expressed by a sentence is simply a matter of grasping the meaning of the sentence. One may also have to look to what the words refer.

Propositions are abstract items. Logicians are interested in the relation between a proposition or a set of propositions, the premise(s), and a proposition, the conclusion, of an argument. This is apt to make their activity seem divorced from human activity, dealing as they do with such abstract things as propositions. This impression is misleading and one way of seeing that it is so is to consider the phenomenon of belief. Consider Icabod who believes that kings have a divine right to rule. We can focus on his psychological state – that of believing rather than, say, wishing that kings had divine rule. In this case we can ask how long he has believed. Perhaps it was first brought on by doing

British history at Oxford. Or we can focus on the content of his belief – on what it is that he believes. This is expressed by the sentence 'Kings have a divine right to rule'. We can regard belief as a relation between a person and what is expressed by a sentence; namely, a proposition. Thus what we believe and what we deal with in logic is the same thing: propositions.

We can take this connection between logic and belief a step further. A valid argument is one in which if the premises are true the conclusion has to be true. If one comes to believe the propositions which are the premises of the argument, one is committed to believing the conclusion. Of course some of us will on some occasions fail to believe the conclusion when we believe the premises because we fail to see that it follows validly. Thus we have to re-phrase the connection: it is not rational to believe the premises of a valid argument and not to believe the conclusion. Logic then connects with the very human activity of belief through providing a tool for evaluating one aspect of the rationality of beliefs. But one should not expect too much. Logic is not a tool for the determination of just what it is rational to believe. It will at least tell us that if you have certain beliefs, rationality constrains what other beliefs you ought to hold.

EXERCISES

1 Give three sentences which are semantically ambiguous.

2 Give three sentences which are syntactically ambiguous.

3 Why is it not rational to accept the premises of a valid argument and to deny the conclusion?

5 LOGIC AND LINGUISTICS

Why should one be interested in the study of logic? One pat answer to this question frequently given in elementary texts is that the study of logic will improve one's powers of reasoning. Having learned techniques for distinguishing between valid and invalid arguments, one will be less prone to pass from true beliefs to false conclusions and better able to spot the fallacies in the arguments of others. This justification ought at this stage to seem unconvincing. For you are already adept at distinguishing between valid and invalid arguments. You have an intuitive grasp of this distinction by reference to which you were able to see the validity or invalidity as the case was of the sample arguments introduced in this chapter. Of course I could have produced complex examples which you could not see intuitively whether they were valid. However, there would be something artificial about constructing such examples. For anything subtle enough to require study of logic to see whether it is valid is likely to be something you will never encounter in day-to-day life. At the level of elementary logic (the propositional logic which we develop in the next chapter), it is difficult to produce examples of arguments one might encounter the validity of which cannot be ascertained intuitively. I do not make this claim categorically. For when we come to the predicate logic in the latter half of this book we will find arguments which might actually be used the validity of which cannot be easily seen purely intuitively. However, it remains true that those who hope that logic will substantially improve their powers of reasoning are bound to be disappointed. Consequently it is worth developing a reason for being interested in logic even if it will not turn us into demons of rationality. This will be done using an analogy from linguistics.

Any reader of this text is able to distinguish between sequences of words that are sentences of English and sequences of words that are not. Anyone can see and has been able to see from a tender age that 'grass blue green fast' is not a sentence and that 'the grass is blue' is a sentence. I am sure that no reader has encountered the following sequence of words: The Junior Proctor astonished the Professor of Poetry by dancing badly with the Senior Proctor's pink giraffe in the Sheldonian Theatre. Somehow you were able to see that that unfamiliar string of words is a sentence. There are an infinite number of finite sequences of words of English and you can make this discrimination with regard to any one of those sequences (setting aside the occasional border-line case). There is then no question but that we have this skill. The question is: how is it that we make this discrimination? What enables us to exercise that skill? If there is some finite list of rules which determine whether a sequence was a sentence or not we could explain how it is that we have the skill.

For if there is such a system and if we have internalized it we can be applying the rules non-consciously to give the discriminations. If there is no such system of rules it is quite mysterious how we can do what we obviously do. Thus the best explanation of our exercise of this skill involves assuming such a system of rules. Having made this move we will have to try and articulate what those rules are. Of course failure to discover an adequate system of rules ought to make us have reservations about the assumption that there is such a system. And discovering a system is not going to make us really any better at exercising the skill (although it might be appealed to in adjudicating certain border-line cases). The point of articulating the rules is to be able to explain the exercise of the skill we undoubtedly possess. It has, in fact, proved difficult to articulate a system of rules. However, enough progress has been made to make it reasonable to assume that the enterprise will be successful in the end.

There is a similar situation with regard to arguments. We could produce as long a sequence of arguments as you like which you can classify as valid or not. There must be some system of rules that you have implicitly internalized, the possession of which explains your ability to make these discriminations. This explanation can only be sustained if we can specify the system of rules in question. One task of logic is to do just this. Doing this will be of interest even if it does not make one any better at distinguishing between valid and invalid arguments. To the extent that we are successful we will be able to offer an answer to the question: in virtue of what is it that one can recognize an argument as valid? That is, we will develop through the study of logic a technique for doing explicitly and reflectively something that we can do reasonably well for simple arguments implicitly and without reflection.

I hasten to add that I am not saying that logic does not help to improve one's power of reasoning. I am offering a reason for being interested in logic, particularly elementary logic, which would have force even if one did not feel that one's reasoning abilities had been sharpened by the study of logic. We will consider arguments the appraisal of which cannot proceed intuitively but needs explicit appeal to the rules of logic. By making explicit the rules we have a tool for checking our intuitive judgments. And this can be important for there have been arguments used in mathematics which seemed valid at an intuitive level but which turned out not to be so. Perhaps the greatest incentive for the development of contemporary logic was Russell's discovery that intuitively plausible reasoning in the foundations of mathematics led to a contradiction. This increased the desire to have a fully explicit system of rules for checking the validity of arguments. We will return to the question of the importance of logic at the end of the book having articulated some rules for determining the validity or invalidity of arguments and having seen some other uses to which the study of logic can be put.

CHAPTER 2
A propositional language

1 TRUTH-FUNCTIONS AND TRUTH-TABLES

In this chapter we develop a technique for testing the validity of a limited class of arguments. To characterize the class in question we need to consider one way in which indicative sentences of English can be formed. There are words or sequences of words which themselves do not constitute sentences but which can be used to construct sentences if put together in the appropriate way with a sentence or sentences. For instance, the word 'and' can be used to generate a sentence by putting sentences before and after it as in 'Icabod is a student *and* Icabod is rich'. Similarly the phrase 'Icabod believes that' which is not a sentence can be used to generate a sentence if we put a sentence after it as in 'Icabod believes that students are exploited'. We will call such expressions *sentence-forming operators* because they operate on sentences to give more complex sentences. A sentence-forming operator is a word or sequence of words which is not a sentence but which when appropriately concatenated with an indicative sentence or sentences gives an indicative sentence of English. Other examples of sentence-forming operators are: It is not the case that, or, if . . . then . . ., it is possible that, Icabod hopes that, because.

Consider the complex sentence: Icabod likes marcels and Icabod is in love. If I were to tell you the truth-value of the simple sentences which are concatenated with 'and' to give this complex sentence you could, quite trivially, determine the truth-value of the complex sentence. If both sentences are true, the complex sentence is true. If either or both are false the complex sentence must be false. Consider the complex sentence: Icabod believes that an excess consumption of vitamin B causes schizophrenia. If I told you the truth-value of the constituent sentence (an excess consumption of vitamin B causes schizophrenia) you still could not work out the truth-value of the complex sentence. If it is true,

15

Icabod may or may not believe it. If it is false, Icabod may or may not believe it. Its being true does not guarantee that Icabod believes it, nor does it guarantee (happily) that he does not believe it. Its being false (sadly) does not guarantee that he does not believe it.

We will call any sentence-forming operator which is like 'and' in this respect a *truth-functional sentence-forming operator* meaning that given the truth-values of the sentences concatenated with 'and' we can determine on the basis of that information alone the truth-value of the resulting complex sentence. A non-truth-functional sentence-forming operator is one which can be used to construct sentences the truth-value of which cannot be determined solely by means of information about the truth-value of the constituent sentences, the constituent sentences being those which are concatenated with the operator to give the complex sentence.

We noted in Chapter 1 that our concern in logic is with form and not content. It was said that this meant that we could use symbols to represent arguments. We will use symbols in two different ways. Upper-case letters from the middle of the alphabet '*P*', '*Q*', '*R*', . . . will be used to stand for particular propositions. In part the point of this is simply to save us the tedium of writing out a full English sentence to specify a proposition. Just which proposition is being symbolized by what we will call a *propositional letter* will be given in a code called an *interpretation*. Thus, I might say that '*P*' will be used in place of the proposition expressed by the sentence 'Icabod is in love' and '*Q*' in place of the proposition expressed by the sentence 'Icabod is rich'. We will use upper-case letters from the beginning of the alphabet '*A*', '*B*', '*C*', . . . for what will be called *formulae variables*. Formulae variables are not propositions. They indicate where expressions for propositions are to be placed. For instance, if I write '*P* and *Q*' that expresses the proposition that Icabod is in love and Icabod is rich given the interpretation above. If I write '*A* and *B*' I make no assertion. I indicate the form of a possible proposition; namely, one formed from two propositions (or one proposition taken twice) conjoined by 'and'.

[handwritten margin note: Metalogical Variable]

An analogy will be helpful. The expressions '*1*', '*2*', '*3*' stand for particular numbers in a way analogous to that in which '*P*', '*Q*', '*R*', etc., are to be thought of as standing for particular propositions. Combining these symbols with symbols for arithmetical operations gives particular assertions. For instance, $2+3 = 5$ or $2+3 = 3+2$. In algebra one uses variables, i.e. x, y, z, writing, for instance, $x+y=z$. This latter expression does not make an assertion. It makes an assertion only if the variables are replaced by terms for particular numbers and will be true or false depending on the replacement. Thus, $2+3 = 5$ is true but $3+4 = 5$ is not. In a similar way the expression '*A* and *B*' does not make an assertion. It indicates a form and can be converted into an assertion if '*A*' and '*B*' are replaced by terms expressing particular propositions, just as replacing xs and ys in algebraic equations by terms for particular numbers yields an assertion.

Let '*P*' and '*Q*' be understood by the interpretation given above. '*P* and *Q*' is true just in case '*P*' is true, '*Q*' is true. If '*P*' is false and '*Q*' is true, '*P* and *Q*' is false. If '*P*' is false and '*Q*' is true, '*P* and *Q*' is false. And if '*P*' is false and '*Q*' is false, '*P* and *Q*' is false. It is clear that we have covered all the possibilities for truth and falsity with regard to '*P*' and '*Q*'. Writing '*T*' for 'true' and '*F*' for 'false' we can represent the possibilities as follows:

P	*Q*
T	T
T	F
F	T
F	F

We based our determination of the truth-value and '*P* and *Q*' on our intuitive understanding of 'and'. We can represent that knowledge in the following table to be called a *truth-table*.

P	*Q*	*P* and *Q*
T	T	T
T	F	F
F	T	F
F	F	F

'*P*' and '*Q*' have specific content being short-hand for, respectively, 'Icabod is in love' and 'Icabod is rich'. But as the calculation of the truth-value of a conjunction (a *conjunction* being the complex sentence formed by putting sentences before and after an 'and') depends only on the truth-value of the conjuncts (the sentence before and the sentence after the 'and' are called *conjuncts*) we use formulae variables in representing the truth-function 'and' writing its table as follows where '&' is the symbol to be used for 'and':

A B	A & B
T T	T
T F	F
F T	F
F F	F

The phrase 'it is not the case that' is a truth-functional sentence-forming operator. We use the symbol ' ⌐' in place of the English phrase and write its truth-table as follows:

A	⌐A
T	F
F	T

In natural language we often use in place of this cumbersome phrase 'not' or some contraction of 'not'. If we have let '*P*' stand for 'Icabod is in love' we can write ' ⌐*P*' for 'Icabod isn't in love'.

Another important truth-function in English is 'or'. Most often we use 'or' in an *exclusive* sense. If I say that it will rain or it will snow, you will take me to be predicting one or the other but not both. This exclusive sense of 'or' has the following table:

A B	*A* or (exclusive) *B*
T T	F
T F	T
F T	T
F F	F

We will call sentences formed using the operator 'or', *disjunctions* and refer to the sentences before and after the 'or' as *disjuncts*.

There is another weaker sense of 'or' occasionally used in English which we will call the *inclusive* sense. A disjunction formed using the inclusive 'or' is true if either disjunct is true or if both disjuncts are true. Its truth-table is:

A *B*	*A* or (inclusive) *B*
T T	*T*
T F	*T*
F T	*T*
F F	*F*

For an illustration of the use of 'or' in its inclusive sense consider the situation in which you and I have tickets (along with many others) in a lottery with several prizes of equal value. In an optimistic frame of mind I predict: Either you will win or I will win. If, to be even more optimistic, it should turn out that we both win, we would not count what I originally said as false. If 'or' had been used in the exclusive sense my prediction would have been false. We will introduce the symbol '*v*' to stand for 'or' in its inclusive sense. We do not need to introduce a separate symbol for the exclusive sense (we could if we wanted to) for we can express the exclusive sense by using combinations of other symbols. This will be done after we have introduced the notion of *scope*.

Consider the sentence: I will go to town and I will drink beer or I will find some good wine. This might be construed in two ways. I might mean I will go to town and in town I will either spend the time drinking beer or looking for fine wine. I am off to town and have yet to decide which of these things to do when there. Or I might mean that my choice is between going to town and drinking beer on the one hand or not going to town and, say, looking for the fine wine in the countryside, on the other hand. We need a way of representing unambiguously these different construals.

Let '*P*', '*Q*' and '*R*' be given the following interpretation:

P: I will go to town

Q: I will drink beer

R: I will find some good wine

Using this 'code' we might write the original sentence as:
P & Q v R. But with this formalization, this symbolic representation of what was meant in the English, you cannot tell which of the meanings is intended. In spoken English I might have made my intentions clear through the emphasis of my voice. In writing, one might make the intended meaning clear through re-phrasing or punctuation: I will go to town. I will drink beer or I will find good wine. The other construal would be: Either I will find good wine or I will go to town and drink beer.

 To handle such ambiguities in logic we use brackets in a fashion analagous to their use in arithmetic. The arithmetical expression $3+4\times5$ is ambiguous. It may be intended to mean the result of multiplying the sum of 3 and 4 by 5 (i.e. 35). Or, it may be intended to mean the result of adding 3 to the product of 4 and 5 (i.e. 23). We distinguish between these, writing the former as $(3+4)\times5$ and the latter as $3+(4\times5)$. In $(3+4)\times5$ the addition operator works on 3 and 4. This is expressed by saying that its *scope* is the expression $(3+4)$. The multiplication operator works on $(3+4)$ and 5; that is, its scope is the expression $(3+4)\times5$. In $3+(4\times5)$, the multiplication operator has smaller scope than the addition operator. For it works on 4 and 5 and has as its scope the expression (4×5) whereas the addition operator works on 3 and (4×5) and has as its scope the expression $3+(4\times5)$.

To apply these ideas to our example from logic above we write '*P & (Q v R)*' on the first construal indicating both that I will go to town *and either* drink beer *or* find good wine. The brackets indicate that the alternative is between '*Q*' and '*R*', an alternative which is then conjoined with '*P*'. For the second construal we write: $(P \& Q) v R$. This indicates that the alternative is between going to town and drinking beer *or* finding some good wine (perhaps here in the country). In the former case of '*P & (Q v R)*', '*v*' operates on '*Q*' and '*R*' to form the disjunction: *Q v R*.

The scope of 'v' is the expression '$(Q \lor R)$'. '&' operates on the disjunction '$(Q \lor R)$' and 'P' to form the conjunction 'P & $(Q \lor R)$'. Its scope is then the entire expression. In the latter case of '$(P$ & $Q) \lor R$', '&' operates on 'P' and 'Q' to form the conjunction '$(P$ & $Q)$', its scope being the expression '$(P$ & $Q)$'. 'v' then operates on the conjunction '$(P$ & $Q)$' and on 'R' to form the disjunction: $(P$ & $Q) \lor R$. The scope of 'v' is then the entire expression '$(P$ & $Q) \lor R$' and is hence larger than the scope of '&'.

The above account provides only a rudimentary introduction to the notion of scope. This together with the use of bracketing in the examples in this and the next chapter should give an intuitive understanding of the idea of scope which is rigorously defined in Chapter Four (pp.79–80). As a further illustration at this stage let 'P' be interpreted as 'I am happy' and 'Q' as 'Icabod is happy'. We can form the negation of 'P', '$\neg P$', which would say that I am not happy. To conjoin the negation of 'P' with 'Q' gives something which says that I am not happy and Icabod is happy which means something quite different from conjoining 'P' and 'Q' and taking the negation of the resulting conjunction. This would say that it is false that I am happy and Icabod is happy. In the latter case we show that the negation operates on the conjunction of 'P' and 'Q' by putting that conjunction in brackets with the negation operator outside: $\neg(P$ & $Q)$. In the former case we can write brackets around the negation of 'P', '$(\neg P)$' to show that its operation is limited to 'P'. The resulting expression is then '$(\neg P)$ & Q'. In point of fact we adopt the convention that if no brackets are shown negation is taken as operating only on the first propositional letter that follows. Thus we write: $\neg P$ & Q.

Having introduced brackets to indicate scope we can express the exclusive sense of 'or' using the symbols 'v' (inclusive or), '&' and '$\neg$' as follows: 'P or (exclusive) Q' is equivalent to '$(P \lor Q)$ & $\neg(P$ & $Q)$'. The first conjunct says that it is that P or that Q or possibly both. The second conjunct rules out it being both that P and Q. Thus the up-shot is that it is that P or it is that Q but not both.

1 State which of the following sentence-forming operators are truth-functional: until, neither . . . nor, unless, It is certain that, Icabod knows that, It will be that, whenever, It is probable that, It is true that, It is possible that, even though, because, and then.

   Give three further examples of non-truth-functional operators.

2 Define a *partial truth-functional operator* to be a sentence-forming operator for which at least some lines of a truth-table can be filled in. Give partial truth-tables for any such operators in exercise 1.

3 Formalize the following sentences using brackets to display the syntactical ambiguities in the English (be sure to specify your interpretation):

   (a) Icabod will work hard and get a first or Icabod will row for his college.

   (b) I'll be home at 4 and will bring strawberries if and only if it doesn't rain.

   (c) Icabod bought grapes and apples or oranges.

   (d) This is Tweedledum or that is Tweedledee and I'm a Dutchman.

2 CONDITIONALS

We have considered some sentence-forming operators that are definitely truth-functional and others that are definitely not. There are other cases about which there is controversy. One of these is that of the conditional. A conditional is a sentence formed using 'if . . . then . . .' The sentence following the 'if' is called the *antecedent* and the sentence following the 'then' is called the *consequent*. This case is of crucial importance to the development of logic and we cannot avoid the controversy. It will be helpful to consider first an important difference in the ways in which we can evaluate assertions. We can ask if someone's assertion is true or false. We can also consider whether an assertion is misleading even though true. For instance, suppose that I say to you that I will vote for Carter or I will vote for Anderson. Suppose that in fact I have definitely decided to vote for Carter. My assertion to you is true but it may be misleading. You may be led to think that the matter is still open (not surprisingly I have rejected the thought of voting for Reagan) and waste time trying to persuade me to vote for Anderson. The reason that my assertion of the disjunction was misleading in the context is that conversation is generally governed by certain maxims designed to make it helpful. We have learned to expect others to be following these maxims. One of these enjoins us to make the strongest assertion we are in a position to make. The assertion that I will vote for Carter is stronger than the assertion that either I will vote for Carter or I will vote for Anderson. You assume I am following the general maxim and that in asserting the disjunction I made the strongest assertion I was in a position to make. Thus you may take it that the choice between Anderson and Carter is still open. It is not. And thus I have misled you notwithstanding the fact that what I said was true. Saying the truth is not the only goal governing discourse. We also aim at being helpful and generally that involves making the strongest assertion one is warranted in making. Another example of an infelicity of this kind would arise if I answered my mother's question: 'Do you have a girl friend?' by saying that I have a girl friend when in fact I have six. If I have six it is true that I have a girl friend but I have misled my mother about the true nature of my amorous activities. For she will expect me to have not only told the truth but to have made the strongest assertion which I was in a position to do so and that would meaning confessing to six girl friends.

Logicians are interested in the conditions under which sentences are true. For determining the validity of an argument is, as we have seen, a matter of determining whether any conditions that make all the premises true make the conclusion true. Given that interest, we do not discuss in any systematic way the conditions under which the assertion of a sentence is misleading even though true. But it is very important that we recognize this distinction. Otherwise certain moves made by logicians will be puzzling. For instance, consider the sentence-forming operators 'even though', 'but' and 'although'. If I say that we are having a picnic even though it is raining what I said will be true just in case it is true that we are having a picnic and it is raining. In formulating this proposition we will write it as 'P and Q' where 'P' is 'we are having a picnic' and 'Q' is 'it is raining'. Clearly 'P even though Q' does not mean the same as 'P and Q'. The former suggests that one would not expect P given Q. If this condition is not satisfied it would be misleading for me to say 'P even though Q' instead of simply saying 'P and Q'. But from the point of truth 'P and Q' and 'P even though Q' do not differ. We express this by saying that they have the same *truth-conditions*. That is, they are true in precisely the same conditions. The difference in meaning means that it may be misleading in a given context to use one rather than the other. This same point holds with regard to 'although' and 'but'. Since the validity of an argument depends on relations between conditions under which things are true and not on conditions under which things are misleading, we can express 'but', 'although', 'even though', using '&' for this gives sentences with the same truth-conditions even though they differ in other respects.

We return to the thorny topic of conditionals. There is no hiding the fact that logicians do strange things with conditionals! For the moment we restrict attention to conditionals in which both the antecedent and the consequent are in the indicative mode as in the sentence 'If the grass is green then the grass has chlorophyll'. We set aside for the moment conditionals with sentences in the subjunctive mode, such as 'If the grass were to contain chlorophyll it would be green' and counterfactual conditionals such as 'If the grass had contained chlorophyll it would have been green'. Are conditionals in this restricted class truth-functional? Given that 'P' is 'The grass is green' and 'Q' is 'The grass contains chlorophyll' can we complete the truth-table for 'if P then Q'?

P Q	if P then Q
T T	?
T F	F
F T	?
F F	?

We have no hesitation in putting an F in the second line. For if it turns out that the grass is green but does not contain chlorophyll then it is certainly false to say that if the grass is green then it contains chlorophyll. The other lines are more problematic. We certainly would not want to put an F in the first line. But to put a T there would mean that the conditional 'If water is H_2O then grass is green' is true since both the antecedent and the consequent are true. In point of fact we expect that there is some connection between the antecedent and the consequent if the conditional is to be true. Whether or not there is the requisite connection is not something we can determine merely from the truth-values of the antecedent and the consequent.

Consider the third line. We do not want to put an F here. For the conditional 'If the liquid in the glass is beer, then there is alcohol in the glass' is certainly true. But if the liquid in the glass is in fact wine, the antecedent is false and the consequent true. Neither should we agree without qualms to putting a T for this line. Let us make poor Icabod a schizophrenic and let us suppose that it is false that he has a vitamin B excess. That does not seem enough to make it true that if Icabod has a vitamin B excess then he is a schizophrenic. For the conditional suggests that there is a connection, a connection which is in no way established just by the fact that he is a schizophrenic who has no vitamin B excess. Similarly we will have hesitations about putting a T in the final line. We would not think the conditional just given was true just because Icabod happily turns out not to be a schizophrenic and turns out not to have a vitamin B excess. And certainly we would not want to put an F here. To see this consider the conditional above about the liquid in the glass and suppose that the glass is empty. Then both the antecedent and the consequent are false but we would count the conditional as true.

Logicians introduce a symbol '→' which is called the *material conditional* and give it the following truth-table by fiat:

A B	A → B
T T	*T*
T F	*F*
F T	*T*
F F	*T*

We will follow the standard practice of using that symbol to represent the indicative conditional. This means we are treating the conditional as truth-functional even though the above discussion shows that this at the very least is contentious.

Some logicians believe that the conditional in English is indeed truth-functional. In which case they regard the material conditional as an adequate representation of 'if . . . then . . .'. They will argue that when one asserts a conditional in English one *suggests* that there is some connection between the antecedent and the consequent but one does not *actually assert* that there is such a connection. According to them a conditional is true just in case we do not have a true antecedent and a false consequent. We may mislead our audience if we assert a conditional just because we have one of the other three cases for our audience will expect us to have asserted the conditional on the basis of some connection between the antecedent and the consequent. But, on this view, we cannot be accused of having spoken falsely. The proponents of this view may appeal to examples such as the following. Adults have been known to say to children that if they pick guinea pigs up by their tails, their eyes (those of the guinea pig) will fall out. Children, on hearing this, run to the cage to put this to the test, assuming that there is some mysterious mechanism connecting eyes and tails. Finding that there are no tails on guinea pigs they are apt to complain. Adults defend themselves by saying that *if* you pick them up by their tails their eyes drop out. In this case the conditional is being asserted simply on the grounds of a false antecedent. It is misleading to assert it on these grounds but it is not actually false (or so some logicians would claim).

Within the confines of this work we cannot go into all the pros and cons of the debate (for further discussion see readings given on p. 48). Probably the majority of philosophers would maintain that the conditional is rarely used in English in a truth-functional way. That is, that in most cases of even the indicative conditional, the truth of the conditional requires that some connection obtain between the antecedent and the consequent. That being so we cannot determine the truth-value of the conditional just on the basis of knowing the truth-values of the antecedent and the consequent. Notwithstanding this we will *treat* the conditional as truth-functional.

Those who think that the conditional is not truth-functional may be inclined to be dismissive of our entire enterprise at this point. Three pleas can be entered in mitigation. *First*, we are in the process of setting up an abstract model language to be used in testing arguments in English for validity. An abstract model can be of interest even if it does not model its subject matter perfectly. For instance, scientists study ideal gas models. Actual gases do not behave precisely like ideal gases in the scientists' model. However, there is enough of an approximation to make it worth developing the ideal models. And something is learned about actual gases by seeing how their behaviour departs from that of an ideal gas. Even if we think that English differs from the ideal formal language we are developing we should still explore our ideal model for it may approximate adequately enough for us to obtain useful results. If no sentence-forming operators in English were truth-functional it might be absurd to develop a logic in which all operators were truth-functional. But some operators ('and', 'or', 'not') are clearly truth-functional and we may obtain a model that is not totally distorting if we treat the conditional as a truth-functional operator. *Secondly*, it turns out that virtually every argument that comes out valid in English, is still valid if we treat the conditional as a truth-function. And virtually every argument that is valid if we treat the conditional truth-functionally turns out to be valid. And many philosophers (including those who object that the conditional is not truth-functional) would hold that there are no cases where questions of validity get answered differently depending on whether the conditional is treated truth-functionally or not. Thus in so far as our concern is with validity, the alleged distortion is not significant. *Thirdly*, it turns out to be very difficult to give a systematic formal treatment of logic without treating the conditional as a truth-function. There are logics that do not do this. However, one cannot run logically without first walking logically and we ought to begin at the beginning with a simple logic. Having mastered it the diligent student can go on to study more sophisticated logics in which there is no crude equation of the conditional in English with the logician's material conditional.

3 TESTING FOR VALIDITY: THE SEMANTICAL METHOD

Having introduced propositional symbols, brackets and symbols for certain truth-functional operators we are in a position to represent many arguments of English in our symbolic language. We call the result of producing such a representation, a *formalization*. In giving a formalization we always specify our interpretation of the propositional symbols. To illustrate let us apply this to the following simple argument:

> Icabod is rich.
> If Icabod is rich then Icabod is happy.
> Therefore, Icabod is happy.

We give the interpretation as:

> P: Icabod is rich.
>
> Q: Icabod is happy.

The argument is represented as:

> $P, P \rightarrow Q$. Therefore, Q.

In what follows we will replace 'therefore' by '$\vDash$' which we will call for reasons to be explained the *semantic turnstile*. The resulting expression for the argument (i.e. $P, P \rightarrow Q \vDash Q$) will be called a *semantic sequent*. As a check on our formalization we can apply the interpretation as a code and translate back into English.

But in an argument the premisses are asserted, whereas in $P, P \rightarrow Q \vDash Q$, neither P nor $P \rightarrow Q$ is asserted

   The next step in developing our first test for validity involves
learning how to construct truth-tables for complex formulae
where by a *formula* we mean an expression in our new, developing, formal language (this notion will be given a very precise
characterization in the next chapter). We defined a truth-
functional sentence-forming operator as one generating
sentences the truth-value of which could be determined from a
knowledge of the truth-values of the constituent sentences.
We have considered the truth-tables for the simplest type of
formulae: $P \lor Q$, $P \& Q$, $\neg P$, $P \rightarrow Q$. We can build more
complex formulae using our operators to give formulae the truth-
value of which will be determined by the truth-value of the
constituents — for example: $P \lor \neg P$, $(P \lor Q) \& (R \lor S)$, $(P \& Q)$
$\rightarrow R$. If a formula contains two variables, say P and Q, there are
the following four possibilities for combinations of truth-values:

P	Q
T	T
T	F
F	T
F	F

We call each possibility a *circumstance* and we can say for a
complex formula containing as variables only 'P' and 'Q' under
what circumstances that formula is true. Consider the formula
'$(P \lor Q) \& P$'. Using the table for '$\lor$' we compute the value of
'$(P \lor Q)$' for each circumstance and write that value under the
'$\lor$':

P	Q	$(P \lor Q)$
T	T	T
T	F	T
F	T	T
F	F	F

We transcribe the values of 'P' under the 'P' and then by
reference to the table for '$\&$' we compute the value of the entire

formulae writing the result under the main connective:

P	Q	(P v Q)	&	P
T	T	T	T	T
T	F	T	T	T
F	T	T	F	F
F	F	F	F	F

In carrying out such a computation we have had to pay close attention to scope. We start with connectives of smallest scope and work to those of larger scope. An analogy will be helpful. In arithmetic we use brackets to indicate scope writing, say, (2+3)×6 or 2+(3×6). The brackets tell us to carry out the computations within the brackets using that result in computing with the 6 in the first case or the 2 in the second case. We proceed in the same way in constructing truth-tables. Some students may find it helpful to transcribe the values of the propositional variables for each circumstance under their occurrences in the complex formulae before carrying out the computation. Doing this would have given:

P	Q	(P v Q)			&	P
T	T	T	T	T	T	T
T	F	T	T	F	T	T
F	T	F	T	T	F	F
F	F	F	F	F	F	F

Others may find it harder to see the woods if the page is littered with *T*s and *F*s. A *T* or an *F* should be placed under each operator, even if one does not put *T*s and *F*s under each propositional letter. As a further illustration of these computations consider the following complex truth-tables:

P	P	v	¬P
T	T	T	F
F	F	T	T

P	Q	(P v Q)	→	P
T	T	T	T	T
T	F	T	T	T
F	T	T	F	F
F	F	F	T	F

For formulae with three propositional variables 'P', 'Q', 'R' there will be not four but eight different circumstances to be considered. We illustrate this below in giving a complex truth-table for the formula (P v Q) & R:

P Q R	(P v Q) & R
T T T	T T T
T T F	T F F
T F T	T T T
T F F	T F F
F T T	T T T
F T F	T F F
F F T	F F T
F F F	F F F

An argument is valid if whenever all the premises are true the conclusion is true. The truth-table device enables us to determine whether this condition obtains for an important class of arguments. Consider the argument formalized at the beginning of this section. The truth-tables will allow us to determine in which circumstances both premises are true. Thus we write:

P Q	P, P → Q ⊨ Q
1. T T	T T T
2. T F	T F F
3. F T	F T T
4. F F	F T F

The only circumstances in which all premises are true are those represented by line 1. We ask if the conclusion is true in just those circumstances. It is. Q has the value T in line 1.

Determining the validity of those arguments which can be adequately formalized within the resources we have developed so far is a matter of constructing what we call a *circumstance surveyor*. A circumstance surveyor lists the propositional letters and the possible circumstances with regard to truth and falsity for them. It then gives for each circumstance the truth-value of each premise and of the conclusion. A valid argument is one in which each line of the circumstance surveyor that makes each premise true is one which makes the conclusion true. Or, equivalently, one in which there is no line which makes all premises true and the conclusion false. Notice that we use truth-tables for individual formulae and a circumstance surveyor for arguments. The reason for this is that a truth-table gives the truth-value of a formula in each circumstance. Arguments do not have truth-values. It is only premises and conclusions that have truth-values. Arguments are valid or invalid, not true or false. It helps to keep this difference before our attention by referring to truth-tables for formulae and circumstance surveyors for arguments. Of course in writing down our circumstance surveyor for an argument we write a truth-table for each premise and for the conclusion. We write these linearly so we can survey the circumstances to see whether all those which make the premises true make the conclusion true. The construction of circumstance surveyors for simple arguments is illustrated below.

Example 2.3.1

Argument

> Either Icabod is a Balliol student or Icabod is stupid.
> Icabod is not a Balliol student.
> Therefore, Icabod is stupid.

Interpretation

> P: Icabod is a Balliol student.
> Q: Icabod is stupid.

Formalization

> $P \vee Q,\ \neg P \vDash Q$

Circumstance surveyor

P Q	$P \vee Q,$	$\neg P \vDash$	Q
T T	T	F	T
T F	T	F	F
F T	T	T	T
F F	F	T	F

We will draw a line whenever the possible circumstances make all the premises true. The only such case is the third line. As that circumstance also makes the conclusion true the argument is valid.

Example 2.3.2

Argument

> If Eclipse wins the 2.30 I will win £400.
> If I win £400 I will settle my debts.
> Therefore if Eclipse wins the 2.30,
> I will settle my debts.

Interpretation

> *P*: Eclipse wins the 2.30.
> *Q*: I will win £400.
> *R*: I will settle my debts.

Formalization

$$P \rightarrow Q, Q \rightarrow R \vDash P \rightarrow R$$

Circumstance surveyor

P Q R	$P \rightarrow Q, Q \rightarrow R \vDash P \rightarrow R$		
T T T	*T*	*T*	*T*
T T F	*T*	*F*	*F*
T F T	*F*	*T*	*T*
T F F	*F*	*T*	*F*
F T T	*T*	*T*	*T*
F T F	*T*	*F*	*T*
F F T	*T*	*T*	*T*
F F F	*T*	*T*	*T*

Each line of the circumstance surveyor that makes all the premises true makes the conclusion true. Thus the argument is valid. Remember that we calculate the truth-value of the

premises and the conclusion by reference to the truth-tables for
→, &, *v* and ⌐. In this particular case we only need the truth-table for the conditional.

Example 2.3.3

Argument

> Either Icabod is a Balliol student or Icabod is rich.
> Therefore Icabod is rich.

Interpretation

> *P*: Icabod is a Balliol student.
> *Q*: Icabod is rich.

Formalization

$P \lor Q \vDash Q$

Circumstance surveyor

P	Q	P v Q	⊨Q
T	T	T	T
T	F	T	F
F	T	T	T
F	F	F	F

This argument turns out unsurprisingly to be invalid. There are circumstances in which the premise is true and the conclusion false; namely, when Icabod is a Balliol student but not rich.

Example 2.3.4

Argument

> If Icabod is a Balliol student than Icabod is clever.
> Icabod is clever.
> Therefore, Icabod is a Balliol student.

Interpretation

> *P*: Icabod is a Balliol student.
> *Q*: Icabod is clever.

Formalization

$P \rightarrow Q, Q \vdash P$

Circumstance surveyor

P	Q	$P \rightarrow Q, Q \vdash P$		
T	T	T	T	T
T	F	F	F	T
F	T	T	T	F
F	F	T	F	F

The argument is displayed to be invalid. For the circumstance surveyor gives a condition under which the premises are true and the conclusion false. Some invalid argument forms which are sometimes confusedly taken to be valid have been given names. This form is called *the fallacy of affirming the consequent.*

Not all valid arguments can be shown to be valid using circumstance surveyors as we will see in Chapter 5. This device tests for validity any argument that can be expressed within the limited language we have developed. That is, it is adequate for testing arguments the validity of which turns on the way that truth-functional operators function in the premises and in the conclusion. Validity is a purely general notion defined in regard to any type of argument. We give a restricted definition which is approximate for our restricted language. We define a semantic sequent to be a *tautologous sequent* just in case any line of a circumstance surveyor for the sequent which gives all of the formulae on the left of the semantic turnstile the value *T* also gives the formula on the right of the semantic turnstile the value *T*. A semantic sequent represents the form and structure of an argument (taken with an interpretation it will give a particular argument) and it represents a valid argument form just in case it is a tautologous sequent.

On first working with circumstance surveyors students frequently say that an argument is sometimes valid and sometimes not. They are inclined to say that the argument in Example 2.3.4 is correct for line 1 but not for line 3. This is wrong. An argument is valid or invalid. It is not valid for some lines and invalid for others. There is a feeling that it is unfair to an argument to reject it because it goes wrong on some lines of the circumstance surveyor. One can simply cite the definition of validity (or the more specialized definition of a tautologous sequent) in showing that this is wrong. However, it may be helpful to think of the situation as follows. For the argument expressed by '$P \rightarrow Q$, $Q \vdash P$', only 50 per cent of the circumstances in which the premises are true are ones in which the conclusion is true. That there is at least one line in which the premises are true but the conclusion false shows that in some circumstances you will be led from true premises to a false conclusion. On the other hand in the argument expressed by 'P, $P \rightarrow Q \vdash Q$' any circumstances in which the premises are true the conclusion is true. You will never be led into error if you start with true premises and use this argument form. We reject any argument with even a single line in the circumstance surveyor that makes the premise true and the conclusion false for we are looking for arguments which *guarantee* the preservation of truth. That is, argument forms which if applied to true premises guarantee true conclusions. From the point of view of validity, one bad line ruins an argument.

EXERCISES

1 Construct truth-tables for the following formulae:

(a) $P \lor \neg P$

(b) P

(c) $P \rightarrow \neg P$

(d) $(P \rightarrow Q) \rightarrow (\neg Q \rightarrow \neg P)$

(e) $(P \rightarrow Q) \rightarrow (Q \rightarrow P)$

(f) $(P \rightarrow Q) \rightarrow (\neg P \lor Q)$

(g) $P \rightarrow (P \& Q)$

(h) $(P \& (Q \lor \neg Q)) \rightarrow ((P \& Q) \lor (P \& \neg Q))$

2 Define $A \leftrightarrow B$ as $(A \rightarrow B) \& (B \rightarrow A)$. We call this the *bi-conditional* and use it to express the English phrase 'if and only if'. Construct a truth-table for $A \leftrightarrow B$. Give truth-tables for

the following formulae:

(a) $P \leftrightarrow \neg P$

(b) $(P \rightarrow Q) \leftrightarrow (\neg P \vee Q)$

(c) $(P \rightarrow Q) \leftrightarrow (Q \rightarrow P)$

(d) $(P \mathbin{\&} Q) \leftrightarrow (Q \mathbin{\&} P)$

3 A truth-functional sentence-forming operator which requires a concatenation of n sentences to form a sentence will be said to be an *n-place operator*. On this definition $\neg$ is a one-place operator and & is a two-place operator. A one-place operator has a truth-table with two lines, a two-place operator has a truth-table with 4 lines. How many lines would a three-place operator and four-place operators have in their truth-tables? Let $\Phi\,(P,Q,R)$ be the three-place operator representing: if P and Q then R. Construct its truth-table. Let $\Psi\,(P,Q,R,S)$ be the four-place operator representing: if P and Q then R or S. Construct its truth-table. How many lines would there be in a truth-table for an n-place operator. Justify your answer.

4 Use circumstance surveyors to determine whether the following sequents are tautologous:

(a) $P \rightarrow Q,\ \neg Q \vDash P$

(b) $P \rightarrow \neg Q \vDash Q \rightarrow \neg P$

(c) $P \rightarrow \neg Q \vDash \neg(P \rightarrow Q)$

(d) $P \vDash P \rightarrow Q$

(e) $P \vDash Q \rightarrow P$

(f) $P \rightarrow Q \vDash Q \rightarrow P$

(g) $P \mathbin{\&} Q \vDash P \vee Q$

(h) $P \vee Q \vDash P \mathbin{\&} Q$

(i) $P \vee Q,\ \neg\neg P \vDash Q$

(j) $P \rightarrow \neg Q,\ \neg\neg Q \vDash P$

(k) $((P \vee Q) \rightarrow S) \vDash P \rightarrow S$

(l) $(S \rightarrow (P \vee Q)) \vDash S \rightarrow P$

(m) $P \vee Q \vDash \neg(\neg P \mathbin{\&} \neg Q)$

(n) $P \& Q \vDash \neg(\neg P \vee \neg Q)$

(o) $(P \rightarrow Q) \& (P \rightarrow \neg Q) \vDash \neg P$

5 Formalize the following arguments and test for validity using circumstance surveyors to determine whether the formalizations are tautologous sequents:

(a) Icabod is not both a Balliol student and a modest person. Therefore, Icabod isn't a Balliol student or he isn't modest.

(b) Icabod is a Balliol student. So he is either a Balliol student or he is modest.

(c) Icabod is a Balliol student or he is modest. But he is modest. So he is not a Balliol student.
(Is there a construal of this argument which renders it valid? How would you express this construal using &, *v* and $\neg$?)

(d) If Reagan is assassinated there will be chaos. But if Reagan is not assassinated there will be chaos. So there's going to be chaos.

(e) Either the male (human) lead of Bed Time for Bonzo is President of the United States or there is no threat of war. There is a threat of war. Hence, the male (human) lead of Bed Time for Bonzo is President of the United States.

(f) If Icabod diets, then Icabod will get thin. Icabod diets. So Icabod gets thin.

(g) Either way you look at it we're in for trouble. It's either Reagan or Carter. For Anderson hasn't got a chance. If it's Reagan we're in for trouble. Just look at his views on defence! If it's Carter we're in for trouble. How can a peanut farmer manage an economy?

(h) There is no freedom in communist countries. So you shouldn't visit East Germany.

(i) God is all good and all powerful. But if he is all powerful and all good there can be no evil. But there is plenty of evil. So God is not all good or God is not all powerful.

(j) If the Devil has no redeeming graces, he is thoroughly

bad. Hence, if he is thoroughly bad, he has no redeeming graces.

4 FURTHER DEVELOPMENTS

Consider the following formulae and their truth-tables:

P	$P \lor \neg P$
T	T $\boxed{T}$ F
F	F $\boxed{T}$ T

P Q	$(P \,\&\, Q) \to P$
T T	T $\boxed{T}$ T
T F	F $\boxed{T}$ T
F T	F $\boxed{T}$ F
F F	F $\boxed{T}$ F

P Q	$P \to (P \lor Q)$
T T	T $\boxed{T}$ T
T F	T $\boxed{T}$ T
F T	F $\boxed{T}$ T
F F	F $\boxed{T}$ F

These formulae take the value T for each assignment of truth-values. That is, these formulae come out true for each possible circumstance. This result holds independently of the interpretation that we might give of the propositional letters. Such formulae are called *tautologies*. Some philosophers have said that tautologies say nothing about the world. We can see the justice in this description. For we do not have to look at the world to see that any tautology must be true. If I say that it is raining or it is snowing you have to look at the weather to find out if what I said is true. If on the other hand I say that it is raining or it is not raining (with the caveat below), you do not need to consult a weather man. The caveat is that there may be circumstances in the actual world in which we would hesitate to say that it is true that it is raining but also hesitate to say that it is true that it is not raining. This hesitation arises not from any ignorance about what is going on (we can be standing out in the weather and clearly perceiving the state of things) but from the vagueness involved in what counts as raining. As a further example consider baldness. Just how many hairs does someone have to have before he is no longer bald? Since there is no answer to this question there are situations in which we do not want to say that someone is bald nor do we want to say that he is not bald. In the logic we are developing we are assuming that any proposition is true or is false. This is shown by the fact that we do not set up tables with T, F and, say, ? for the borderline cases. Opinions will differ about how widespread and significant the phenomenon of vagueness is. Those who are impressed by it will regard our logic as at best making an idealizing assumption. There are logicians who attempt to develop logics which do not make this assumption. The sign of an argument, $\vDash$, is also used as the sign of a tautology: $\vDash (P \& Q) \rightarrow P$.

Consider the formulae below and their truth-tables:

P	P	$\&$	$\neg P$
T	T	$\boxed{F}$	F
F	F	$\boxed{F}$	T

P	Q	$\neg P$	$\&$	$(Q$	$\&$	$(Q \rightarrow P))$
T	T	F	$\boxed{F}$	T	T	T
T	F	F	$\boxed{F}$	F	F	T
F	T	T	$\boxed{F}$	T	F	F
F	F	T	$\boxed{F}$	F	F	T

P	Q	$(P \leftrightarrow Q)$	$\&$	$(\neg P \leftrightarrow Q)$
T	T	T	$\boxed{F}$	F
T	F	F	$\boxed{F}$	T
F	T	F	$\boxed{F}$	T
F	F	T	$\boxed{F}$	F

These formulae take the value F for each possible circumstance. That is, there is no way that any one of them could be true. Such formulae are called *inconsistencies*. We shall define a formula to be *semantically inconsistent* just in case there is no possible circumstance which would make it true. That is, there is no assignment of truth-values to the constituent propositions that makes the formula true. A formula which has the value T for at least one circumstance and the value F for at least one circumstance is said to be *contingent*.

The notion of semantical inconsistency as defined applies to a single formula. It can be extended to cover sets of formulae. A semantically inconsistent set of formulae will be one for which there is no assignment of truth-values to the constituents that makes all the formulae in the set true simultaneously. For instance, consider the set of formulae:

$$\{P, P \to Q, \neg Q\}$$

Consider the truth-tables below:

P	Q	P	$P \to Q$	$\neg Q$
T	T	T	T	F
T	F	T	F	T
F	T	F	T	F
F	F	F	T	T

There is no possible circumstance which makes all three true together. This notion of semantic inconsistency has an important connection with the notion of a tautologous sequent. For if a sequent is tautologous any way of making the premises true is a way of making the conclusion true. This means that if we form a set consisting of the premises and the negation of the conclusion that set will be semantically inconsistent. For if we try to make each formula in that set true by finding a possible circumstance we will find that any circumstance that makes the premises true makes the conclusion true and hence (by the truth-table for negation) makes the negation of the conclusion false.

There are two reasons for being interested in the question of the semantical consistency of a set. *First*, we want to have consistent beliefs. We want the set of propositions that we believe true to be consistent. And using the truth-table technique will enable us to test at least a limited class of types of propositions for consistency. *Secondly*, we have seen that there is an equivalence between the validity of an argument and the inconsistency of a related set of propositions. We used the truth-table technique above to display the inconsistency of a set of propositions. Note that we cannot draw any conclusion about the validity of a sequence from finding a set to be consistent.

To illustrate and further develop the techniques introduced in this chapter we will analyse a number of sample arguments.

Example 2.4.1

Argument

> John is a bachelor.
>
> John is not a bachelor.
>
> Therefore Icabod is rich.

Interpretation

> P: John is a bachelor.
> Q: Icabod is rich.

Formalization

> $P, \neg P \vDash Q$

Circumstance surveyor

P	Q	P	,	$\neg P$	$\vDash$	Q
T	T	T		F		T
T	F	T		F		F
F	T	F		T		T
F	F	F		T		F

There are no lines in which the premises are both true and the conclusion false. Hence the argument is valid for its formalization is a tautologous sequent. This may come as a surprise. For the conclusion has nothing to do with the premise. But it is a consequence of our definition of validity that any conclusion follows from a premise set which is semantically inconsistent. For in such a case there is no possibility of the premises all being true and the conclusion false. The fact that anything at all follows validly from inconsistent premises is one of the reasons we do not like inconsistencies. A person who accepts an inconsistency is committed to accepting anything!

Example 2.4.2

Argument

> Only if Eclipse wins the 2.20 will I pay my debts.
> My creditors won't be happy unless I will pay my debts.
> Therefore, Eclipse wins the 2.20 or my creditors will be unhappy.

Interpretation

> P: Eclipse wins the 2.20.
> Q: I will pay my debts.
> R: My creditors will be happy.

Formalization

> $Q \rightarrow P, \; \neg Q \rightarrow \neg R \vDash P \vee \neg R$

Notice that the first premise contains the operator *only if*. '$P \rightarrow Q$' formulates 'if P then Q'. The following situation illustrates the difference between 'if' and 'only if'. I might assert the first premise because I have no means at present to pay my debt. If Eclipse wins I will have the means. But I am not saying that I will pay. I may come to have the means and decide to spend the money on further gambling. Hence the premise is not to be formulated as '$P \rightarrow Q$' but rather as '$Q \rightarrow P$', meaning that if I do pay then Eclipse did win. Notice that the second premise contains the operator '*unless* . . .?' 'Unless P, Q' is formulated as '$\neg P \rightarrow Q$'. That my creditors will not be happy unless I pay my debts means if I do not pay my debts they will not be happy. Finally, notice that negation of a proposition is sometimes expressed by prefixing 'un' to the predicate, as in the conclusion.

Circumstance surveyor

P	Q	R	$Q \to P$,	$\neg Q \to \neg R$	$\vDash P \vee \neg R$
T	T	T	T	T	T
T	T	F	T	T	T
T	F	T	T	F	T
T	F	F	T	T	T
F	T	T	F	T	F
F	T	F	F	T	T
F	F	T	T	F	T
F	F	F	T	T	T

The argument is valid as the formalization is a tautologous sequent.

Example 2.4.3

Argument

> Either Eclipse or Morning Star will win the 2.30.
> If Eclipse wins, Icabod will be happy.
> So, if Morning Star wins, Icabod won't be happy.

Interpretation

> P: Eclipse will win the 2.30.
> Q: Morning Star will win the 2.30.
> R: Icabod will be happy.

Formalization

> $P \vee Q, P \to R \vDash Q \to \neg R$

Notice that in the formalization and interpretation we have had to render less idiomatic the formulation of the first premise.

Circumstance surveyor

P	Q	R	P v Q,	P →R ⊨	Q → ⌐R
T	T	T	T	T	F
T	T	F	T	F	T
T	F	T	T	T	T
T	F	F	T	F	T
F	T	T	T	T	F
F	T	F	T	T	T
F	F	T	F	T	T
F	F	F	F	T	T

The argument is not valid as there is a circumstance which would make the premises are true and the conclusion false.

EXERCISES

1 Use truth-tables to determine whether each of the following is a tautology, a contingent formula or an inconsistency.

(a) $P \to \lnot P$

(b) $(P \mathbin{\&} Q) \leftrightarrow (Q \mathbin{\&} P)$

(c) $(P \to Q) \leftrightarrow (Q \to P)$

(d) $(P \to Q) \leftrightarrow \lnot(P \mathbin{\&} \lnot Q)$

(e) $(Q \lor \lnot Q) \mathbin{\&} \lnot(P \lor \lnot P)$

(f) $(P \to (Q \to R)) \to ((P \to Q) \to (P \to R))$

(g) $(P \to Q) \to ((P \lor R) \to Q)$

(h) $(P \to Q) \to (P \to (Q \lor R))$

(i) $P \mathbin{\&} (P \to Q) \mathbin{\&} (P \to \lnot Q)$

2 Determine whether the following sets of formulae are semantically consistent. In the case of any set that is semantically inconsistent, form a tautologous sequent with the negation of one formula as conclusion and the remaining formulae as premises.

(a) $\{\neg Q, P, \neg(Q \rightarrow R)\}$

(b) $\{Q \rightarrow Q, P \rightarrow R, P, \neg(Q \vee R)\}$

(c) $\{P \rightarrow Q, Q, \neg P\}$

(d) $\{P, Q \rightarrow R, \neg(P \rightarrow R)\}$

3 Formalize the following arguments and test for validity using circumstance surveyors to determine if the formalization is a tautologous sequent.

(a) Realism leaves no room for miracles. Under normal weather conditions, the *Luftwaffe* would gain undisputed mastery of the air; and in that event, the BEF would be destroyed on the beaches of Dunkirk. If the realists were right, the retreating army could not be saved.

(b) There is no time unless there is change. There is no change unless some objects exist to change. Therefore either some objects exist to change or there is no time.

(c) Logic is either too boring or too difficult. For either it is part of mathematics or it is part of philosophy. And unless it isn't part of mathematics it is too difficult. Only if it is too boring will it be part of philosophy.

(d) The cow is not there unless I see it. If the cow is not there then the fields and, indeed, the earth, are not there. If the fields and the earth are not there then I cannot exist. But I can only see the cow if I exist. Obviously, then, I do not exist.

(e) If there is some empirical way of distinguishing between absolute rest and absolute motion, Newton was right to think that there is absolute, and not only relative space. Also, if there is absolute space, there is really a difference between absolute rest and absolute motion – whether or not they are empirically distinguishable. So if, as some people argue, there cannot really be a difference between absolute rest and absolute motion unless they are empirically distinguishable, there is absolute space if and only if there is some empirical way of distinguishing between absolute rest and absolute motion.

4 Show the following:

   (a) A, B, C $\vDash$ D if and only if $\vDash$ A & B & C $\rightarrow$ D.

   (b) If A $\vDash$ B and B $\vDash$ C then A $\vDash$ C.

   (c) Any sequent with a contradictory premise is tautologous.

   (d) Any sequent with a tautology as conclusion is tautologous.

5 To determine whether a formula is a tautology using truth-tables becomes tedious as the number of propositional letters increases. There is an alternative procedure which in many cases is more efficient. Suppose we wish to determine if the formula $((P \rightarrow Q)$ & $(Q \rightarrow R)) \rightarrow (P \rightarrow R)$ is a tautology. Assume for the sake of argument that it is not. In that case there is some line of its truth-table which has an F under the main connective, the arrow. This means that the sub-formula on the left must take the value T and the sub-formula on the right must have the value F for that. If $(P \rightarrow R)$ is F, P must be T and R must be F. If $((P \rightarrow Q)$ & $(Q \rightarrow R))$ is T, $(P \rightarrow Q)$ is T and $(Q \rightarrow R)$ is T. We have determined that R is F, then as $(Q \rightarrow R)$ is T, Q must be F. But $(P \rightarrow Q)$ is T and P is T, making Q T. We have a contradiction; Q is both T and F. Hence we conclude that there can be no such line, i.e. a line in which the entire formula is F. Therefore the formula is a tautology. We can record the procedure as follows:

$$((P \rightarrow Q) \; \& \; (Q \rightarrow R)) \rightarrow (P \rightarrow R)$$

$$F$$

$$\qquad\qquad T \qquad\qquad\qquad\quad F$$

$$\quad T \qquad\qquad T$$

$$\qquad\qquad\qquad\qquad\qquad T \quad F$$

$$\quad T \quad\; T \quad\; F \quad\; F$$

If we do not obtain a contradiction we know that the formula is either contingent or inconsistent. How might we determine without constructing a full truth-table whether a formula is inconsistent? Use these techniques to answer question 1 above. In some cases one cannot conclude that the propositional letters have a particular value and must consider the different possible values as illustrated below:

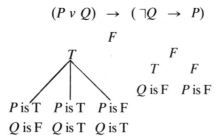

Apply this method to answer question 1 above. Devise a technique for determining whether a sequent is tautologous which does not involve constructing a full circumstance surveyor. Use this technique to determine whether your formalizations in question 3 above are tautologous sequents.

FURTHER READING

On 'if . . . then . . .' and '→':

A. C. Grayling, *An Introduction to Philosophical Logic* (Brighton: Harvester, 1982).

James D. McCawley, *Everything That Linguists Have Always Wanted to Know about Logic But Were Ashamed to Ask*) (Oxford: Blackwell, 1982).

P. F. Strawson, *An Introduction to Logical Theory* (London: Methuen, 1967).

CHAPTER 3
A propositional calculus

1 THE RULES OF NATURAL DEDUCTION

In the last chapter a technique was given for rigorously determining the validity of arguments of our propositional language. The reader is unlikely to have encountered anything even remotely like this technique outside of the study of logic. One is more likely to be familiar with attempts to show that a certain conclusion follows validly from a set of premises by *deriving* that conclusion from the premises. For instance, in Euclidean geometry one seeks to establish that certain results (the theorems) follow validly from certain premises (Euclid's axioms) by manipulating the premises in various ways to obtain the conclusion. In this chapter we will develop this sort of procedure for rigorously establishing the validity of arguments by deriving the conclusion of the argument from the premises using a system of rules. We introduce the symbol '⊢' called the *syntactic turnstile* writing, for instance, '$P \vee Q$, $\neg P \vdash Q$' to express the claim that 'Q' can be derived from the premises using the system of rules to be introduced.

In a valid argument if the premises are true the conclusion must be true. If our system of rules is to be such that it only permits us to derive a conclusion if the conclusion does follow validly from the premises, the rules will have to be *truth-preserving*. That is, if a rule allows us to derive a formula C from a pair of formulae, A and B, C will have to be true if A and B are true. It will be shown that each rule is truth-preserving in any simple direct application. In the next chapter we will show that the system of rules is truth-preserving in *all* applications. At that time we will also consider the reasons for developing this alternative approach to the investigation of arguments.

Conjunction Elimination (&E)
A pair of rules will be introduced for each operator of our

49

propositional language. The rule of *conjunction elimination*, cited as &E, allows us to derive from any formula of the form *A* & *B* either the formula *A* or the formula *B*. If *A* & *B* is true, our truth-table for & shows that *A* is true and that *B* is true. Thus this rule is truth-preserving in a single simple application.

Our aim is to establish a procedure whereby we pass step by step from a premise or premises to a conclusion, each step being licensed by some rule. To this end we set out the derivations as a sequence of numbered lines, indicating the source of each line, for instance:

Prem   (1)   *P* & *Q*

indicates that *P* & *Q* has been introduced as a premise and is the first line in our derivation. Applying the &E rule we write:

Prem   (1)   *P* & *Q*
1   (2)   *P*   1 &E

The entry to the right of line (2) shows that that line was obtained from the first line by the application of the &E rule. The fact that line (2) depends on *P* & *Q* as a premise is shown by writing the number of the line at which the premise *P* & *Q* was introduced to the left of the line number (2). The line to which &E is applied may not be a premise itself having been obtained from another premise or premises. We indicate this by writing the number of the line (lines) in which the premise(s) were introduced to the left of the line number for the line where the rule has been applied. By this procedure we can see at each stage of a proof whether a line represents a premise (in which case Prem is written to the left of the line number) or whether it depends on other lines as premises in which case the numbers to the left of the line number indicate those premises. The numbers to the left of a line taken with the formula of that line indicates what has been established. For instance, in the mini-proof given above *P* occurs as line (2). The 1 to the left of (2) indicates that *P* depends on line (1), i.e. on *P* & *Q* as premise. Thus the proof shows *P* & *Q* ⊦ *P*. Further examples will make clear the style in which proofs are to be set out.

Conjunction Introduction (&I)

The rule of *conjunction introduction* (&I) states that from *A* and from *B* we can infer *A* & *B* or *B* & *A*. Any individual application of this rule will be truth-preserving. For if *A* is true and *B* is true, the table for & shows that *A* & *B* will be true as will *B* & *A*. The result of applying the rule, *A* & *B*, will depend on whatever premise(s) *A* depends on and on whatever premise(s) *B* depends on. If *A* (*B*) is itself a premise we cite the number of the line at which *A*(*B*) is introduced as a premise on the left of the line number for *A* & *B*. If *A*(*B*) is not a premise but has been derived from other premises we cite the lines in which that premise(s) was (were) introduced. To the right of the line we cite the rule and the lines to which the rule was applied. For instance, below are proofs of the sequents *P*,*Q* ⊢ *P* & *Q* and *P*,*Q* ⊢ *Q* & *P*:

Prem	(1)	*P*	
Prem	(2)	*Q*	
1,2	(3)	*P* & *Q*	1,2 &I

Prem	(1)	*P*	
Prem	(2)	*Q*	
1,2	(3)	*Q* & *P*	1,2 &I

Negation elimination (¬E)

The *negation elimination* rule, to be cited as ¬E, allows us to derive *A* from ¬¬*A*. The result of applying the rule, *A*, will rest on whatever premises ¬¬*A* rests on or will rest on ¬¬*A* if ¬¬*A* was itself a premise. The proof of the sequent ¬¬*P* ⊢ *P* is:

Prem	(1)	¬¬*P*	
1	(2)	*P*	1 ¬E

In citing the rule we give the number of the line to which it has been applied, writing, as above, 1 ¬E. The truth-tables below show that the rule is truth-preserving in individual applications.

P	$\neg P$	$\neg\neg P$
T	F	T
F	T	F

Negation Introduction ($\neg$I)

The rule of *negation introduction*, cited as $\neg$I, says that if from some formula A as premise we can derive B & $\neg B$ we can infer $\neg A$. The conclusion, $\neg A$, rests on whatever premises are used in the derivation of B & $\neg B$ (excepting A itself). This is a version of the style of argumentation called proof by *reductio ad absurdum*. We reject a premise A (i.e. assert its negation) on the grounds that taking A as a premise leads to the absurd contradictory result B & $\neg B$. Assuming that the premises used (excepting A) are true and that the other rules used are truth-preserving, we can infer that $\neg A$ is true. For if $\neg A$ were false, A would be true and given the proof of B & $\neg B$ from A, both B and $\neg B$ would be true and this is impossible. This rule is used to derive the sequent $P \vdash \neg(\neg P\ \&\ \neg Q)$:

Prem	(1)	$\neg P\ \&\ \neg Q$	
Prem	(2)	P	
1	(3)	$\neg P$	1 &E
1,2	(4)	$P\ \&\ \neg P$	2,3 &I
2	(5)	$\neg(\neg P\ \&\ \neg Q)$	1,4 $\neg$I

As illustrated in the above derivation, in citing the rule of $\neg$I, we give the line number of the premise which is negated in the application of the rule and the number of the line on which the derived contradiction occurs.

Material Conditional Elimination ($\rightarrow$E)

Our next rule is *material conditional elimination* which is cited as $\rightarrow$E. It licenses us to pass from a pair of formulae of the form A, $A \rightarrow B$ to the formula B. B will rest on whatever premises A and $A \rightarrow B$ rest on. Clearly if A is true and $A \rightarrow B$ is true, B must be true thus the rule is truth-preserving in individual applications. The following examples illustrate the use of this rule which is called traditionally *modus ponendo ponens*.

$$P, P \to Q, Q \to R \vdash R$$

Our goal is to obtain R from the formulae to the left of the turnstile. To this end we begin our proof by writing these as premises:

Example 3.1.1

Prem	(1)	P	
Prem	(2)	$P \to Q$	
Prem	(3)	$Q \to R$	
1,2	(4)	Q	1,2 →E
1,2,3	(5)	R	3,4 →E

Notice that in citing the rule we give the number of the two lines to which it is applied. Our premises for line (4) are lines (1) and (2) which are therefore cited to the left of the turnstile in line (4). In line (5) →E has been applied to lines (3) and (4). (3) is a premise and (4) depends on (1) and (2) as premises. Hence we write 1, 2, 3 to the left of line (5).

Example 3.1.2

$$P \to Q, \neg Q \vdash \neg P$$

Prem	(1)	$P \to Q$	
Prem	(2)	$\neg Q$	
Prem	(3)	P	
1,3	(4)	Q	1,3 →E
1,2,3	(5)	$Q \And \neg Q$	2,4 &I
1,2	(6)	$\neg P$	3,5 ¬I

Notice that we assumed as a premise P in addition to the premises of the sequent. We then used the *reductio ad absurdum* style of arguing to reject that premise.

Material Conditional Introduction (→I)

The rule of material conditional introduction cited as →I, says that if we have derived a formula B from a formula A as a premise we can conclude that $A \to B$ citing any premises introduced in the course of the derivation of B from A. We do not cite A as a premise in concluding $A \to B$. The rule is truth-preserving. For if our other rules preserve truth and if we have derived B from A as a premise we know that if A is true then B is true and that means that $A \to B$ will be true. We drop the assumption of A in deriving the conclusion $A \to B$. Having derived B with A as premise, in effect we sum this up by making the conditional assertion $A \to B$ which says what has been shown; namely, that if A then B. In citing the rule we give the line at which the antecedent of the conditional was taken as a premise and the line at which the consequent of the conditional was obtained as illustrated below. For the application of the rule the consequent must be obtained from the antecedent as premise.

Example 3.1.3

$$P \to Q, Q \to R \vdash P \to R$$

Prem	(1)	$P \to Q$	
Prem	(2)	$Q \to R$	
Prem	(3)	P	
1,3	(4)	Q	1,3 $\to$E
1,2,3	(5)	R	2,4 $\to$E
1,2	(6)	$P \to R$	3,5 $\to$I

Notice that in establishing a conditional we proceed by assuming the antecedent of the conditional hoping to be able to derive the consequent from the antecedent as premise. If we are able to do this we can derive the material conditional using the rule of $\to$I.

Example 3.1.4

$$P \to Q \vdash \neg Q \to \neg P$$

Prem	(1)	$P \to Q$	
Prem	(2)	$\neg Q$	
Prem	(3)	P	
1,3	(4)	Q	1,3 $\to$E
1,2,3	(5)	$Q \, \& \, \neg Q$	2,4 &I
1,2	(6)	$\neg P$	3,5 $\neg$I
1	(7)	$\neg Q \to \neg P$	2,6 $\to$I

Disjunction Introduction (vI)

The rule of *disjunction introduction* licenses the conclusion *A v B* or the conclusion *B v A* from *A*. The conclusion will depend on whatever premises *A* depends on and will depend on *A* if *A* is a premise. Clearly it is truth-preserving in an individual application. From the truth-table for disjunction it is seen that both *A v B* and *B v A* will be true if *A* is true. In citing the rule we give the line at which *A* occurs as illustrated in the proof below of the sequent *P* ⊢ *P v Q*:

```
Prem   (1)   P
1      (2)   P v Q          1 vI
```

Disjunction Elimination (vE)

Suppose we have a formula of the form *A v B*, and that we can show that *C* can be derived from *A* and that *C* can also be derived from *B*. In that case we can derive *C* from *A v B* as premise using the rule of *disjunction elimination vE*. To illustrate this style of argument suppose I know that Jones smokes heavily or that Jones drinks heavily. I do not know which it is that he does (perhaps he does both). Suppose that on the basis of various other premises I derive from the premise that Jones smokes that he has a lower than average life expectancy. And suppose further that with the help of other premises I derive from the premise that Jones drinks that he has lower than average life expectancy. In this case I can conclude that Jones has a lower than average life expectancy on the basis of the premise that Jones drinks heavily or that Jones smokes heavily (taken with the various subsidiary premises). The conclusion will not depend on the premise that Jones smokes heavily nor will it depend on the premise that Jones drinks heavily. In using the *v*E rule to derive a conclusion *C* from a premise *A v B*, we carry out two preliminary derivations. We derive *C* from *A* and we derive *C* from *B*. On the basis of these successes we conclude *C* given *A v B*. Our conclusion does not depend on *A* nor does it depend on *B*. It will depend on any premises introduced in the course of the derivation of *C* and from *A* and *C* from *B* (except *A* and *B* themselves). In order to represent the workings of *v*E most perspicuously our preliminary derivations will be set out side-by-side as illustrated below. We number the lines consecutively through the derivation on the left-hand side and continue the numbering through the derivation on the right-hand side. We could set out the right-hand derivation below the left-hand derivation. However, setting out the proofs in this branching fashion helps to remind us that we are exploring alternatives in applying vE. In citing vE we give the numbers of five lines: that of the disjunction $A \lor B$, that of the assumption of the first disjunct A, that where C is obtained from A, that of the assumption of the second disjunct B, that where C is obtained from B. The conclusion C will depend on $A \lor B$ and on any premises introduced in the course of the two preliminary derivations, these all being cited to the left of the number of the conclusion.

(see opposite page)

Notice that in the above proof we started preliminary derivations using P and using Q preparatory to applying the vE rule. In the course of carrying out the derivation from Q we have applied a further step of vE in relation to the disjunction $(P \lor R)$. This means that given our convention for laying out proofs the right-hand branch of the proof itself branches. The derivations above have established: $P \lor (Q \& R) \vdash (P \lor Q) \& (P \lor R)$ and $(P \lor Q) \& (P \lor R) \vdash P \lor (Q \& R)$. Where a derivation goes through from the left to the right and vice versa (as in this case) we will write: $(P \lor Q) \& (P \lor R) \dashv\vdash P \lor (Q \& R)$.

Bi-conditional Elimination ($\leftrightarrow$E)

The *bi-conditional elimination* rule licenses us to derive from a formula of the form $A \leftrightarrow B$ the formula $(A \to B) \& (B \to A)$. The conclusion will rest on whatever premises the formula $A \leftrightarrow B$ rests on and in citing the rule we cite the line on which that formula occurs writing for the rule $\leftrightarrow$E. The truth-table for the bi-conditional shows that individual applications of this rule to be truth-preserving.

Example 3.1.5

P v (Q & R) ⊢ (P v Q) & (P v R)

Prem	(1)	P v (Q & R)	
Prem	(2)	P	
2	(3)	P v Q	2 vI
2	(4)	P v R	2 vI
2	(5)	(P v Q) & (P v R)	3,4 &I
Prem	(6)	(Q & R)	
6	(7)	Q	6 &E
6	(8)	(P v Q)	7 vI
6	(9)	R	6 &E
6	(10)	(P v R)	9 vI
6	(11)	(P v Q) & (P v R)	8,10 &I
1	(12)	(P v Q) & (P v R)	1,2,5,6,11 vE

Example 3.1.6

(P v Q) & (P v R) ⊢ P v (Q & R)

Prem	(1)	(P v Q) & (P v R)	
1	(2)	(P v Q)	1 &E
Prem	(3)	P	
3	(4)	P v (Q & R)	3 vI
Prem	(5)	Q	
1	(6)	(P v R)	1 &E
Prem	(7)	P	
7	(8)	P v (Q & R)	7 vI
Prem	(9)	R	
5,9	(10)	(Q & R)	5,9 &I
5,9	(11)	P v (Q & R)	10 vI
1,5	(12)	P v (Q & R)	6,7,8,9,11 vE
1	(13)	P v (Q & R)	2,3,4,5,12, vE

Bi-conditional Introduction ($\leftrightarrow$I)

The *bi-conditional introduction* rule licenses us to derive a formula of the form $A \leftrightarrow B$ from formulae of the form $A \rightarrow B$ and $B \rightarrow A$. $A \leftrightarrow B$ will rest on whatever premises $A \rightarrow B$ rests on and on whatever premises $B \rightarrow A$ rests on. In citing the rule we write $\rightarrow$I and give the number of the lines at which $A \rightarrow B$ occurs and $B \rightarrow A$ occurs.

This completes our introduction to the rules which will be more precisely stated in the next chapter. Further examples of the uses of the rules in constructing proofs are given below. For easy reference a summary of the rules is given at the end of this chapter on pages 75–77.

Example 3.1.7

$$P \leftrightarrow Q, Q \leftrightarrow R \vdash P \leftrightarrow R$$

Prem	(1)	$P \leftrightarrow Q$	
Prem	(2)	$Q \leftrightarrow R$	
1	(3)	$(P \rightarrow Q)$ & $(Q \rightarrow P)$	$1\leftrightarrow$E
1	(4)	$(P \rightarrow Q)$	3 &E
1	(5)	$(Q \rightarrow P)$	3 &E
2	(6)	$(Q \rightarrow R)$ & $(R \rightarrow Q)$	$2\leftrightarrow$E
2	(7)	$(Q \rightarrow R)$	6 &E
2	(8)	$(R \rightarrow Q)$	6 &E
Prem	(9)	P	
1,9	(10)	Q	4,9 $\rightarrow$E
1,2,9	(11)	R	7,10 $\rightarrow$E
1,2	(12)	$(P \rightarrow R)$	9,11 $\rightarrow$I
Prem	(13)	R	
2,13	(14)	Q	8,13 $\rightarrow$E
1,2,13	(15)	P	5,14 $\rightarrow$E
1,2	(16)	$(R \rightarrow P)$	13,15 $\rightarrow$I
1,2	(17)	$(P \rightarrow R)$ & $(R \rightarrow P)$	12,16 &I
1,2	(18)	$(P \leftrightarrow R)$	17$\leftrightarrow$I

Example 3.1.8

$(P \rightarrow R) \& (Q \rightarrow R) \vdash (P \vee Q) \rightarrow R$

Prem	(1)	$(P \rightarrow R) \& (Q \rightarrow R)$	
Prem	(2)	$(P \vee Q)$	
Prem	(3)	P	
1	(4)	$(P \rightarrow R)$	1 &E
1,3	(5)	R	3,4 →E
1,2	(9)	R	2,3,5,6,8 vE
1	(10)	$(P \vee Q) \rightarrow R$	2,9 →I

Prem	(6)	Q	
1	(7)	$(Q \rightarrow R)$	1 &E
1,6	(8)	R	6,7 →E

60.Logic: An introductory course

Notice that since what we wish to establish is a conditional it is advisable to assume as a premise the antecedent (line (2)) and to derive the consequent as conclusion (line (9)) and then we obtain the conditional by using a stage of →I.

Example 3.1.9

$(P \to Q) \dashv \vdash \neg (P \& \neg Q)$

(a) $(P \to Q) \vdash \neg(P \& \neg Q)$

Prem	(1)	$(P \to Q)$	
Prem	(2)	$P \& \neg Q$	
2	(3)	P	2 &E
1,2	(4)	Q	1,3 →E
2	(5)	$\neg Q$	2 &E
1,2	(6)	$Q \& \neg Q$	4,5 &I
1	(7)	$\neg(P \& \neg Q)$	2,6 ¬I

Since we are deriving a formula the main operator of which is ' ¬ ' it is worth attempting to do this by taking as premise the formula without ' ¬ ' with a view to using ¬I.

(b) $\neg(P \& \neg Q) \vdash (P \to Q)$

Prem	(1)	$\neg(P \& \neg Q)$	
Prem	(2)	P	
Prem	(3)	$\neg Q$	
2,3	(4)	$(P \& \neg Q)$	2,3 &I
1,2,3	(5)	$(P \& \neg Q) \& \neg(P \& \neg Q)$	1,4 &I
1,2	(6)	$\neg\neg Q$	3,5 ¬I
1,2	(7)	Q	6 ¬E
1	(8)	$(P \to Q)$	2,7 →I

(see opposite page)

1 Derive the following sequents:

(a) $P \& Q \vdash Q \& P$

(b) $P v Q \vdash Q v P$

(c) $P v (Q v R) \vdash (P v Q) v R$

Example 3.1.10

$P \& Q \vdash \lnot(\lnot P \lor \lnot Q)$

Prem	(1)	$P \& Q$	
Prem	(2)	$(\lnot P \lor \lnot Q)$	
Prem	(3)	$\lnot P$	
1	(4)	P	1 &E
1,3	(5)	$P \& \lnot P$	3,4 &I
3	(6)	$\lnot(P \& Q)$	1,5 ¬I
Prem	(7)	$\lnot Q$	
1	(8)	Q	1 &E
1,7	(9)	$Q \& \lnot Q$	7,8 &I
7	(10)	$\lnot(P \& Q)$	1,9 ¬I
2	(11)	$\lnot(P \& Q)$	2,3,6,7,10 vE
1,2	(12)	$(P \& Q) \& \lnot(P \& Q)$	1,11 &I
1	(13)	$\lnot(\lnot P \lor \lnot Q)$	2,12 ¬I

(d) $P \& (Q \& R) \vdash (P \& Q) \& R$

(e) $P \& (Q \vee R) \dashv \vdash (P \& Q) \vee (P \& R)$

(f) $P \dashv \vdash (P \& Q) \vee (P \& \neg Q)$

(g) $P \dashv \vdash P \vee (Q \& \neg Q)$

(h) $((P \rightarrow Q) \rightarrow P) \vdash P$

(i) $(P \rightarrow (Q \rightarrow R)) \vdash ((P \rightarrow Q) \rightarrow (P \rightarrow R))$

(j) $(P \rightarrow Q) \vdash (Q \rightarrow R) \rightarrow (P \rightarrow R)$

(k) $P \rightarrow (Q \rightarrow R) \dashv \vdash P \& Q \rightarrow R$

(l) $P \leftrightarrow Q \dashv \vdash \neg P \leftrightarrow \neg Q$

2 Derive the sequents corresponding to those of Exercise 4 on p. 37.

2 TESTING ARGUMENTS FOR VALIDITY:
THE SYNTACTICAL APPROACH

In employing the technique introduced in the previous section we are assuming that the rules when taken together preserve truth in the derivations constructed using them. And we assume that any valid argument that can be expressed in our limited language can be represented by a derivable sequent. The vindication of these claims is given in the next chapter. It is the most sophisticated thing we do in this book and for the moment the adequacy of the rules is taken for granted. Study the following examples carefully.

Example 3.2.1

> If we give Icabod arsenic he'll either get very ill or he'll die. If he is very ill he won't be able to run for president and if he is dead he certainly won't be able to run. So if we give him arsenic he won't be able to run.

Interpretation

> *P*: We give Icabod arsenic.
> *Q*: Icabod will get very ill.
> *R*: Icabod will be dead.
> *S*: Icabod is able to run for the presidency.

Formalization

$P \rightarrow Q \vee R, Q \rightarrow \neg S, R \rightarrow \neg S \vdash P \rightarrow \neg S$

(see next page)

Example 3.2.2

Argument

Icabod will have time to row and get a first? That must be wrong. If he works hard he won't have time to row. If he doesn't work hard he's not going to get a first.

Interpretation

P: Icabod will have time to row.
Q: Icabod will get a first.
R: Icabod works hard.

Formalization

$R \rightarrow \neg P, \neg R \rightarrow \neg Q \vdash \neg(P \& Q)$.

Derivation

Prem	(1)	$R \rightarrow \neg P$	
Prem	(2)	$\neg R \rightarrow \neg Q$	
Prem	(3)	$(P \& Q)$	
Prem	(4)	R	
1,4	(5)	$\neg P$	1,4 $\rightarrow$ E
3	(6)	P	3 &E
1,3,4	(7)	$P \& \neg P$	5,6 &I
1,3	(8)	$\neg R$	4,7 $\neg$I
1,2,3	(9)	$\neg Q$	2,8 $\rightarrow$E
3	(10)	Q	3 &E
1,2,3	(11)	$Q \& \neg Q$	9,10 &I
1,2	(12)	$\neg(P \& Q)$	3,11 $\neg$I

Students are often puzzled about the rule of $\neg$-introduction. In using that rule we derive a contradiction from a number of

Derivation

Prem	(1)	$P \rightarrow (Q \lor R)$	
Prem	(2)	$Q \rightarrow \neg S$	
Prem	(3)	$R \rightarrow \neg S$	
Prem	(4)	P	
1,4	(5)	$(Q \lor R)$	1,4 →E
Prem	(6)	Q	
2,6	(7)	$\neg S$	2,6 →E
Prem	(8)	R	
3,8	(9)	$\neg S$	3,8 →E
1,2,3,4	(10)	$\neg S$	5,6,7,8,9 ∨E
1,2,3	(11)	$P \rightarrow \neg S$	4,10 →I

premises (possibly just one but often several). The rule does not tell us which premise is to be rejected. All we know is that we have to reject one of them. Which one we actually reject depends on what we are trying to establish. If we reject the 'wrong' one our move is still legitimate but we will not establish what we sought to prove. If one has done this, one can then without re-deriving the contradiction, cite the line at which it was obtained in negating another of the premises. In which case, of course, the rejected premise will be re-introduced.

Example 3.2.3

Argument

> If God is supremely good and all powerful there is no evil in the world. God is supremely good and all powerful but there is evil in the world. Therefore the church should be suppressed.

Interpretation

> *P*: God is supremely good and all powerful.
> *Q*: There is evil in the world.
> *R*: The church should be suppressed.

Formalization

> $P \to \neg Q, P \& Q \vdash R$

Derivation

Prem	(1)	$P \to \neg Q$	
Prem	(2)	$P \& Q$	
Prem	(3)	$\neg R$	
Prem	(4)	$Q \& \neg R$	
4	(5)	Q	4 &E
2	(6)	P	2 &E
1,2	(7)	$\neg Q$	1,6 $\to$E
1,2,4	(8)	$Q \& \neg Q$	5,7 &I
1,2	(9)	$\neg(Q \& \neg R)$	4,8 $\neg$I
2	(10)	Q	2 &E
2,3	(11)	$(Q \& \neg R)$	3,10 &I

1,2,3	(12)	$(Q \,\&\, \neg R) \,\&\, \neg(Q \,\&\, \neg R)$	9,11 &I
1,2	(13)	$\neg\neg R$	3,12 $\neg$I
1,2	(14)	R	13 $\neg$E

We have given various rules of thumb which are worth bearing in mind in constructing derivations (e.g. when faced with a sequent, the conclusion of which is a conditional, assume the antecedent as a premise with a view to using →I). These are but rules of thumb and not mechanical rules which guarantee that a derivation of a derivable sequent will be forthcoming. And the above derivation indicates how ingenuity may be needed if one wants to construct a short proof. For this reason such derivations as the above are not particularly easy. However, one can check mechanically that the derivation is correct by reference to the rules once it has been produced. It should be clear that *any* conclusion can be derived from the premises used in the above derivation. The premises are inconsistent. Line (1) and (2) give us the conclusion $Q \,\&\, \neg Q$ and the derivation reveals that any conclusion can be derived from a contradiction, this being the syntactical counterpart of the semantical result cited on p.47 that any argument with inconsistent premises is valid.

EXERCISES

1 Derive the tautologous sequents of question 5 on p. 38, and of question 3 on p.48.

2 Formalize the following and derive the resulting sequent:

(a) There will be scandal unless the *RCMP* acted legally. If there is a scandal, they will be discredited in the public eye. If they did give *LSD* to prisoners they acted illegally. So, if they did do this, they will be discredited.

(b) The *RCMP* do not deserve their reputation for integrity. For whether or not they acted legally in giving prisoners *LSD*, they certainly acted immorally. And they deserve their reputation for integrity only if they did not act immorally.

(c) The *RCMP* officers will be convicted unless the judge is a political appointee. So they'll get off because the judge is a friend of the Prime Minister.

(d) If I am a brain in a vat, I could not believe I was not. For I could only believe I was not if I had a language. And if I were a brain in a vat I couldn't have a language. And furthermore, since I do believe I am not a brain in a vat, I am not a brain in a vat.

(e) There is evil unless God exists. There is evil only if the devil exists. God exists if and only if the devil does. But God does not exist and hence there is no devil.

(f) It is raining. So either it is snowing or it is not.

(g) There will be peace only if there is good will on both sides. Whether or not Reagan wins there will be peace. And in any event there is no good will on either side. So Reagan likes Andropov.

3 (a) Show that A,B,C ⊢ D if and only if A ⊢ B & C → D.

(b) Show that if A ⊢ B and B ⊢ C then A ⊢ C.

(c) Show that A ⊢ A and that if A ⊢ C then A,B ⊢ C.

(d) Show that any sequent with a contradictory premise is derivable. Show that any sequent with a tautology as conclusion is derivable.

3 THEOREMS, SUBSTITUTION AND DERIVED RULES

Consider the derivation below:

Example 3.3.1

Prem	(1)	⌐(P ∨ ⌐P)	
Prem	(2)	P	
2	(3)	(P ∨ ⌐P)	2 ∨I
1,2	(4)	(P ∨ ⌐P) & ⌐(P ∨ ⌐P)	1,3 &I
1	(5)	⌐P	2,4 ⌐I
1	(6)	P ∨ ⌐P	5 ∨I
1	(7)	(P ∨ ⌐P) & ⌐(P ∨ ⌐P)	1,6 &I
	(8)	⌐⌐(P ∨ ⌐P)	1,7 ⌐I
	(9)	P ∨ ⌐P	8 ⌐E

It is easy to check that each step is licensed by the rules. Note that the conclusion rests on *no* premises. In constructing the derivation two premises were introduced but by using the rule of ⌐I the dependencies were reduced from two to one premise and then from one premise to no premises. When we can construct a derivation of a conclusion that rests on no premises we will refer to the conclusion as a *theorem*. We write ⊢ A with nothing on the left-hand side of the turnstile to mean that A can be obtained as the conclusion of a derivation not resting on any premises. We will show in the next chapter that the set of all theorems is exactly the same as the set of all tautologies.

If we have a derivation of a theorem such as ⊢ $P \& Q \rightarrow P$ we could use exactly the same form of derivation to establish as a theorem any other formula of the same form. For example, consider the derivations given below:

Example 3.3.2

$P \& Q \rightarrow P$

Prem	(1)	$P \& Q$	
1	(2)	P	1 &E
	(3)	$P \& Q \rightarrow P$	1,2 →I

The formula $R \& S \rightarrow R$ has the same form as the theorem $P \& Q \rightarrow P$ and we can generate a proof of this formula as a theorem by simply replacing each occurrence of '*P*' by '*R*' and each occurrence of '*Q*' by '*S*' in the above derivation to obtain the following proof of ⊢ $R \& S \rightarrow R$:

Prem	(1)	$R \& S$	
1	(2)	R	1 &E
	(3)	$R \& S \rightarrow R$	1,2→I

It is easy to confirm that this result is not affected if one takes more complex formula of the same form. For instance, construct a derivation of the formula $(Y \vee \neg(U \rightarrow \neg V)) \& (W \rightarrow X) \rightarrow (Y \vee \neg(U \rightarrow \neg V))$.

We define a substitution instance of a formula A to be a formula obtained by replacing each occurrence of a propositional letter in *A* by some other formula. In obtaining a substitution instance we can carry out this substitution on some or all of the propositional letters and we may substitute the same or a different formula for different propositional letters. But if we replace one occurrence of a propositional letter by a formula we must put that formula in place of each occurrence of the propositional variable. If we did not obey this constraint we could take '*S* v ⅂*Y*' as a substitution instance of '*P* v ⅂*P*'. While '*P* v ⅂*P*' is a theorem. '*S* v ⅂*Y*' is not a theorem. Given this understanding of a substitution instance we can see that if *A* is a theorem, any substitution instance of *A* is a theorem. Similarly, if we have any sequent which is derivable such as *P* v *Q*, ⅂*Q* ⊢ *P* any sequent obtained by carrying out the uniform substitution of formulae for propositional letters throughout the sequent will be derivable. For instance, it is easily verified that the substitution instance of the above sequent, (*R* & *S*) v (*V* → *W*), ⅂(*V* → *W*) ⊢ (*R* & *S*) can be proved by taking the derivation of the former sequent and substituting '(*R* & *S*)' for '*P*' and '(*V* → *W*)' for '*Q*' throughout.

We express the above claims in the following pair of *metarules*:

Theorem Instance (*TI*). Any substitution instance of a theorem is a theorem.

Sequent Instance (*SI*). Any substitution instance of a derivable syntactic sequent is a correct syntactic sequent. These are not part of our system of rules but rather represent claims about what can be done using the rules we have. It is to be noted that they are redundant in the sense that anything that we might prove by appeal to them can be proved without them. They do not extend our powers of proving but do save us a considerable amount of tedium.

In, say, Euclidean geometry one proves theorems which are appealed to in the proof of further theorems. Of course any theorem could be proved from the axioms but to do so would simply mean tediously writing out previously produced proofs as part of the proof in question. Similarly it is convenient to be able to make use of previous results in establishing new theorems and sequents. Consider the following derivation:

Example 3.3.3

$P \rightarrow Q \vdash \neg P \lor Q$

Prem	(1)	$P \rightarrow Q$				
	(2)	$P \lor \neg P$	TI $(P \lor \neg P)$			
Prem	(3)	P		Prem	(6)	$\neg P$
1,3	(4)	Q	1,3 $\rightarrow$E	5	(7)	$\neg P \lor Q$ 5 $\lor$I
1,3	(5)	$\neg P \lor Q$	4 $\lor$I			
1	(8)	$\neg P \lor Q$	2,3,5,6,7 $\lor$E			

At line (2) we have written a theorem previously proved and employed in the derivation. We know that we could have derived $P \lor \neg P$ in the course of the proof resting on no assumption. But to avoid this repetition we use the rule of *theorem introduction* which allows us to write as a line of a proof a previously proved theorem or a substitution instance of a previously proved theorem not resting on any premises. If we are introducing a theorem we will cite TI to the right. If we are introducing a substitution instance of a theorem we will write TI( ) with the original theorem in brackets to the right of the TI.

Suppose that formulae $A_1, A_2, \ldots, A_n$ occur as the lines of a proof and that we have proved the sequent $A_1, A_2 \ldots, A_n \vdash B$. The rule of *sequent introduction* (to be cited as *SI*) licenses us to conclude B resting on whatever premises the lines $A_1, A_2, \ldots A_n$ rest on. As with theorem introduction this rule does not allow us to prove anything that could not be proved without it. It simply takes some of the tedium out of logic. The justification for the rule lies in the fact that we could always simply run through our original proof of B from $A_1, A_2, \ldots A_n$ in the course of the new proof. It is easily seen that if we have a proof of a sequent, we can generate a proof of any substitution instance of that sequent. Consequently, our rule of sequent introduction is to be taken to cover either a previously proved sequent (*SI*) or a substitution instance (*SIS*). In both cases we cite the original sequent in brackets following '*SI*' or '*SIS*' as illustrated below:

(see opposite page)

Example 3.3.4

¬P v Q ⊢ P → Q

Prem	(1)	¬P v Q	
Prem	(2)	P & ¬Q	
Prem	(3)	¬P	
2	(4)	P	2 &E
2,3	(5)	P & ¬P	3,4 &I
3	(6)	¬(P & ¬Q)	2,5 ¬I
Prem	(7)	Q	
2	(8)	¬Q	2 &E
2,7	(9)	Q & ¬Q	7,8 &I
7	(10)	¬(P & ¬Q)	2,9 ¬I
1	(11)	¬(P & ¬Q)	1,3,6,7,10 vE
1	(12)	P → Q	11 SI (¬(P & ¬Q) ⊢ P → Q)

EXERCISES

1 Derive the following theorems:

(a) ⊢ (P & P) ↔ P
(b) ⊢ (P v P) ↔ P
(c) ⊢ P ↔ ⌐⌐P
(d) ⊢ ⌐(P & ⌐P)
(e) ⊢ P → ((P & Q) ↔ Q)
(f) ⊢ ⌐P → ((P v Q) ↔ Q)
(g) ⊢ (P → Q) v (Q → P)
(h) ⊢ P v (P → Q)
(i) ⊢ (P → Q) v (Q → R)
(j) ⊢ (P v (P & Q)) ↔ P
(k) ⊢ (P & (P v Q)) ↔ P)
(l) ⊢ ((P & Q) v (P & ⌐Q)) ↔ P
(m) ⊢ ((P v Q) & (P v ⌐Q)) ↔ P
(n) ⊢ (P ↔ (Q ↔ R)) ↔ ((P ↔ Q) ↔ R)

4 FURTHER APPLICATIONS OF THE RULES

There are an infinite number of different theorems and sequents which can be derived. Not all are of equal interest. The following derivable sequents (some of which have been derived above) are of particular interest:

$$P → Q ⊣⊢ ⌐P v Q$$
$$P → Q ⊣⊢ ⌐(P & ⌐Q)$$
$$P v Q ⊣⊢ ⌐(⌐P & ⌐Q)$$
$$P & Q ⊣⊢ ⌐(⌐P v ⌐Q)$$
$$P ↔ Q ⊣⊢ (P → Q) & (Q → P)$$

These derivations license us to pass from formulae with one particular main connective to formulae in which this operator does not occur. In fact, it can be proved, for example using repeated application of these results that any formula is interderivable with a formula containing only & and $\neg$. We will pursue the significance of this and related results in section 2 of Chapter 4. In preparation for this two further derivations are given below:

(see next page)

Example 3.4.2

$\neg(\neg P \vee \neg Q) \vdash P \& Q$

Prem	(1)	$\neg(\neg P \vee \neg Q)$	
Prem	(2)	$\neg P$	
2	(3)	$(\neg P \vee \neg Q)$	$2 \vee$I
1,2	(4)	$(\neg P \vee \neg Q) \& \neg(\neg P \vee \neg Q)$	1,3 &I
1	(5)	$\neg\neg P$	2,4 $\neg$I
1	(6)	P	5 $\neg$E
Prem	(7)	$\neg Q$	
7	(8)	$\neg P \vee \neg Q$	$7 \vee$I
1,7	(9)	$(\neg P \vee \neg Q) \& \neg(\neg P \vee \neg Q)$	1,8 &I
1	(10)	$\neg\neg Q$	7,9 $\neg$I
1	(11)	Q	10 $\neg$E
1	(12)	$P \& Q$	6,11 &I

The analogy between logic and Euclidean geometry (see p.69) can be taken a step further by developing a version of the logic which uses *axioms* in place of *rules*. To achieve this we drop all the rules except that of $\rightarrow$ elimination and introduce the following axioms:

A_1 $P \rightarrow (Q \rightarrow P)$

A_2 $(P \rightarrow (Q \rightarrow R)) \rightarrow ((P \rightarrow Q) \rightarrow (P \rightarrow R))$

A_3 $P \& Q \rightarrow P$

A_4 $P \& Q \rightarrow Q$

A_5 $P \rightarrow (Q \rightarrow (P \& Q))$

A_6 $P \rightarrow (Q \rightarrow (Q \& P))$

A_7 $P \rightarrow (P \vee Q)$

A_8 $P \rightarrow (Q \vee P)$

A_9 $((P \rightarrow R) \& (Q \rightarrow R)) \rightarrow ((P \vee Q) \rightarrow R)$

Example 3.4.1

$P \& Q \vdash \lnot(\lnot P \lor \lnot Q)$

Prem	(1)	$P \& Q$	
Prem	(2)	$\lnot P \lor \lnot Q$	
Prem	(3)	$\lnot P$	
1	(4)	P	1 &E
1,3	(5)	$P \& \lnot P$	3,4 &I
3	(6)	$\lnot(P \& Q)$	1,5 ¬I
Prem	(7)	$\lnot Q$	
1	(8)	Q	1 &E
1,7	(9)	$Q \& \lnot Q$	7,8 &I
7	(10)	$\lnot(P \& Q)$	1,9 ¬I
2	(11)	$\lnot(P \& Q)$	2,3,6,7,10 vE
1,2	(12)	$(P \& Q) \& \lnot(P \& Q)$	1,11 &I
1	(13)	$\lnot(\lnot P \lor \lnot Q)$	2,12 ¬I

A_{10} $\neg\neg P \rightarrow P$

A_{11} $P \rightarrow \neg\neg P$

A_{12} $((P \rightarrow Q) \, \& \, (P \rightarrow \neg Q)) \rightarrow \neg P$

A_{13} $(P \leftrightarrow Q) \rightarrow ((P \rightarrow Q) \, \& \, (Q \rightarrow P))$

A_{14} $((P \rightarrow Q) \, \& \, (Q \rightarrow P)) \leftarrow (P \rightarrow Q)$

To call a formula an axiom means that it or any substitution instance of it can be introduced as a line of a proof not resting on any premises. It can be shown that exactly the same theorems and sequents can be derived in the above axiomatic system as can be derived in our natural deduction system. To illustrate axiomatic proof techniques we derive the sequent $\neg(\neg P \lor \neg Q)$ $\vdash P \, \& \, Q$.

(*see next page*)

By the same pattern of argument we can derive Q resting on premise (1) and then using the axiom $P \rightarrow (Q \rightarrow (P \, \& \, Q))$ we can obtain the desired result. The complexity of axiomatic proofs (compare with natural deduction proof on p. 73) is a clear reason for preferring a natural deduction system.

NATURAL DEDUCTION RULES FOR THE PROPOSITIONAL LOGIC

& Elimination

> Given $A \, \& \, B$ we can derive A or we can derive B resting on whatever premises $A \, \& \, B$ rest on.

& Introduction (&I)

> Given A and given B we can derive $A \, \& \, B$ resting on whatever premises A rests on and B rests on.

$\neg$ *Elimination* ($\neg$E)

> Given $\neg\neg A$ we can derive A resting on whatever premises $\neg\neg A$ rests on.

$\neg$ *Introduction* ($\neg$I)

> Given a proof of $B \, \& \, \neg B$ resting on A as premise we can derive $\neg A$, resting on whatever premises $B \, \& \, \neg B$ rests on except A.

Example 3.4.3

Prem	(1)	$\neg(\neg P \lor \neg Q)$	
	(2)	$\neg P \to (\neg P \lor \neg Q)$	Ax 7 (S)
	(3)	$\neg(\neg P \lor \neg Q) \to (\neg P \to \neg(\neg P \lor \neg Q))$	Ax 1(S)
1	(4)	$\neg P \to \neg(\neg P \lor \neg Q)$	1,3 →E
	(5)	$((\neg P \to (\neg P \lor \neg Q)) \,\&\, (\neg P \to \neg(\neg P \lor \neg Q))) \to \neg\neg P$	Ax 12 (S)
	(6)	$(\neg P \to (\neg P \lor \neg Q)) \to ((\neg P \to \neg(\neg P \lor \neg Q)) \to ((\neg P \to (\neg P \lor \neg Q)) \,\&\, (\neg P \to \neg(\neg P \lor \neg Q))))$	Ax 5 (S)
	(7)	$(\neg P \to \neg(\neg P \lor \neg Q)) \to ((\neg P \to (\neg P \lor \neg Q)) \,\&\, (\neg P \to \neg(\neg P \lor \neg Q)))$	2,6 →E
1	(8)	$(\neg P \to (\neg P \lor \neg Q)) \,\&\, (\neg P \to \neg(\neg P \lor \neg Q))$	4,7 →E
1	(9)	$\neg\neg P$	5,8 →E
	(10)	$\neg\neg P \to P$	Ax 10 (S)
1	(11)	P	9,10 →E

→ *Elimination* (→E)

Given A and $A \rightarrow B$ we can derive B resting on the premises on which A rests and on which $A \rightarrow B$ rests.

→ *Introduction* (→I)

Given a proof of B resting on A as premise we can derive $A \rightarrow B$ resting on whatever premises B rests on excepting A.

v Elimination (*v*E)

Given a proof of C resting on A as premise and a proof of C resting on B as premise we can derive C resting on $A \vee B$ and all premises used in the derivations of C excepting those of A and of B.

v Introduction (*v*I)

Given A we can derive $A \vee B$ or $B \vee A$ resting on whatever premises A rests on.

↔ *Elimination* (↔E)

Given $A \leftrightarrow B$ we can derive $(A \rightarrow B)$ & $(B \rightarrow A)$ resting on whatever premises $A \leftrightarrow B$ rests on.

↔ *Introduction* (↔I)

Given $A \rightarrow B$ and $B \rightarrow A$ we can derive $A \leftrightarrow B$ resting on whatever premises $A \rightarrow B$ rests on and $B \rightarrow A$ rests on.

EXERCISES

1 Derive the sequents on p. 72 which have not been derived in the text.

2 In the natural deduction system establish as theorems the axioms given on pp. 73–5. This shows that any theorem or sequent which can be established in the axiomatic system can be established in the natural deduction system.

FURTHER READING

On the axiomatic approach:

E. Mendelson, *An Introduction to Mathematical Logic* (New York: Van Nostrand, 1968), chapter 1.

On the tableau approach:

W. Hodges, *Logic* (Harmondsworth: Penguin, 1977). This provides yet another syntactical approach for establishing validity.

CHAPTER 4
Elementary meta-theory for the propositional calculus

1 THE PROPOSITIONAL LANGUAGE AND THE PROPOSITIONAL CALCULUS

We have developed two techniques for establishing the validity of those arguments the validity of which depends on the role of truth-functional sentence-forming operators. This involved giving a symbolic representation of arguments in English. We can establish the validity of the symbolized argument using circumstance surveyors or by manipulating the premises in accord with the rules of natural deduction to obtain the conclusion. As noted, this symbolic approach is fruitful just because validity is a matter of form and not content. We developed our symbolic language and our system of rules by abstracting from the English language and from natural reasoning. This creation developed to study arguments expressed in English can itself in turn become an object of study. In this chapter we investigate the system itself one result of which will be to show that the two approaches match up in the appropriate way. To begin this meta-study we need a precise characterization of what it is that we are investigating.

We have first to characterize our language. The vocabulary consists of the following symbols: &, v, $\daleth$, $\rightarrow$, $\leftrightarrow$, (,), together with the infinite list of symbols of: $P_0, P_1, P_2, \ldots P_n, \ldots$. We will use this last list rather than the eleven letters: $P, Q, R, \ldots$ as our propositional letters for we do not want to have any limit on the number of propositions that can be represented in our language. To specify a language we need not only a vocabulary but a system of rules enabling us to determine which combination of expressions from the vocabulary are to count as sentences of the language. In the case of English the articulation of rules distinguishing sequences of words that are sentences from sequences of words that are not is a difficult task which has yet to be successfully completed. For our formal propositional language a precise and terse characterization is available, of what is called a *well-formed-formula* or *wff*. Until this juncture we have used the term "formula" for expressions of the language with the understanding that the expressions counted as a sentence of that language. From henceforth formula will mean *any* sequence of expressions from the vocabulary. Formulae which are analogues of sentences of English will be referred to as well-formed formulae. Thus, for example, '$((P_1P_2P_1 \ v \ \&$' and '$P_1P_2 \ \&))$' are formulae but not well-formed formulae whereas '$((P_1 \ v \ P_2) \ \& \ P_1)$' and '$((P_1 \ \& \ P_2) \rightarrow P_3)$' are well-formed formulae. The following clauses characterize the *wff*s of our propositional language:

1 Any propositional letter is a *wff*.

2 If A is a *wff* then $\neg A$ is a *wff*.

3 If A and B are *wff*s, $(A \ \& \ B)$ is a *wff*.

4 If A and B are *wff*s, $(A \ v \ B)$ is a *wff*.

5 If A and B are *wff*s, $(A \rightarrow B)$ is a *wff*.

6 If A and B are *wff*s, $(A \leftrightarrow B)$ is a *wff*.

7 The only formulae that are *wff*s are those that are so in virtue of clauses 1 to 6.

Consider the examples of *wff*s given above in relation to these clauses. In the case of '$((P_1 \ v \ P_2) \ \& \ P_1)$', '$P$'$_1$ and 'P'$_2$ are *wff*s in virtue of clause 1. '$(P_1 \ v \ P_2)$' is therefore a *wff* in virtue of clause 4 and '$((P_1 \ v \ P_2) \ \& \ P_1)$' is then a *wff* in virtue of clause 3. In the case of '$((P_1 \ \& \ P_2) \rightarrow P_3)$', '$P$'$_1$,$P_2$', '$P_3$' are *wff*s by clause 1. Thus by clause 3, '$(P_1 \ \& \ P_2)$' is a *wff*. Therefore, '$((P_1 \ \& \ P_2) \rightarrow P_3)$' is a *wff* by clause 5. On the other hand it is clear that on these clauses the formulae '$))P_1P_2P_3 \ v \ \&$' and '$P_1P_2P_3 \ \& \ ()$' are not *wff*s.

We introduced the device of bracketing to indicate scope and thereby to prevent certain syntactical ambiguities arising in our propositional language. For example '$(P_1 \ \& \ (P_2 \rightarrow P_3))$' makes it clear that '$P_1$' is conjoined with the conditional '$(P_2 \rightarrow P_3)$'. '$((P_1 \& P_2) \rightarrow P_3)$' makes it clear that '$(P_1 \& P_2)$', the antecedent of the conditional, is the conjunction of 'P_1' and 'P_2'. If we followed explicitly the clauses above our *wff*s would bristle with brackets even when this is not necessary to prevent ambiguity. For instance, we should write '$(P_1 \rightarrow P_2)$' even though writing '$P_1 \rightarrow P_2$' does not give rise to ambiguity. While it is of utmost importance that we have a means of constructing *wff*s which cannot give rise to ambiguity, we can in practice depart from the details by following certain conventions to obtain expressions that are more pleasing to the eye and pen. For instance, no confusion will arise if we do not bother to write the outer brackets (i.e. the brackets at the extreme left and extreme right) of any *wff*. We will also adopt the conventions that '&' and 'v' have smaller scope than '$\rightarrow$', '&' smaller than 'v' and ' $\neg$' has smaller scope than any other operator. This means that in place of '$((P_1 v P_2) \rightarrow P_3)$' we will write simply '$P_1 v P_2 \rightarrow P_3$.' If we wish to form the disjunction of 'P'$_1$ with the conditional '$P_2 \rightarrow P_3$' we have to write this as '$P_1 v (P_2 \rightarrow P_3)$'. By these conventions we can write for '$((P_1 \& P_2) \rightarrow (P_1 v P_2))$', '$P_1 \& P_2 \rightarrow P_1 v P_2$'. The convention suppressing some bracketing is adopted for convenience and the student should not hesitate to write formulae in the theoretically correct fashion with the full or a fuller complement of brackets if this is found to be less confusing.

The precise definition of a *wff* permits a similarly precise characterization of the scope of a truth-functional sentence-forming operator. The scope of the occurrence of such an operator is the shortest *wff* within the formula containing that operator. In the *wff* '$P_1 v \neg P_2$', the shortest *wff* contained within that *wff* in which ' $\neg$' occurs is ' $\neg P'_2$ and hence this *wff* is the scope of ' $\neg$'. *The shortest wff* containing 'v' is the *wff* itself making the scope of 'v' the entire *wff*. In this case 'v' has greater scope than ' $\neg$'. For the *wff* giving its scope contains as a part the *wff* giving the scope of ' $\neg$'. The main operator is the one having as its scope the entire *wff*.

The propositional calculus is the propositional language together with the rules for constructing proofs of syntactic sequent. A syntactic sequence $A_1, A_2, \ldots A_n \vdash B$ obtains just in case there is a proof of B from $A_1, \ldots A_\nu$ as premises. A proof is a sequence of lines the last of which is B such that:

1 Each line is either a premise (A_i or **other**) or obtained from other lines in accord with the given rules of natural deduction.

2 B rests on no premise not included in $A_1, A_2, \ldots A_n$.

EXERCISES

1 Which of the following formulae are *wff*s? Justify your answer by reference to the definition of a *wff*.

(a) $((P_1 \vee \neg(P_2)) \leftrightarrow P_3)$

(b) $(\neg(\neg(P_3)) \rightarrow P_3))$

(c) $((P_1 \rightarrow P_2) \rightarrow ((P_3 \rightarrow P_1) \rightarrow (P_3 \rightarrow P_2)))$

(d) $((P_2 \rightarrow (P_2 \rightarrow P_3)) \rightarrow (P_1 \rightarrow P_2 \rightarrow P_1P_3))$

(e) $((P_1 \mathbin{\&} \neg(P_2)) \rightarrow (P_3 \vee \neg(P_4)))$

(f) $((P_1P_2) \rightarrow (P_2P_1))$

2 Re-write the *wff*s of 1 using the conventions for the suppression of brackets.

3 Give three examples of sentences of English which display ambiguities of scope of truth-functional operators. Give alternative formalizations of each sentence and state the scope of each operator.

2 EXPRESSIVE ADEQUACY

The first question we ask of our creation concerns the propositional language and not the propositional calculus. The truth-functional operators were introduced to represent the functioning in our language of certain words of English. We can, however, take a more abstract turn and consider truth-functional sentence-forming operators whether or not they represent some truth-functional sentence-forming operator for which there is a simple expression in English. For we defined such an operator to be one used to form sentences whose truth-value can be calculated from an assignment of truth-values to the constituent propositions. We define the following pair of binary truth-functional operators O and U which we can imagine being considered as possible additions to our propositional language (Remember our language by definition has only the vocabulary given. The only sentence-forming operators are: &, v, ⌐, → , ↔ .)

A B	$A\ O\ B$		A B	$A\ U\ B$
T T	F		T T	F
T F	F		T F	F
F T	F		F T	F
F F	T		F F	F

The operator O has the same truth-table as the binary operator 'neither . . . nor . . .' and we might well wish to be able to express it. The operator U on the other hand would be singularly useless in a natural language. For any sentence formed by it counts as false regardless of the truth-values of the constituent sentences! It would be simply boring to form and use sentences which by definition were false. However, it remains a truth-functional sentence forming operator even if singularly useless which could be added to our propositional language or to English for that matter.

Before actually adding an operator to our language we should check to see if it is already possible to express it in the language. Consider the formula ' ⌐P_1 & ⌐P_2' and the formula '$(P_1$ & ⌐$P_1)$ & $(P_2$ & ⌐$P_2)$' the truth-tables for which are:

$P_1\,P_2$	⌐P_1 & ⌐P_2			$P_1\,P_2$	$(P_1$ & ⌐$P_1)$ & $(P_2$ & ⌐$P_2)$						
T T	F	F	F		T T	T	F	F	F	T	F	F
T F	F	F	T		T F	T	F	F	F	F	F	T
F T	T	F	F		F T	F	F	T	F	T	F	F
F F	T	T	T		F F	F	F	T	F	F	F	T

The truth-tables reveal that these *wff*s take the same values, respectively, as do the formulae '$P_1\ O\ P_2$' and '$P_1\ U\ P_2$'. Consequently these formulae express the truth-functions expressed by O and U. This means that there is indeed no necessity of adding to our vocabulary special signs for these functions. Of course it might be convenient to have a simple sign for them but adding such a sign does not increase the expressive power of our language.

This reflection prompts the question: are there any truth-functions that cannot be expressed in our propositional language as it stands? The answer is no. For this reason we say that the language is *truth-functionally adequate* meaning that all truth-functions of any number of places can be expressed in it. It is easy to verify that this is so in the case of one–place and two-place truth functions. The following represent all the possible truth-functions for one variable:

P	f_1	f_2	f_3	f_4
T	T	T	F	F
F	T	F	T	F

Constructing truth-tables for the following formulae reveals that they express the above truth-functions:

f_1: $P \lor \neg P$

f_2: P

f_3: $\neg P$

f_4: $P \& \neg P$

In the case of two place truth-functions we have the following sixteen possibilities.

P	Q	f_1	f_2	f_3	f_4	f_5	f_6	f_7	f_8
T	T	T	T	T	T	F	T	T	F
T	F	T	T	T	F	T	T	F	F
F	T	T	T	F	T	T	F	F	T
F	F	T	F	T	T	T	F	T	T

P	Q	f_9	f_{10}	f_{11}	f_{12}	f_{13}	f_{14}	f_{15}	f_{16}
T	T	T	F	F	F	F	T	F	F
T	F	F	T	T	F	T	F	F	F
F	T	T	T	F	T	F	F	F	F
F	F	F	F	T	F	F	F	T	F

The student should construct truth-tables to verify that the *wffs* listed below express the truth-functions above:

f_1: $P \& Q \lor P \& \neg Q \lor \neg P \& Q \lor \neg P \& \neg Q$

f_2: $P \& Q \lor P \& \neg Q \lor \neg P \& Q$

f_3: $P \& Q \lor P \& \neg Q \lor \neg P \& \neg Q$

f_4: $P \& Q \lor \neg P \& Q \lor \neg P \& \neg Q$

f_5: $P \& \neg Q \lor \neg P \& Q \lor \neg P \& \neg Q$

f_6: $P \& Q \lor P \& \neg Q$

f_7: $P \& Q \lor \neg P \& \neg Q$

f_8: $\neg P \& Q \lor \neg P \& \neg Q$

f_9: $P \& Q \lor \neg P \& Q$

f_{10}: $P \& \neg Q \lor \neg P \& Q$

f_{11}: $P \& \neg Q \lor \neg P \& \neg Q$

f_{12}: $\neg P \& Q$

f_{13}: $P \& \neg Q$

f_{14}: $P \& Q$

f_{15}: $\neg P \& \neg Q$

f_{16}: $P \& \neg P \lor Q \& \neg Q$

The sixteen formulae have been mechanically generated. To see how consider the truth-table for f_6. There are two and only two circumstances that make it true; namely, when '*P*' is true and '*Q*' is true and when '*P*' is true and '*Q*' is false. But '*P* & *Q*' is true just in case '*P*' is true and '*Q*' is true. And '*P*' is true and '*Q*' is false just in case '*P* & $\neg Q$' is true. Thus if f_6 is true, either '*P* & *Q*' is true or '*P* & $\neg Q$' is true. That is, if f_6 is true, '*P* & *Q* $\lor$ *P* & $\neg Q$' is true. Similarly one can see that if '*P* & *Q* $\lor$ *P* & $\neg Q$' is true, then no matter which of the disjuncts is true, f_6 is true. So the *wff* '*P* & *Q* $\lor$ *P* & $\neg Q$' is true if and only if f_6 is true. To generalize, for any line of the truth-table in which the *wff* has the value *T* one forms a conjunction each conjunct of which is a propositional letter in the *wff* if that letter has the value *T* in that line. If that letter has the value *F* one puts the negation of the letter in the conjunction. One then forms the disjunction of all such conjunctions. If the formula has no line at which it gets the value T it is an inconsistency and one simply forms a disjunction of conjunctions of the form 'P & $\neg P$' for each propositional letter 'P'. This procedure can be used for a truth-function having any number of propositional letters as is shown below.

The fact that we have used only '&', 'v', '$\neg$' in the *wff*s above suggests that our language in overly rich. We could in fact have used '&', 'v', '$\neg$' to express all truth-functions of any number of places. This prompts the question as to whether further reductions in the number of symbols in the vocabulary would be possible while preserving the expressive adequacy of the language. The fact that '$P \ v \ Q$' is equivalent to '$\neg(P$ & $\neg Q)$' shows that we could make do with just '&' and '$\neg$'. And the equivalence of 'P & Q' and '$\neg(\neg P \ v \ \neg Q)$' shows that '$v$' and '$\neg$' would do on their own. The precise definition of equivalence being used is the following: A and B are equivalent just in case $\vDash A \leftrightarrow B$. That is, $A \leftrightarrow B$ is a tautology. Equivalent *wff*s take the same truth-value for the same assignments of values to the constituent propositional letters and thus express the same truth-function.

To have established as we did above that '&', 'v', and '$\neg$' are adequate to express all truth-functions of two variables is not to show that our language is expressly adequate. For that we need to consider all truth-functions of all numbers of places. Let '$*(P_1, P_2, \ldots P_n)$' be an n-place truth-function having the truth-table:

P_1	P_2	$P_3 \ldots$	P_n	$*(P_1, P_2, P_3, \ldots, P_n)$
T	T	T	F	T
T	T	F	F	T
T	T	F	F	F

Consider the first line of the truth-table. The following *wff* will be true just in case its variables are assigned the values given in the first line: P_1 & P_2 & $\ldots$ & P_{n-1}, & $\neg P_n$. Consider the next line. The following *wff* is true just in case its variables have the values given in line two: P_1 & P_2 & $\ldots$ & $\neg P_{n-1}$ & $\neg P_n$. In a similar fashion we can form an expression (take the propositional letter if it is assigned the value true in the line and take its negation if it is assigned the value false, then form the conjunction of these) corresponding to each line of the table in which the *wff* has the value T. Next we form this disjunction of all such *wff*s. There will be one disjunct for each line which has the value T. The formula '$*(P_1, \ldots, P_n)$' is true if and only if its variables have the values given in one of these lines. Thus it will be true in just those cases in which the disjunction of the *wff* corresponding to the true lines is true. This is purely general procedure for finding a *wff* which is equivalent to a given truth-function of n-places using only '&', 'v' and '$\daleth$'. Hence any language containing these connectives is truth-functionally adequate. If there are no lines of the truth-table with a T we take as our formula: P_1 & $\daleth P_1$. The equivalences noted above show that we can find expressions containing only '&' and '$\daleth$' or 'v' and '$\daleth$' which are equivalent to the *wff*s obtained using the above procedure and so languages with '&' and '$\daleth$' and 'v' and '$\daleth$' are truth-functionally adequate.

We have shown that our propositional language is richer than is necessary. For a more modest vocabulary would still have sufficed for expressive adequacy. Call our language and system of rules, L. If we had restricted our vocabulary to 'v', '&', '$\daleth$' our only rules would be $\daleth$I, $\daleth$E, vI, vE, &I, and &E. Call this system L^*. L^* with its restricted vocabulary and smaller system of rules is none the less equivalent to L in a sense. If we regard expressions of the form $\daleth(A$ & $\daleth B)$ in L^* as abbreviations of $A \rightarrow B$ on the grounds that they have the same truth-table anything that can be proved in L can be proved in L^* (as we show below). As anything which can be proved in L^* can obviously be proved in L (L has all the rules of L^* and more), whatever can be proved in one can be proved in the other. To show that whatever can be proved in L can be proved in L^* we have to show that the rules of $\rightarrow$ I and $\rightarrow$ E can be obtained in L^* as derived rules. That is, anything that could be proved if they were added to L can be proved without their addition (provided we treat $A \rightarrow B$ as abbreviating $\daleth(A$ & $\daleth B)$). To establish this we need to prove a sequent in L^* corresponding to the rule of $\rightarrow$ E; that is A, $A \rightarrow B \vdash B$ which on the understanding of '$\rightarrow$' means showing that A, $\neg(A \ \& \ \neg B) \vdash B$. The requisite derivation is as follows:

Prem	(1)	P	
Prem	(2)	$\neg(P \ \& \ \neg Q)$	
Prem	(3)	$\neg Q$	
1,3	(4)	$(P \ \& \ \neg Q)$	1,3 & I
1,2,3	(5)	$(P \ \& \ \neg Q) \ \& \ \neg(P \ \& \ \neg Q)$	2,4 & I
1,2	(6)	$\neg \neg Q$	3,5 $\neg$I
1,2	(7)	Q	6 $\neg$E

It is slightly more complicated to show that anything proved in L using $\rightarrow$ I can be proved in L^*. The rule of $\rightarrow$ I in L states that if from a premise A together with a set of premises Γ we have derived a conclusion B (resting on A and on the members of Γ) we may infer $A \rightarrow B$ resting on the set of premises Γ. We have to show that under these conditions we can infer in L^* $\neg(A \ \& \ \neg B)$. We know on assumption that there is a derivation of B from premise A and the set of premises Γ. Extend that derivation by taking an additional premise $(A \ \& \ \neg B)$. There is now a derivation from A, Γ and $(A \ \& \ \neg B)$ of B (adding additional premises has no effect). In addition there is a derivation of $\neg B$ from $A \ \& \ \neg B$ by use of &E. Thus we have by &I a derivation of $B \ \& \ \neg B$ from A, Γ, $(A \ \& \ \neg B)$ and hence by $\neg$I we can derive $\neg(A \ \& \ \neg B)$ from A and Γ which is what we had to establish to show that $\rightarrow$ I is a derived rule in L^*.

In the design of a logic, a system for carrying out derivations, there is considerable variation possible which does not generate any essential difference. For instance, we can select a number of different sets of truth-functional operators so long as that set is truth-functionally adequate. We can opt for economy in the number of operators and a corresponding economy in the number of rules. This economy will be purchased at the cost of greater complexity in the derivations of theorems and sequents. In this book we have opted for a rich set of operators and rules to simplify the derivations. We will make use of the fact that more economical but essentially equivalent systems could have been used later in this chapter. For some results can more easily be proved with regard to an economical language and logic than with regard to the rich logic and language we introduced.

1 Give *wff*s containing &, v, $\neg$ as their only operators which express the truth-functions f_1, f_1, f_3, f_4:

P Q R	f_1 f_2 f_3 f_4
T T T	T T T T
T T F	F F F T
T F T	F T F T
T F F	F F F F
F T T	T T F F
F T F	F F F F
F F T	F T F T
F F F	F F F F

2 Show that a propositional language with $\neg$, $\rightarrow$ as its only truth-functional operators is expressively adequate. Show that a language with O as its only operator is expressly adequate (truth-table for O is given on p.82).

3 TURNSTILES AND MATERIAL IMPLICATION

Turnstiles are the signs of arguments. The semantic sequent A_1, . . . ,$A_n \vDash B$ says that B follows validly from A_1, . . . ,A_n. In any circumstances in which each of A_1, . . . ,A_n is true, B is true. The syntactic sequent A_1, . . . ,$A_n \vdash B$ says that B can be obtained from A_1, . . . ,A_n using the rules of our natural deduction system. In a well-designed logic syntactic sequents mirror semantic sequents in the sense that a semantic sequent is correct just in case the corresponding syntactic sequent is correct. The main result of this chapter is a proof that our logic for the propositional language is well-designed. Of these two notions it is the semantical one that is most basic. For it is based *directly* on our fundamental characterization of what it is for an argument to be valid. That is the basic notion in terms of which arguments are evaluated is that of validity not derivability. This means that the signs $\vdash$ and $\vDash$ are very different from $\rightarrow$. For $\rightarrow$ is a sentence-forming operator. It occurs within our propositional language and is used to construct sentences which are to be evaluated as true or false.

It is not a sign for an argument. ⊨ and ⊢, being the signs of arguments are not part of our language. They are used to make assertions *about* the relation between sentences of the language. $A_1, \ldots, A_n \vDash B$ says that whenever the sentences $A_1, \ldots, A_n$ are true B is true. $A_1, \ldots, A_n \vdash B$ says that the sentence B can be obtained from the sentences $A_1, \ldots, A_n$ using our rules of derivation. While the signs ⊢ and ⊨ play a very different role from the sign → there is an important relation between them which we establish in this section as a preliminary to exploring the relationship between ⊢ and ⊨.

First we show that $A_1, \ldots, A_n \vDash B$ if and only if $A_1, \ldots, A_{n-1} \vDash A_n \to B$. Suppose that $A_1, \ldots, A_{n-1} \vDash A_n \to B$. This means that if $A_1, \ldots, A_{n-1}$ are all true, $A_n \to B$ is true. Given the truth-table for → it follows that if $A_1, \ldots, A_{n-1}$ are all true and A_n is true, B is true. Thus, if $A_1, \ldots, A_n$ are all true, B is true and by the definition of ⊨ we have: $A_1, \ldots, A_n \vDash B$. This argument establishes that if $A_1, \ldots, A_{n-1} \vDash A_n \to B$ then $A_1, \ldots, A_n \vDash B$. To establish the converse suppose that $A_1, \ldots, A_n \vDash B$. If $A_1, \ldots, A_{n-1}$ are all true $A_n \to B$ is true. For suppose that in these circumstances $A_n \to B$ was false. In which case A_n is true, B is false (by the truth-table for →). But this means that $A_1, \ldots, A_n$ are all true and by the supposition that $A_1, \ldots, A_n \vDash B$, B is true. Since the supposition made for the sake of argument that $A_n \to B$ is false has given rise to a contradiction (B is true and B is false), it follows that $A_n \to B$ is true. Hence if $A_1, \ldots, A_n \vDash B$ then $A_1, \ldots, A_{n-1} \vDash A_n \to B$.

By repeating the steps in the above argument n-times we establish that $A_1, \ldots, A_n \vDash B$ if and only if $\vDash A_1 \to (A_2 \to (A_3 \to \ldots (A_n \to B))) \ldots$. A simple application of the above result is: $A \lor B \vDash \neg(\neg A \, \& \, \neg B)$ if and only if $\vDash (A \lor B) \to \neg (\neg A \, \& \, \neg B)$. This says that the conclusion $\neg(\neg A \, \& \, \neg B)$ follows validly from the premise $A \lor B$ just in case the conditional $A \lor B \to \neg (\neg A \, \& \, \neg B)$ is a tautology. In general terms, the argument formed by taking the antecedent of a conditional as premise and the consequent as conclusion is valid if and only if the conditional is true in all circumstances, i.e. the conditional is a tautology. Notice that it is not enough for the conditional to be true. It has to be a tautology. If the conditional is true but not a tautology, there will be circumstances in which the antecedent is true and the conclusion false. Hence the argument formed with the antecedent as premise and the consequent as conclusion cannot be valid. For in these circumstances the premises would be true and the conclusion false.

The corresponding result holds for $\vdash$; namely, $A_1, \ldots, A_n \vdash B$ if and only if $A_1, \ldots, A_{n-1} \vdash A_n \rightarrow B$. This is a different result from the one established above. That $A_1, \ldots, A_n \vdash B$ if and only if $A_1, \ldots, A_{n-1} \vdash A_n \rightarrow B$ means that there is a derivation of B from the premises $A_1, \ldots, A_n$ just in case there is a derivation of $A_n \rightarrow B$ from $A_1, \ldots, A_{n-1}$. To show that if $A_1, \ldots, A_{n-1} \vdash A_n \rightarrow B$ then $A_1, \ldots, A_n \vdash B$ suppose that $A_1, \ldots, A_{n-1} \vdash A_n \rightarrow B$. On this assumption there is a derivation of $A_n \rightarrow B$ from the set of premises $A_1, \ldots, A_{n-1}$. Then given the premise set $A_1, \ldots, A_{n-1}, A_n$ there is, *ex hypothesi*, a derivation of $A_n \rightarrow B$ from $A_1, \ldots, A_{n-1}$. Using A_n and $A_n \rightarrow B$ and a step of $\rightarrow$ E we extend this derivation to obtain B. Thus, if $A_1, \ldots, A_{n-1} \vdash A_n \rightarrow B$ then $A_1, \ldots, A_n \vdash B$. To establish the converse we assume $A_1, \ldots, A_n \vdash B$. Suppose that B rests on A_n. Given this we extend the derivation of B from $A_1, \ldots, A_n$ by a step of $\rightarrow$ I to obtain $A_n \rightarrow B$ resting on $A_1, \ldots, A_{n-1}$. If B does not rest on A_n as a premise (it may not do so for A_n could be an extra premise not used in the derivation of B), in which case we have a derivation of B from $A_1, \ldots, A_{n-1}$. You proved that $P \vdash Q \rightarrow P$ (see p.62). Thus by introducing a substitution instance of this sequent ($P \vdash Q \rightarrow P$) we extend the derivation to obtain $A_n \rightarrow B$ resting on $A_1, \ldots, A_{n-1}$. Hence $A_1, \ldots A_{n-1} \vdash A_n \rightarrow B$.

4 CONSISTENCY

A valid argument is one which if the premises are true the conclusion must be true. Given that definition we developed a test for determining the validity of arguments expressible in a propositional language. Using circumstance surveyors, we have a mechanical procedure to ascertain whether any circumstance that makes all members of a premise set $A_1, \ldots, A_n$ true also makes a conclusion B true. In such a case we say that B is a *semantic consequent* of $A_1, \ldots, A_n$ and express this in a semantic sequent: $A_1, \ldots, A_n \vDash B$. We also developed a technique which is intended to show that an argument is valid by showing that the conclusion B can be obtained from the premises $A_1, \ldots, A_n$ using the rules of natural deduction. When B can be so obtained we call it a *syntactic consequent* of $A_1, \ldots, A_n$ and we express this in the syntactic sequent: $A_1, \ldots, A_n \vdash B$.

To talk of semantics is to talk of meanings and $\vDash$ is called a semantical notion because in explicating it reference is made to the meaning of the symbols 'v', '&', '$\rightarrow$', '$\neg$', '$\leftrightarrow$'. For in determining whether a semantical sequent is correct we have to use truth-tables. And truth-tables can be viewed as explicating the meaning of the symbols in question. That '&' is to be interpreted as '*and*' and not, say, '*or*' is shown by the fact that sentences constructed using '&', 'P & Q', are true if and only if both 'P' is true and 'Q' is true and not if and only if, say at least one of 'P', 'Q' is true. One who failed to understand the rules for determining the truth-values of 'P and Q' and 'P or Q' as a function of the truth-values of 'P' and of 'Q' would have failed to understand what we mean by '*and*' and '*or*'. In calling the notion a syntactical one on the other hand we are signalling the fact that it can be understood without reference to the meaning of the symbols of the language. It is true that we did refer, for example, to the interpretation of '&' as meaning the same as '*and*' in motivating the acceptance of the rule of &E. However, we can specify that rule and the other rules without reference to meaning by simply stating that the rule licenses one to write 'A' or write 'B' as a line of a proof given a line of the form 'A & B'. Indeed, one could teach someone to construct proofs as a simple game played with marks on paper in accord with the rules without explicitly or even implicitly conveying what the point of the activity was. Thus the notions of a semantic consequent and of a syntactic consequent are very different and independent of one another in the sense that someone could learn how to ascertain whether $A_1, \ldots, A_n \vdash B$ by learning how to construct proofs without having any idea how to ascertain whether $A_1, \ldots, A_n \vDash B$ by constructing circumstance surveyors and vice versa.

The notion of a correct semantic sequent represented by the

semantic turnstile, $\vDash$, is more basic than the notion of a correct syntactic sequent represented by the syntactic turnstile, $\vdash$ (as was noted above). For the former notion is a direct result of making the general definition of validity precise for our particular propositional language. If it turned out that in the design of our system of rules for natural deduction some sequent was semantically correct but not syntactically correct we would endeavour to extend our system of rules in order to carry out the derivation in question. We use the technique of derivation as an alternative tool for establishing the validity of arguments and we have to ensure that the system of rules is indeed adequate to that task. On the other hand, in designing a system of rules it could have turned out that we could derive a conclusion B from premise $A_1, \ldots, A_n$ where in fact it could be that all the premises were true and the conclusion false. In this event we would seek to weaken the system of rules to block the derivation. For instance, suppose we had a rule $\neg E^*$ licensing the derivation of A from $\neg A$ as a premise, the conclusion A resting on whatever premises the premise $\neg A$ rested on (or on $\neg A$ if it was itself a premise). In this case we could derive anything.:

	(1)	$P \vee \neg P$ (TI)			
Prem	(2)	P	Prem	(3)	$\neg P$
				(4)	$P \ 3 \neg E^*$
	(5)	P	1,2,2,3,4	vE.	

If every single sentence is a derivable theorem of the system, every sequent is derivable. Thus it is clear that this would not be an astute rule to adopt.

In fact, in introducing our system of rules we looked to the intended interpretation of the symbols '&', 'v', '$\neg$', '$\rightarrow$', '$\leftrightarrow$' and we checked to make sure that individual applications of the rules were truth-preserving. However, we have to check to see that the rules when used in sequence still preserve truth. That is, we must consider whether it is the case that whenever we have a syntactically valid sequent $A_1, \ldots, A_n \vdash B$ we have a semantically valid sequent $A_1, \ldots, A_n \vDash B$. The proof given below that this is so for our system of rules is called the *consistency proof* of our logic. In addition, we have to check to see if we can indeed derive a sequent $A_1, \ldots, A_n \vdash B$ whenever we have a semantically valid sequent $A_1, \ldots, A_n \vDash B$. This result which is called the *completeness proof* does hold for our logic as is shown in the next section. These two results together show that $A_1, \ldots, A_n \vdash B$ if and only if $A_1, \ldots, A_n \vDash B$; that is, these very different notions, $\vdash$, and, $\vDash$, do indeed match up.

The proof that if we have a derivable sequent $A_1, \ldots, A_n \vdash B$, the corresponding semantic sequent $A_1, \ldots, A \vDash B$ holds proceeds by what is called *mathematical induction*. We show that this result holds for the special case, a derivation that is only one line long (Lemma A below). We then establish the conditional (Lemma B below): if the result holds for any derivation of m or less lines, then the result holds for any derivation of $m+1$ lines. We then conclude that the result holds for any derivation whatsoever. To see why the general result follows from the two particular claims note that establishing the conditional above means that we have the following particular cases:

If the result holds for a derivation of one or less lines, it holds for a derivation of two lines.

If the result holds for a derivation of two or less lines, it holds for a derivation of three lines.

If the result holds for a derivation of three or less lines, it holds for a derivation of four lines.

And so on.

Then, if we show that the result holds for one line derivations, taking that with the first conditional above shows that it holds for a derivation of two or less lines. That taken with the second conditional shows that the result holds for derivations of three or less lines. And that in turn taken with the third conditional shows that the result holds for four lines. Clearly, iterating this procedure shows that the desired result holds for a derivation of any number of lines and as a syntactically correct sequent must be derivable in a finite number of lines we have shown that any syntactically correct sequent corresponds to a semantically correct sequent.

Lemma A

Using only primitive rules, any derivation whatsoever must have a first line of the form

Prem   (1) A.

Remember that what has been established as a syntactical sequent at each step in a derivation is a sequent with the premises on which that line depends listed to the left of the syntactic turnstile and the *wff* of that line on the right of the turnstile. After one line of derivation we have then established a sequent of the form $A \vdash A$. To show that the desired result holds we have to show that $A \vDash A$. But trivially, whenever A is true, A is true. Thus $A \vDash A$.

Lemma B

Assume that for any derivation of m or less lines establishing $A_1, \ldots, A_n \vdash B$ that the result holds, i.e. that $A_1, \ldots, A_n \vDash B$. We will show that under this assumption the desired result holds for any derivation $m+1$ lines in length. We do this by establishing that any way of extending a derivation of m lines to a derivation $m+1$ lines long is such that the resulting syntactically correct sequent corresponds to a semantically correct sequent. This strategy means that we have to consider each rule in turn, checking that if it is used to extend a derivation, the result still holds.

(1) &E

Suppose there is a derivation of m or less lines of B from premises $A_1, \ldots, A_n$ such that $A_1, \ldots, A_n \vDash B$. If we extend the derivation using &E we derive a *wff* C or a *wff* D from a *wff* of the form $C \& D$ resting on whatever premises $C \& D$ rests on. In this case either B is of the form $C \& D$ or some other line in the derivation is of that form. First, assume that B is of the form $C \& D$ and that the derivation is extended to give C. *Ex hypothesi* any circumstances that make $A_1, \ldots, A_n$ true make B and hence, as this means that $C \& D$ is true, C is true (given the truth table for &). Second, assume that some line in the derivation is of the form $C \& D$. Consider the derivation to that point. It will have less than m lines. Hence, *ex hypothesi*, any circumstance which makes $A_1, \ldots, A_n$ true makes C & D true and hence makes C true. Therefore, $A_1, \ldots, A_n \vDash C$ Thus the result assumed to hold for derivations of m or less lines (i.e. that if $A_1, \ldots, A_n \vdash B$ then $A_1, \ldots, A_n \vDash B$) holds if that derivation is extended to one of $m+1$ lines long using &E.

(2) &I
Suppose we have a derivation of B from $A_1, \ldots, A_n$ which is m or less lines long and that $A_1, \ldots, A_n \vDash B$ and that this result holds for any derivation of m or less lines. To extend the derivation using &I means that we conclude C & D where C and D occur as lines somewhere in the derivation. The derivation to the line at which C occurs and the line at which D occurs have m or less lines. Thus we know that $A_1, \ldots, A_n \vDash C$. And $A_1, \ldots, A_n \vDash D$. Thus any circumstances that make $A_1, \ldots, A_n$ true make C and make D true. Hence C & D is true. Therefore $A_1, \ldots, A_n \vDash C$ & D.

(3) ⅂E
Assume that $A_1, \ldots, A_n \vDash B$ for any derivation of B from $A_1, \ldots, A_n$ of m or less lines. If such a derivation is extended using the rule of ⅂E we will have a final line of the form C obtained from some line of the form ⅂⅂C. At the point where ⅂⅂C occurs we have a derivation of m or less lines. Hence, *ex hypothesi*, we have $A_1, \ldots, A_n \vDash C$ (note: we may not have used all the premises $A_1, \ldots, A_n$ to that point. However, we can add extra premises. Whenever $A_1, \ldots, A_n$ are all true ⅂⅂C is true and by the table for ⅂, C is true. Hence we have the desired result: $A_1, \ldots, A_n \vDash C$.

(4) ⅂I.
As before assume that $A_1, \ldots, A_n \vDash B$ for any derivation of B from $A_1, \ldots, A_n$ which had m or less lines. To extend a derivation using ⅂I there must be a line in the derivation of the form C & ⅂C. Whether or not all of the premises $A_1, \ldots, A_n$ have been used to that point it is the case that $A_1, \ldots, A_n \vdash C$ & ⅂C and, by assumption, $A_1, \ldots, A_n \vDash C$ & ⅂C. Using ⅂I we

extend the derivation to obtain $\daleth A_i$ for some premise on which the conclusion $C \& \daleth C$ depends. Assume for the sake of argument that $A_1, \ldots, A_{i-1}, A_{i+1}, \ldots, A_n \vDash A_i$. This means that there is a circumstance that makes the premises $A_1, \ldots A_{i-1}, A_{i,1}, \ldots A_n$ true and $\daleth A_i$ false. Then A_i is true. In which case $C \& \daleth C$ is true since $A, \ldots A_n \vDash C \& \daleth C$. This is absurd. Therefore we reject $A_1, \ldots A_{i-1}, A_{i,1}, A_n \vDash A_i$ and conclude $A_1, \ldots, A_{i-1}, A_i, A_{i+1}, \ldots, A_n \vDash \daleth A_i$ obtaining the desired result.

(5) → E.

To extend a derivation of m lines using the rule of $\rightarrow$ E, there has to be a line of the form $C \rightarrow D$ and a line of the form C. In which case we have $A_1, \ldots, A_j \vdash C$ and $A_k, \ldots, A_n \vdash C \rightarrow D$, each derivation having m or less lines. Given (as before) the assumption that if B can be derived from $A_1, \ldots, A_n$ in m or less lines, then $A_1, \ldots, A_n \vDash B$, we can conclude that $A_1, \ldots, A_j \vDash C$ and $A_k, \ldots, A_n \vDash C \rightarrow D$. Applying $\rightarrow$E to extend the derivation we establish: $A_1, \ldots, A_j, \ldots, A_n \vdash D$. Consider any circumstance that makes $A_1, \ldots, A_j, A_k, \ldots, A_n$ all true. In virtue of $A_1, \ldots, A_j$ being true C is true and in virtue of $A_k, \ldots, A_n$ being true $C \rightarrow D$ is true. By the truth-table for $\rightarrow$, D is true. Hence, we have the required result: $A_1, \ldots, A_j, A_k, \ldots, A_n \vDash D$.

(6) → I.

Suppose for any derivation of m or less lines of B from $A_1, \ldots, A_n$ that $A_1, \ldots, A_n \vDash B$. Extending such a derivation using $\rightarrow$ I means writing as the next line $A_i \rightarrow B$ for some A_i. In which case we have derived the sequent $A_1, \ldots A_{i-1}, A_{i+1}, \ldots A_n \vdash A_i \rightarrow B$. Suppose that there is a circumstance making $A_1, \ldots, A_{i-1}, A_{i+1}, \ldots, A_n$ true and $A_i \rightarrow B$ false. If $A_i \rightarrow B$ is false, A_i is true and B false. In which case all of $A_1, \ldots, A_{i-1}, A_j, A_{i+1}, \ldots, A_n$ are true and *ex hypothesi* B is true. In view of the contradiction we reject the supposition and conclude that $A_1, \ldots, A_{i-1}, A_{i-1}, \ldots A_n \vDash A_i \rightarrow B$.

To complete the proof similar arguments are needed for the rules of vI, vE, $\leftrightarrow$I and $\leftrightarrow$E. This is left as an exercise. If this is done it will have been shown that if for any derivation of B from $A_1, \ldots, A_n$ in m or less lines we have $A_1, \ldots, A_n \vDash B$, then any derivation of B in $m+1$ lines provides a semantically correct sequent with the B as conclusion. Since we have shown that any derivation of one or less lines has the property of giving a semantically correct sequent, by the inductive argument outlined above (cf. p.93) we can conclude that any derivation of a *wff* B from premises $A_1, \ldots, A_n$ of any length corresponds to a semantically correct sequent: $A_1, \ldots, A_n \vDash B$.

What we have established is a *meta-theorem*. It is not a proof within the system but a proof about the system showing that any syntactically correct sequent corresponds to a semantically correct sequent. The result is often called the proof of the *consistency* of our logic as it can be used to show the consistency of the logic. By definition a *syntactically consistent* logic is one in which one cannot derive both B and $\neg B$ for any B. The result we have established shows that if $\vdash B$ then $\vDash B$. For this is just a special case of the general result that if $A_1, \ldots, A_n \vdash B$ then $A_1, \ldots, A_n \vDash B$. Suppose that our logic is inconsistent. In which case, $\vdash B$ and $\vdash \neg B$ for some B. But then by the meta-theorem $\vDash B$ and $\vDash \neg B$. But if B is a tautology, $\neg B$ is not a tautology. Therefore it is not the case that $\vdash B$ and $\vdash \neg B$. Thus our logic is consistent.

The notion of syntactic consistency is also applied to sets of *wff*s:

A set Γ of *wff*s is syntactically consistent if and only if there is no *wff* A such that $\Gamma \vdash A$ and $\Gamma \vdash \neg A$.

The notation $\Gamma \vdash A$ means that there is a derivation of A from premises contained in the set Γ. In addition we define a semantic counter-part to syntactic consistency:

A set Γ of *wff*s is semantically consistent if and only if there is at least one assignment of truth-values to propositional variables of the *wff*s in Γ which makes all the *wff*s true.

Any such assignment is said to provide a model for the set of *wff*s.

The above argument shows that any theorem is a tautology. This is halfway to our goal of showing that the syntactical notion of a theorem matches up with the semantical notion of a tautology in the sense that whatever is a theorem is a tautology and vice versa. Once this conclusion is established it can be used to transfer results proved at the syntactic level to the semantical level. For instance, it was shown (cf. p.49) that any substitution instance of a theorem is itself a theorem (a substitution instance being the result of uniformly replacing some or all propositional variables in a *wff* by *wff*s). Given the match of ⊢ and ⊨ we could conclude from this that any sustitution instance of a tautology is itself a tautology. For tautology is a theorem (by the result to be proved in the next section) and the substitution instance will be itself a theorem and as all theorems are tautologies it will be a tautology. This result can also be established without looking ahead as follows. Let A be a tautology containing propositional variables $P_1, P_2, P_3, \ldots P_n$. The lines of a truth-table for A cover all possible combinations of assignments of truth-values to the P_i's. In each the resulting value for A is T. If a wff B_i is substituted for a propositional variable P_i, it will when evaluated be T or F. But we already know that whether a T or an F is entered the value of A will be T. For it will merely replicate one of the lines of the original truth-table as is illustrated below:

> *wff*: $(\neg P \mathbin{\&} (P \vee Q)) \rightarrow Q$
> substitution: $\neg(R \vee S)$ for Q

P	Q		$(\neg P \mathbin{\&} (P \vee Q)) \rightarrow Q$			
T	T		F	F	T	T
T	F		F	F	T	T
F	T		T	T	T	T
F	F		T	F	F	T

The result of the substitution is:
$(\neg P \mathbin{\&} (P \vee \neg(R \vee S))) \rightarrow \neg(R \vee S)$. A truth-table for this new *wff* would have eight lines. However, we need not construct the new table for we see that if '$\neg(R \vee S)$' has the value T, the result will be the same as line 1 or 3 (depending on whether 'P' is T or F). And if '$\neg(R \vee S)$' is F the result will be the same as line 2 or 4 depending on whether 'P' is T or F.

A semantically inconsistent *wff* is one that takes the value F no matter what values are taken by its consistituent propositonal variables. A similar argument to the above shows that any substitution instance of a semantically inconsistent *wff* is itself semantically inconsistent. Contingent *wff*s (i.e. *wff*s which sometimes take the value *F* and sometimes take the value *T*) do not have this nice stability. Their substitution instances may be contingent, tautologous or inconsistent. Consider the *wff* '*P* v (*Q* → *P*)' and its truth-table below:

P *Q*	*P* v (*Q* → *P*)
T *T*	*T* *T* *T*
T *F*	*T* *T* *T*
F *T*	*F* *F* *F*
F *F*	*F* *T* *T*

In the first line of the table '*P*' is *T* and '*Q*' is *T* and the *wff* in question is *T*. To produce a substitution instance of the *wff* which is a tautology we substitute for '*P*' some *wff* that is always *T* (i.e. a tautology, say, '(*R* v ⌐*R*)'. Similarly for '*Q*' we substitute, say '*S* v ⌐*S*'. Clearly the resulting *wff* will always have the value *T*.

To produce an inconsistent substitution instance of a contingent *wff* we consider a line of its truth-table which gives the *wff* the value *F*. In the case of the *wff* above the only such line is the third. For that line '*P*' is *F* and '*Q*' is *T*. If we substitute for '*P*' an inconsistency, say, '*R* & ⌐ *R*' and for '*Q*' a tautology, say, '*S* v ⌐*S*' we generate a *wff* which is an inconsistency. No matter what values '*S*' and '*R*' have we end up with '*R* & ⌐*R*' having the value *F* and '*S* v ⌐*S*' have the value *T*. And computing the value of the *wff* will then be as line 3.

EXERCISES

1 Determine whether the *wff*s below are contingent, tautologous or inconsistent. Find a tautologous substitution instance and an inconsistent substitution of each contingent *wff*.

(a) *P* → (*Q* → *P*)

(b) *P* → (*P* & *Q*)

(c) $(P \to Q) \to (Q \to P)$

(d) $P \& ((P \to Q) \& (P \to \neg Q))$

(e) $(P \to Q) \& (\neg P \to Q)$

(f) P

(g) $(P \to Q) \to ((Q \to R) \to (R \to P))$

(h) $(P \to Q) \to ((S \to P) \to (S \to Q))$

5 COMPLETENESS

We have shown that if $A_1, \ldots, A_n \vdash B$ then $A_1, \ldots, A_n \vDash B$. To establish that $\vdash$ and $\vDash$ match-up we have to establish the converse of this result. We do this in this section by establishing the *completeness theorem*: if A is a tautology A is a theorem, i.e., if $\vDash A$ then $\vdash A$. From this it follows that if $A_1, \ldots, A_n \vDash B$ then $A_1, \ldots, A_n \vdash B$. For suppose that $A_1, \ldots, A_n \vDash B$. Then by the theorem established on p. 89 it follows that $\vDash (A_1 \to (A_2 \to (A_3 \to \ldots (A_n \to B)))) \ldots$. Then given that we can show that any tautology can be derived as a theorem we can conclude that $(A_1 \to (A_2 \to (A_3 \to \ldots (A_n \to B)))) \ldots$ and by the theorem of page 90 we have $A_1, \ldots, A_n \vdash B$.

There are a number of different ways of showing completeness. The proof to be given has been selected as it is the one which can be most easily generalized to provide a completeness proof of the predicate logic. It is the most sophisticated result given in this book and requires a number of definitions and lemmas. We show first that the result does follow from two lemmas and then proceed to prove the lemmas.

First we define a particularly nice, large kind of set of *wff*s called a maximally consistent set of *wff*s:

> A set S of *wff*s is *maximally consistent* if and only if:
>
> (1) for no *wff* A is it the case that $S \vdash A \& \neg A$
>
> (2) for any *wff* A either A is a member of S or $\neg A$ is member of S.

A maximally consistent set of *wff*s is a set which is as big as can be without generating inconsistency. If you have such a set you cannot add anything else to it without generating an inconsistency. Suppose you thought of adding some *wff B*. Either *B* is already in the set or if it is not then by (2) ⌐*B* is in the set and thus adding *B* would make it inconsistent. One can build up such a set by starting with some *wff*, say, *P* and then going through the set of all *wffs* in some systematic fashion adding each *wff* or its negation and ensuring at each point that consistency is preserved. If one started with the *wff* ⌐*P* one would get a different maximally consistent set.

The completeness result follows from the following lemmas:

> Lemma C_1: Any consistent set of *wffs* of the propositional logic can be extended to a maximally consistent set of *wffs*.

> Lemma C_2: Any maximally consistent set of *wffs* has a model. That is, there is a possible circumstance (an assignment of truth-values to propositional letters) that makes every sentence in the set true.

To establish the completeness result on the basis of these lemmas, let ⌐ be the set of all theorems of the propositional logic. Suppose that some *wff A* is a tautology but not a theorem. Since *A* is not a theorem ⌐*A* can consistently be added to ⌐ to give the set ⌐∪ { ⌐*A* } (this is the notation for a set formed by taking members of ⌐ and adding ⌐*A*). If ⌐*A* when added generated an inconsistency, we could infer that ⌐ ⌐*A* and, hence *A*, contrary to our supposition that *A* is not a theorem by ⌐E. Let ⌐̄ be a maximally consistent extension of the set ⌐∪ { ⌐*A* } (by Lemma C_1 we know that there is such a set). By Lemma C_2, there is a model for ⌐̄. That means there is an interpretation which makes all members of ⌐̄ true including ⌐*A*. But if ⌐*A* is true than *A* is false contrary to our assumption that *A* is a tautology. In view of the contradiction we reject the assumption that *A* is not a theorem and infer that any tautology can be established as a theorem. And, hence, for reasons given above we infer that any semantically correct sequent $A_1, \ldots, A_n \vDash B$ corresponds to a derivable sequent $A_1, \ldots, A_n \vdash B$.

Lemma C_1

To establish that any consistent set of *wffs* can be extended to a maximally consistent set we need to make use of the fact that all *wff*s of the propositional language can be ordered in a sequence and labelled by their position in that sequence using the counting numbers 1,2,3, ... Let $A_1, A_2, A_3, \ldots$ be such a sequence.

Let Γ be a consistent set of *wff*s of the propositional language. By reference to the listing of the *wff*s of the language $A_1, A_2, A_3, \ldots$ we define the following infinite sequence of sets of *wff*s $\Gamma_1, \Gamma_2, \Gamma_3, \ldots$:

$\Gamma_0 = \Gamma$

$\Gamma_1 = \Gamma_0 \cup \{A_1\}$ if $\Gamma_0 \cup \{A_1\}$ is consistent,
  $= \Gamma_0 \cup \{\neg A_1\}$ otherwise.

$\Gamma_2 = \Gamma_1 \cup \{A_2,\}$ if $\Gamma_1 \cup \{A_2,\}$ is consistent,
  $= \Gamma_1 \cup \{\neg A_2,\}$ otherwise

$\Gamma_{n+1} = \Gamma_n \cup \{A_{n+1}\}$ if $\Gamma_n \cup \{A_{n+1}\}$ is consistent
  $= \Gamma_n \cup \{\neg A_{n+1}\}$ otherwise.

This procedure involves enlarging Γ_0 to produce Γ_1 by adding the first *wff* A_1, if A_1, can be consistently added (if A_1, is already in Γ_0 then $\Gamma_1 = \Gamma_0$). If A_1 cannot be consistently added, we add instead $\neg A_1$. The procedure is repeated with $A_2,, A_3$ and so on.

At each stage the set formed Γ_i is consistent. *Ex hypothesi* Γ_0 is consistent. $\Gamma_1 = \Gamma_0 \cup \{A_1\}$ if A_1, can be consistently added. If $\Gamma_0 \cup \{A_1,\}$ is not consistent then $\Gamma_0 \cup \{A_1,\} \vdash B$ and $\Gamma_0 \cup \{A_1,\} \vdash \neg B$ for some B. Then, by $\neg$E, we have $\Gamma_0 \vdash \neg A_1$ and hence $\neg A_1$ can be consistently added to Γ_0 to give Γ_1, and so on for $\Gamma_1, \Gamma_2, \ldots$

Let $\bar{\Gamma}$ be the union of all sets in the sequence $\Gamma_0, \Gamma_1, \Gamma_2, \ldots$. That is, we form a new set $\bar{\Gamma}$ the members of which are all the members of Γ_0, of Γ_1, of $\Gamma_2, \ldots$. $\bar{\Gamma}$ is maximally consistent. That is, for each *wff* B either B or $\neg B$ is a member of $\bar{\Gamma}$ and for no *wff* B is it the case that $\Gamma \vdash B \& \neg B$. To establish that for no *wff* B is it the case that $\Gamma \vdash B \& \neg B$ we assume the contrary. In which case there is a derivation of some *wff* B & $\daleth B$ from some finite list of members of $\bar{\Gamma}$. No more than a finite list of members is required as derivations are by definition of finite length. Let A_n be the *wff* with the largest number in our enumeration which is used in the derivation. Then $\Gamma_n \vdash B \,\&\, \daleth B$. That is, Γ_n is inconsistent contrary to the fact that each member of the sequence of sets $\Gamma_0, \Gamma_1, \Gamma_2, \ldots, \Gamma_n, \ldots$ is consistent. Therefore we reject the assumption that $\bar{\Gamma} \vdash B \,\&\, \daleth B$.

To see that for any *wff* B, B is in $\bar{\Gamma}$ or $\daleth B$ is in $\bar{\Gamma}$, note that any B occurs somewhere in the enumeration of all *wff*s. Suppose B is A_n, in which case either A_n is in Γ_n or $\daleth A_n$ is in Γ_n. Thus, A_n (i.e. B) is in $\bar{\Gamma}$ or $\daleth A_n$ (i.e. $\daleth B$) is in $\bar{\Gamma}$. Hence $\bar{\Gamma}$ is maximally consistent.

Lemma C_2

To show that any maximally consistent set has a model we define the following assignment of truth-values to all propositional letters occurring in *wff*s in $\bar{\Gamma}$ and show that on that assignment all *wff*s in $\bar{\Gamma}$ are true: a propositional letter P is assigned the value true if and only if P is a *wff* in $\bar{\Gamma}$. We next show that a *wff* A has the value true if and only if A is in $\bar{\Gamma}$. The proof proceeds by mathematical induction on the number, n, of truth-functional operators in A. Suppose $n = 0$ in which case A is a propositional letter and by the definition of the assignment of values, A is true if and only if A is in $\bar{\Gamma}$. Next we assume that any *wff* A having n or less operators is true if and only if A is in $\bar{\Gamma}$ and show on this basis that any *wff* A with $n + 1$ or less operators is true and only if A is in $\bar{\Gamma}$. This, taken with the fact that for $n = 0$ A is true if and only if A is in $\bar{\Gamma}$, shows that for any number of operators and hence for any *wff* A, A is true if and only if A is in $\bar{\Gamma}$.

Assuming any *wff*, A, with n or less operators is true if and only if A is in $\bar{\Gamma}$, we consider a *wff*, A, with $n + 1$ operators, and deal in turn with the different possible main operators in A.

(1) $\daleth$. Suppose the main operator is $\daleth$, in which case A has the form $\daleth B$. B has then n operators. Hence, *ex hypothesi*, B is true if and only if B is in $\bar{\Gamma}$. Then B is false if and only if B is not in $\bar{\Gamma}$. Since $\bar{\Gamma}$ is maximally consistent, B is not in $\bar{\Gamma}$ if and only if $\daleth B$ is

in Γ. Therefore B is false if and only if $\neg B$ is in Γ. Also, B is false if and only if $\neg B$ is true. Therefore $\neg B$ is true if and only if $\neg B$ is in Γ, i.e., A is true if and only if A is in Γ.

(2) →. Suppose '→' is the main operator in A. That is, A is of the form $B \to C$. By the truth-table for '→', $B \to C$ is true if and only if B is false or C is true. Since B and C have less than n operators, B is true if and only if B is in Γ, and C is true if and only if C is in Γ. Then B is false if and only if B is not in Γ. Therefore $B \to C$ is true if and only if B is not in Γ or C is in Γ. We prove below that $B \to C$ is in Γ if and only if B is not in Γ or C is in Γ. That having been done we will have shown that $B \to C$ (i.e. A) is true if and only if $B \to C$ (i.e. A) is in Γ.

(i) Assume $B \to C$ is in Γ.
   Assume it is false that B is not in Γ or C is in Γ.
   Therefore, B is in Γ and C is not in Γ.
   $B, B \to C \vdash C$.
   Since B and $B \to C$ are in Γ, Γ $\vdash C$.
   But C is not in Γ. Therefore $\neg C$ is in Γ (Γ is maximally consistent) and Γ is inconsistent. In the face of this contradiction we reject the assumption that it is false that B is not in Γ or C is in Γ and conclude that B is not in Γ or C is in Γ.

(ii) Assume B is not in Γ or C is in Γ.

   Assume B is not in Γ.
   ∴ $\neg B$ is in Γ
   Assume $B \to C$ is not in Γ.
   ∴ $\neg(B \to C)$ is in Γ.
   $\neg B \vdash B \to C$
   ∴ Γ $\vdash B \to C$
   But $\neg(B \to C)$ is in Γ.
   ∴ Γ inconsistent
   ∴ We reject the assumption that $B \to C$ is not in Γ and conclude that $B \to C$ is in Γ.

   Assume C is in Γ.
   Assume $B \to C$ is not in Γ.
   ∴ $\neg(B \to C)$ is in Γ
   $C \vdash B \to C$
   ∴ Γ $\vdash B \to C$
   But Γ $\vdash \neg(B \to C)$
   ∴ Γ is inconsistent
   ∴ We reject the assumption that $B \to C$ is not in Γ and conclude that $B \to C$ *is in* Γ.

   Therefore, $B \to C$ is in Γ.

To complete the proof of the lemma the cases where A has one of the following forms need to be considered: $B \,\&\, C$, $B \vee C$, $B \leftrightarrow C$. This is left as an exercise.

We have established that ⊦ *A* if and only if ⊧ *A* and that $A_1, \ldots A_n \vdash B$ and only if $A_1, \ldots A_n \vDash B$. This means that the two approaches, the syntactical and the semantical, match-up. Consequently, if one wants simply to establish the validity of arguments expressible in the propositional language, one can use either the semantical approach testing with circumstance surveyors or the syntactical approach deriving sequents using the rules of natural deduction. On the basis of what has been presented the former will seem the more attractive procedure as it is purely mechanical. As things stand we have not provided any mechanical procedure guaranteed to produce a proof of anything provable in finite time. However, there are other versions of the completeness proof which have as a bi-product such a mechanical technique for proving any tautology or semantically correct sequent. See in this regard Lemmon op. cit., pp. 88–9.

EXERCISES

1 Show that a set *S* of *wff*s is consistent if and only if every finite sub-set of *S* is consistent.

2 Show that a set *S* of *wff*s has a model if and only if every finite sub-set of *S* has a model.

3 Show that if a set *S* of *wff*s has a model than *S* is consistent.

CHAPTER 5
A predicate language

1 INSIDE THE PROPOSITION: REFERENCE AND PREDICATION

The propositional logic we have developed puts us in a position to rigorously evaluate only a very limited class of arguments, arguments the validity of which turns on the role of truth-functional operators. This means that attention has been limited to arguments that depend for their validity on the relation between simple and compound propositions. We have as yet no tools for investigating arguments the validity of which depends on what is going on inside simple propositions; that is, propositions that do not contain other propositions. For instance, consider the following valid arguments:

All persons are mortal.
Socrates is a person.
Therefore, Socrates is mortal.

All Balliol students are clever.
Icabod is a Balliol student.
Therefore, Icabod is clever.

All zemindars are powerful.
Icabod is a zemindar.
Therefore, Icabod is powerful.

Our recognition of the validity of these arguments arises from our grasp of their form and not their specific content. One does not need to know the meaning of, say, 'zemindar' to see the validity of the last argument. This gives rise to the hope that we may be able to systematically characterize that aspect of form which gives rise to the validity. To do this we will have to look inside the proposition. Our aim is thus to develop a notation for representing the internal form of propositions and we will no longer represent propositions only by the simple symbols, '*P*', '*Q*', '*R*', ...

Consider simple subject-predicate sentences such as: Icabod is happy, Reagan is a loser, Thatcher is stubborn, Everest is high. Two things are to be noted. First, one who asserts such a sentence is picking out someone or something to talk about (Icabod, Reagan, Thatcher, Everest). Secondly, one is ascribing some property to the person or thing picked. One is saying that the thing in question is happy, is a loser, is stubborn, is high. The first activity is called *referring* and the second *predicating*.

Referring is something done by the speaker. There are a variety of linguistic devices which he or she can use to successfully pick something out for the purpose of talking about it. One may use *proper names* as in the above examples. Generally speaking, if a proper name does stand for something (and it may not. After all, there is not and never has been a flying horse called 'Pegasus'), it stands for the same thing on each occurrence of its use (the exception being the use of the same name of different things as in the case of common names like "Joe Smith"). We may also use *singular personal pronouns* to refer to something or someone: I, you, he, she, it. These terms do not refer to the same thing on all occasions of use. We all pick out, for instance, a different person in our use of the word 'I'. We may also use *demonstratives* such as 'this' and 'that'. These words may be used on their own as in 'That is the winner' or in conjunction with a general term which helps us ascertain what is being referred to as in 'This car is for sale'. In both cases, to determine what is being referred to by a speaker we have to pay attention to the situation in which the term is used.

Another device for referring is the *definite description*. The definite description is formed by taking the word 'the' together with some general term as in:

The winner is happy.
The road is slippery.
The lake is dry.

Closely related to definite descriptions are the use of possessive pronouns together with a general term as in:

> My dog is sad.
> Your cat is wicked.
> Their tiger is fierce.

In the course of this and subsequent chapters we will consider these and other devices for referring. For the moment we restrict attention to proper names used to refer to people or things. This restriction means, for instance, that we will not be interested in sentences such as 'Butter is convenient' or 'Ice is nice'. For the names 'butter' and 'ice' are not used as a name of a thing or a person. Butter and ice are best thought of as stuff rather than objects. This is revealed in the fact that you cannot count butter or ice. It makes no sense to ask how many butters you need or how many ices are in Oxford. That is, the indication that a term is for an object as opposed to a stuff is whether it makes sense to think of counting what it designates.

We will use lower case letters from the middle of the alphabet ('m', 'n', 'o', . . .) as proper names. Combining this bit of notation with English we write: n is happy, o is a loser. In introducing letters to function as names we will have to specify what the letters stand for, e.g. 'n' stands for Icabod, 'o' stands for Reagan.

Consider the simple sentences: Icabod is happy, Reagan is a loser, Thatcher is stubborn, Everest is high. The expression we obtain by deleting the name from such sentences is to be called a *predicate*. Thus we might write: – is happy, – is a loser, – is stubborn, – is high. The blank indicates that something must be put therein to form a sentence. In fact we will use lower case letters from the end of the alphabet to indicate the presence of blanks that need filling if we are to have a sentence. Thus we write: x is happy, x is a loser, x is stubborn, x is high. A predicate is to be thought of as expressing a property which is ascribed to something when a sentence is formed by completing the predicate with a name for the thing.

We will call 'x', 'y', 'z', . . . *object variables*. One reason for this label is that the variables show that a sentence about an object will be obtained if the variable is replaced by a name for that object. Not all predicates are so simple. The next level of complexity involves predicates that arise from the deletion of more than one name from a sentence. Consider the sentence: Icabod loves Isabel. The predicate ascribes the property or relation of loving between Icabod and Isabel. We use different variables in place of the different names obtaining: x loves y. This enables us to distinguish the general relation of loving which may obtain between the the same or different people from the relation of self-love which is a property applying to only one person. Thus, from the sentence: Icabod loves himself (i.e. Icabod loves Icabod) we obtain the predicate: x loves x. The repetition of the 'x' means that it must be replaced by the same name in generating a sentence. From the predicate, 'x loves y', we may either generate such sentences as 'Icabod loves Isabel' or 'Icabod loves Icabod'. There is no presumption that different variables must be replaced by different names. However, the same variable must always be replaced by the same name.

A predicate may require more than two names for completion. For instance, the predicate 'x is between y and z' might be completed with the names 'Oxford', 'London' and 'Bristol' to obtain the sentence: Oxford is between London and Bristol. Predicates requiring even more names are rarer but do occur, particularly in mathematical contexts. Predicates requiring n-names for completion will be said to be n-place predicates. Thus, 'x is red,' 'x loves x,' are one-place predicates. 'x is taller than y', 'x loves y' are two-place predicates and 'x is between y and z' is a three-place predicate. In our symbolic notation we will use upper case letters, 'F', 'G', 'H', . . . to represent predicates. In introducing predicates in formulating arguments our interpretation must specify what property or relation the letter is being used to express. In English the names are usually placed before and after the predicate in completing it for any predicate other than one-place one. We will, however, for reasons that will become clear, place the variables used in expressing the predicate after the upper case letters 'F', 'G', 'H', . . . For instance we might write 'Hx' for 'x is happy' and 'Lxy' for 'x loves y'. If we use 'n' for Icabod and 'm' for Isabel, we can complete these predicates to express the sentences 'Icabod is happy' and 'Icabod loves Isabel' as, respectively, *Hn* and *Lnm*. These are sentences expressing propositions which are true or false as the case may be. The expressions *Hx* and *Lxy*, on the other hand, do not make assertions. They are not to be thought of as being true or being false. They do not say that something called '*x*' is happy or that someone *x* loves someone *y*. '*x*' and '*y*' in these contexts are not names. Their role is to indicate the gaps in the predicates to be filled and to indicate whether same or different names may be put in the gaps. They should be thought of as expressing what would be expressed by the English expression 'is happy' 'loves' with the added information our notation conveys about how many names are needed to complete these to make sentences. Such an expression with a gap needing filling to make a sentence are called *open* sentences. Sentences without gaps are said to be *closed*.

2 THE UNIVERSAL AND THE EXISTENTIAL QUANTIFIERS

A more interesting way from the logician's point of view of forming sentences from predicates involves completing them not with names but with *quantifiers*, such as 'everyone'. For instance, adding this to the predicates *x* is happy, *x* loves *y*, gives: Everyone is happy, everyone loves everyone. Of course, if I say that everyone is happy I am very unlikely to mean that literally every person is in this happy state. Using this sentence at a party is likely to convey the thought that everyone at the party is happy. That is, in using this expression I refer to all the members of some set. Just what set I have in mind is likely to be clear from the context. The set intended will be called the *domain of quantification*.

Adding the quantifier 'everyone' to a predicate gives a sentence that says that the predicate applies to each object in the domain ('everyone' carries the implication that the domain is a domain of persons). Thus 'everyone' functions in a very different way from a name. A name standardly picks out a particular person and a predicate completed with the name states that that person had the property expressed by the predicate. Completing a predicate with 'everyone' leads to a sentence which makes a general assertion; namely, each person in the domain has the property expressed by the predicate.

We use an up-side down *A*, $\forall$, to express what is called the *universal quantifier*. When used to complete a predicate it expresses the idea that everything in the domain has the property expressed by the predicate. In English we use 'everyone' if the intended domain is persons, 'everything' if the domain is objects. $\forall$ is not restricted in its application to a particular type of domain. Any restriction to a particular type of domain can be handled through the specification of the domain. One might think of writing '*H*$\forall$*x*' for 'everyone is happy' which parallels most closely writing '*Hn*' for 'Icabod is happy'. Instead, for reasons that will become clear below we write '$(\forall x)Hx$' which is read as: Take anything you like (i.e. anything in the domain): *it* is happy.

Equally important to the analysis of arguments is the *existential quantifier*. This is expressed in English by such expression as 'some' 'something', 'someone'. Adding these expression to a predicate gives a sentence which can be used to assert that there is at least one person or object in the domain which has the property expressed by the predicate. This is expressed in our notation by a backwards '*E*', '$\exists$' and we write for 'someone is happy': $(\exists x)Hx$. This can be read as: You can find something in the domain such that it is happy. It is taken that this means 'at least one' and not necessarily more than one.

We have given examples but no definition of a quantifier. It is just too fundamental a notion to admit of any straightforward definition. Grammatically a quantifier is an expression which attaches to a predicate to generate either a sentence or a new predicate having a smaller number of places. For example, the quantifier 'everyone' attached to the predicate '*x* is happy' generates the sentence 'everyone is happy'. Attaching this quantifier to the second gap in the two-place predicate '*x* loves *y*' gives the new one-place predicate '*x* loves everyone'. This predicate expresses a property which it is supposed is possessed by God. Adding a second quantifier, say, 'someone' to this predicate gives the sentence 'someone loves everyone'. The function of a quantifier is to indicate something about the number of things in the domain to which predicate applies. For instance, this may be quite precise as in 'everyone is happy'. This says that the predicate 'x is happy' applies to each object in the domain. It may be non-specific as in 'some are happy' which conveys the idea that at least one object in the domain has the property of being happy without indicating which object or objects it is. It may be vague as in the quantifiers 'most', 'a few', 'several', 'a lot', etc. There is no definite percentage of things in a domain that have to have the property of being, say, happy before it is true that most of the people in the domain are happy. In this work our focus will be on the universal quantifier, everything, and the existential quantifier, something, and on quantifiers definable in terms of these.

To move to the next stage in our discussion of quantifiers we need to return to predicates to consider another way in which we can generate complex predicates. First it will be convenient to introduce in a preliminary way an idea that will also need refinement later. We say of an object in a given domain that possesses the property expressed by the predicate '*Fx*' that that object *satisfies* the predicate. In the case of a relational predicate such as '*x* loves *y*' we say that a pair of objects *a, b taken in that order* satisfies the predicate '*x* loves *y*' just in case *a* loves *b*. Note that the order is important. The pair of objects — Caesar, Brutus — satisfies the predicate '*x* loves *y*' if Caesar loves Brutus but if, as is said, Brutus did not love Caesar, the pair — Brutus, Caesar — does not satisfy the predicate.

To this juncture we have dealt only with simply unstructured predicates. The operators of our propositional language can be used to build up more complex predicates. Consider the sentence 'Icabod is happy and Icabod is rich'. Deleting the two occurrences of 'Icabod' gives us the complex predicate '*x* is happy and *x* is rich'. This predicate is available for quantification and writing '*Hx*' for '*x* is happy' and '*Rx*' for '*x* is rich' the complex predicate is '*Hx & Rx*' and the result of appending the existential quantifier is '$(\exists x)(Hx \;\&\; Rx)$'. This says that you can find something (in the intended domain of persons) such that it is happy and rich. Or, more idiomatically rendered, we have: 'Someone is happy and rich' or 'There is a happy person who is rich', or 'Some happy people are rich' or 'some rich people are happy'. We have arrived at a symbolic rendering of one very important type of sentence.

Any sentence of the form

Some *F*s are *G*s

is to be rendered as:

$(\exists x)\,(Fx\ \&\ Gx)$

Some *F*s are not *G*s would be rendered as:

$(\exists x)\,(Fx\ \&\ \lnot Gx)$.

This is confirmed by using our pedantic reading of the quantifier and confirming that it has the same sense as the English, i.e. you can find someone who is rich and not happy. This conveys the same as: Some of the rich are unhappy.

Consider the sentence 'If Icabod is a student then Icabod is rich'. Deleting the name 'Icabod' gives the predicate 'If x is a student then x is rich'. Applying the universal quantifier to this complex predicate gives: Take anything you like, if it is a student then it is rich. This captures what is expressed by 'all students are rich'. Thus, any sentence of the form

All *F*s are *G*s

is symbolized as:

$(\forall x)\,(Fx \to Gx)$.

We know from our study of the propositional language that '$P \to Q$' is truth-functionally equivalent to '$\lnot P\ v\ Q$'. Consequently using 'Sx' for 'x is a student' and 'Rx' for 'x is rich', and 'n' for Icabod, 'If Icabod is a student, Icabod is rich' is formulated as '$Sn \to Rn$' which is equivalent to: $\lnot Sn\ v\ Rn$. Thus, something satisfies the predicate '$Sx \to Rx$' if and only if it satisfies the predicate '$\lnot Sx\ v\ Rx$'. This means that the universally quantified sentence '$(\forall x)\,(Sx \to Rx)$' will be true if either there are S's and each of them is an R or there are no S's at all. Thus, in representing 'All Ss are Rs' in the form we have we are not taking it that 'all Ss are Rs' says that there are Ss. That is, we are construing English sentences with the universal quantifier as being implicitly conditional. If one does want to assert not only that if something is an S it is an R but also that there are Ss we can write '$(\forall x)\,(Sx \to Rx)$ $\&\ (\exists x)\,Sx$.

There are various linguistic variants of 'All *F*s are *G*s' all of which symbolized as '∀x(Fx → Gx)':

> Any *F* is a *G*.
> Each *F* is a *G*.
> *F*s are *G*s.
> Every *F* is a *G*.

Some students are sometimes inclined to formulate the above sentences as: (∀x) (Fx & Gx). But this will not do as checking by reading the formulation pedantically back into English reveals: Take anything in the domain that you like: it is both *F* and *G*. Thus, symbolizing 'all students are rich' in this way would lead to the assertion that everything is a student and rich! This tempting error is derived from the fact that in formulating 'some *F*s are *G*s' we use conjunction writing '(∃x) (Fx & Gx)'. Notice that this formulation does commit us to the existence of *F*s whereas the formulation of 'all *F*s are *G*s' as '(∀x) (Fx → Gx)' does not. A similar temptation exists to formulate some *F*s are *G*s as: (∃x) (Fx → Gx). It should be clear that this will not do. For given the equivalence noted above this is the same as '(∃x) (⌐Fx v Gx)' and this would be true if it happens that there are no *F*s in the domain but we would not count it as true to say that 'Some *F*s are *G*s' if there were no *F*s.

There are many other quantifiers in English. Some, as we will see, resist a logical treatment. Others can be explicated in terms of the universal and existential quantifiers. Consider the sentence 'Icabod is over 10 feet tall'. This generates the predicate '*x* is over ten feet tall'. Consider the sentence 'Nobody is over ten feet tall'. If we were to consider that sentence on the model of the former sentence with 'nobody' being treated as a name we would be lead to the 'Lewis Carroll' conclusion that we should get nobody for the basketball team. In fact 'nobody' is a quantifier. The sentence above asserts that you cannot find anything in the domain which is over ten feet tall. Writing '*Ox*' for the predicate in question we can express the sentence as ' ⌐(∃x) Ox.' Or, it can be written equivalently as '(∀x) ⌐Ox'. On our pendantic reading this comes to: take anyone you like from the domain: he or she will not be over ten feet tall.

The quantifiers 'no one', 'nothing', 'no' occur in contexts such as:

> No doctor is a fishmonger.
> No one who wins is lucky.

In formulating these sentences we first re-phrase them as follows:

> Take anything you like, if it is a doctor it is not a fishmonger.
> Take anything you like, if it is a winner it is not lucky.

The correct formulation is then seen to be:

$$(\forall x)(Dx \rightarrow \neg Fx)$$
$$(\forall x)(Wx \rightarrow \neg Lx)$$

Thus far we have dealt with single quantification of increasingly complex predicates such as '$Fx \rightarrow Gx$' and '$Fx \,\&\, Gx$'. A further degree of complexity arises with predicates having two or more places needing filling. Let 'Lxy' be 'x loves y'. Suppose we add the quantifier '$(\exists y)$', to obtain: '$(\exists y)Lxy$'. Notice that this is not a sentence. It has a gap marked by x which has yet to be filled. As it stands it expresses a property – namely that of loving someone. If we fill the blank with the name 'Icabod' we obtain: Icabod loves someone. Suppose we complete this predicate with the quantifier '$(\exists x)$' to obtain '$(\exists x)\,(\exists y)Lxy$' which would say: you can find someone, x, and someone y such that x loves y. Remember that x and y are not names. Here they function like pronouns. We might have phrased the sentence as: You can find someone such that he/she loves someone.

Applying the universal quantifier '$(\forall y)$' to 'Lxy', gives us a predicate '$(\forall y)Lxy$' which expresses the property of loving everyone. We can put the name 'Icabod' in the blank indicated by the 'x' to obtain the sentence: Icabod loves everyone. We can append another universal quantifier '$(\forall x)$' to obtain the sentence '$(\forall x)\,(\forall y)Lxy$' which asserts that anyone you can find loves anyone you can find. Or, in other words, everybody loves everybody. By taking the pedantic readings of '$(\exists x)\,(\exists y)Lxy$' and '$(\exists y)\,(\exists x)Lxy$' together and the readings of '$(\forall x)\,(\forall y)Lxy$' and '$(\forall y)\,(\forall y)Lxy$' you should be able to confirm that in these cases the order in which the quantifiers are appended makes no difference to the sense of what is expressed in the formalization. Notice that we have to add a quantifier containing the same lower case letter as occurs in the predicate. If we wrote, for instance, '(∀x) (∀w)Lxy' we would generate something that is not a sentence and is of dubious sense. Notice too the difference between the predicate '*Lxx*' and '*Lxy*'. The former expresses a relation an object can hold to itself. The latter expresses a relation that may hold between the same or different objects. In quantifying '*Lxx*' universally we obtain '(∀x)Lxx' which says that: take anything you like, it loves itself. '(∃x)Lxx' says that you can find something such that it loves itself. We do not quantify '*Lxx*' using, say, '(∃x)' and '(∃y)' for once '(∃x)' is applied there are no gaps left to filled.

Suppose we wish to formulate the sentence 'Somebody loves everybody'. This says that you can find someone who possesses the property of loving everybody. That property is expressed in our notion by the formula '(∀y)Lxy'. The formalization of the sentence in question is: (∃x) (∀y)Lxy. Consider: 'Everybody loves somebody'. That says: take anyone you like you can find someone who has the property of being loved by them. This property is expressed by '(∃y)Lxy' and thus the formulation of the sentence is: (∀x) (∃y)Lxy. The sentences 'Everyone loves someone' and 'somebody loves everyone' differ in meaning in a way that can be illustrated as follows. Let *A,B,C,D,E* be the members of the domain. Let the arrows represent the relation of loving where the person represented at the head of the arrow is the one who is loved and the one at the tail being the one who does the loving.

I

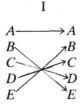

II

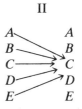

Diagram I represents a situation in which '$(\forall x) (\exists y) Lxy$' is true. For take anyone you like you find someone that they love. Notice that A loves him or herself. If we had to exclude this possibility we should have said: Everyone loves someone else. The formulation of this will be given in section 2 of Chapter 6. '$(\exists y)(\forall x) Lxy$' is false in the situation represented in diagram I for you cannot find someone who is loved by everyone. Diagram II represents a situation in which '$(\exists y) (\forall x) Lxy$'. is true. For you can find someone, lucky C, who is loved by everyone including him – or herself. '$(\forall x) (\exists y) Lxy$' is also true. For take anyone you like you find someone, namely C, that they love. The fact that both sentences are true in the situation represented by diagram II and that one is true and one false in the situation represented in diagram I shows that these sentences are not equivalent in meaning. The order or the quantifiers makes a difference if the quantifiers are mixed; that is, if both universal and existential quantifiers are included. In the case of pure quantifiers (all universal or all existential) the order does not make any difference.

It will already be apparent that a formal language for revealing the internal structure of propositions, to be called a *quantification language*, is of considerably greater complexity than the propositional language. Consequently there are more preliminaries to be covered before we can develop a technique for testing for validity arguments expressed in this language. Translation into the quantificational language (hereafter cited as QL) often requires a subtle grasp of the sense of English sentences and may require quite complex formulae in QL. One complication is that English sentences may involve ambiguities of *scope*. We have seen above that the order of the quantifiers can make a difference to the sense of formula. The difference between '$(\forall x) (\exists y) Lxy$' and '$(\exists y) (\forall x) Lxy$' can be best expressed by saying that '$(\forall x)$' has the larger scope in the first formula and the smaller scope in the latter formula. That is, in the first formula it governs '$(\exists y) Lxy$' and in the latter it governs only 'Lxy'. As we did in the case of PL (the propositional language) , we give later a precise definition of a well-formed formula and of the notion of scope. For the moment we use these notions informally. As a further example of how the scope of quantifiers and operators affects sense consider the formulae '$(\forall x)\ \neg Lxn$' and '$\neg(\forall x)Lxn$' where n is Icabod and 'Lxy' expresses the relation of liking. In the first formula the universal quantifier governs '$\neg Lxn$' and thus has larger scope that '$\neg$' which governs only 'Lxn' and *vice versa* in the second formula. The first says' Take anything in the domain you like, it does not like Icabod. If, on the other hand, the second is true things may not be so bad for Icabod. For it says that it is false that everyone likes Icabod. Thus it may be that some do like Icabod.

We note below some examples of ambiguities of scope that occur in English that can be disambiguated on translation into QL. The sentence 'Everyone in the next room is smoking or drinking' has an ambiguity of scope. It may be construed with the universal quantifier having large scope: Take anyone in the next room, he or she is smoking or drinking. The formalization would be '$(\forall x)\ (Rx \rightarrow (Sx\ v\ Dx))$' with a domain of persons and 'Rx' expressing 'x is in the next room', 'Sx' expressing 'x is smoking', 'Dx' expressing 'x is drinking'. On the other hand it may be construed with the disjunction operator having the larger scope: Everyone in the next room is drinking or everyone in the next room is smoking. In which case the formalization would be: $(\forall x)$ $(Rx \rightarrow Dx)\ v\ (\forall x)\ (Rx \rightarrow Sx)$.

The sentence 'Some people are mugged everyday' might mean: Take any day you like, on that day you can find some people who are mugged. Or, it might mean: You can find some people who are such that if one takes any day, they are mugged on that day. On the latter reading, with its perpetual victims, the existential quantifier 'some people' has the larger scope. On the former reading the universal quantifier 'everyday' has the larger scope. In formulating this sentence we need a domain containing persons and days for we are talking about both. Let 'Px' be 'x is a person' and letting 'Dx' be 'x is a day' and 'Mxy' be 'x is mugged on y'. The formulation on the first reading is: $(\forall x)\ (Dx \rightarrow (\exists y)$ $(Py\ \&\ Myx))$ and the formalization on the latter reading is: $(\exists y)$ $(Py\ \&\ (\forall x)\ (Dx \rightarrow Myx))$.

A fine example of ambiguity of scope is found in a remark of Keynes. Economists often defend their theories against contrary evidence by saying that their predictions will prove correct *in the long run*. Keynes retorted: In the long run we are all dead. This sentence has an ambiguity of scope. The person who asserts the sentence may have in mind the possibility of some holocaust that will obliterate forever the human race. In this case the existential quantifier has large scope: There is a time at which everyone is dead. Or, one might mean only that humans are mortal without asserting that there will ever be a time without any humans. In this case the universal quantifier has larger scope and the reading is: Take anyone you like, there is a time at which he or she is dead.

Examples are given below to illustrate some of the complexities involved in formalizing English sentences in *QL*. Further points will emerge through the exercises at the end of this chapter.

Example 5.2.1

Icabod likes a beautiful girl.

The word 'a' is ambiguous. It may mean a particular girl or it may be functioning as a disguised universal quantifier, i.e. Icabod may like any old beautiful girl. Letting 'n' stand for Icabod and 'Bx' be 'x is a beautiful girl' and 'Lxy' be 'x likes y', the formalization on the first reading is: $(\exists x)\,(Bx\ \&\ Lnx)$. On the second reading it is: $(\forall x)\,(Bx \rightarrow Lnx)$.

Example 5.2.2

Only men are feather-brained.

This says that if anything is feather-brained, it will turn out to be a man. The formalization using 'Mx' for 'x is a man' and 'Fx' for 'x is feather-brained' is: $(\forall x)\,(Fx \rightarrow Mx)$. Note the difference between this and the sentence 'All men are feather-brained' which is formalized as: $(\forall x)\,(Mx \rightarrow Fx)$.

Example 5.2.3

(a) If anyone is late, Icabod will be annoyed.

(b) If everyone is late, Icabod will be annoyed.

Let 'n' stand for Icabod and let 'Lx' be 'x is late' and 'Ax' be 'x

will be annoyed' and let the domain be some set of persons. (i) says that Icabod will be annoyed if even one person is late. (ii) represents him as perhaps more tolerant saying he will be annoyed if all are late. The formalization of (i) is: $(\forall x)$ $(Lx \rightarrow An)$. The formalization of (ii) is $\forall x Lx \rightarrow An$. 'Anyone' generally has a large scope, 'everyone' tends to have smaller scope as this formalization illustrates.

Example 5.2.4

The richer they are, the more he despises them.

'The more' does not refer to some mysterious thing, a particular 'more'. What is meant is that he despises one person more than another if the former is richer than the latter. A three-place relation '$Dxyz$' is needed to represent 'x despises y more than z'. There is no device in our formal language which plays the role of such pronouns as 'he' in this context. To cope we let 'n' be the name of the person who would be referred to by 'he' on the particular occasion of the use of the sentence which we have in mind. Taking as the domain the set of all persons and using 'Rxy' for 'x is richer than y' the formalization is: $(\forall x) (\forall y) (Rxy \rightarrow Dnxy)$.

EXERCISES

1 Formalize the following sentences in QL specifying your domain and the interpretation of the predicate letters:

(a) Icabod is unhappy.

(b) Someone is unhappy.

(c) Everyone is unhappy.

(d) Icabod hates Isabel.

(e) Icabod hates someone.

(f) Someone hates Icabod.

(g) Someone hates someone.

(h) Someone hates himself.

(i) Everyone hates himself.

(j) Icabod hates everyone.

(k) Everyone hates Icabod.

(l) Everyone hates everyone.

(m) Someone hates everyone.

(n) Everyone hates someone.

(o) All zemindars are powerful.

(p) No zemindar is powerful.

(q) Some zemindars are powerful.

(r) Some zemindars are not powerful.

(s) All powerful zemindars are lucky.

(t) Some zemindars hate Icabod.

(u) Each zemindar hates Icabod.

(v) Icabod hates lucky zemindars.

(w) Icabod hates only zemindars.

(x) Oxford is between Reading and Bristol.

(y) Some town is between Reading and Bristol.

(z) Some town is between some town and some town.

2 Formalize the following sentences in *QL* (specify a domain and the interpretation of the predicate letters). For any ambigous sentence give the alternative formalizations.

(a) Icabod likes a zemindar.

(b) Some zemindars are insulted everyday.

(c) Every zemindar rides a dragon.

(d) No zemindar likes a dragon.

(e) If everyone is late Icabod is mad.

(f) If anyone is late Icabod is mad.

(g) If someone's late Icabod is mad.

(h) If Icabod is mad then no one is late.

(i) If Icabod is mad then someone is late

(j) If someone is taller than I then I am smaller than someone.

(k) More expensive things are not always nicer.

(l)   Only fascists are more unscrupulous than mafioso.

(m) No one is more unscrupulous than a fascist.

(n)   One is a fascist if and only if one is unscrupulous.

(o)   Only if one is a fascist will one be despised.

(p)   The bigger they are the harder they fall.

(q)   A rolling stone gathers no moss.

(r)   All that glistens is not golden.

(s)   Every cloud has a silver lining.

(t)   Children should be seen and not heard.

(u)   All Cretans are liars.

(v)   Any devil you know is better than any devil you do not know.

(w) Farther pastures are greener.

(x)   Someone wins every lottery.

(y)   Any mother is someone's mother.

(z)   Some love all who love no one.

3 NATURAL DEDUCTION RULES FOR THE UNIVERSAL QUANTIFIER

The proper names of *QL* '*n*', '*m*', . . . denote some fixed individual in the domain of an interpretation. If every object in a domain has a certain property, any particular named object in the domain has that property. In view of this we want a rule which licenses us to pass from a formula of the form '$(\forall x)Ax$' to a formula '*An*' in which '*n*' replaces every occurrence of '*x*' in '*Ax*'. The conclusion '*An*' rests on whatever premises '$(\forall x)Ax$' rests on or on '$(\forall x)Ax$' itself if it is a premise. To illustrate this rule of *universal elimination*, cited as $\forall$E, consider the argument:

> Icabod is a person. All persons are mortal. Therefore, Icabod is mortal.

Using '*n*' for 'Icabod', '*Px*' for '*x* is a person' and '*Mx*' for '*x* is mortal' the formalization is: $Pn, (\forall x) (Px \rightarrow Mx) \vdash Mn$. Notice that we have used the syntactical sign for an argument. There is no analogue of truth-tables which can be used to establish arguments as valid (the reason for this will be given in Chapter 7). We will develop a system of natural deduction rules to be used in showing that arguments are valid. Hence we use ⊢ and not ⊨ in formulating the arguments at this stage. In Chapter 7 we show how to define ⊨ and cite the fact that one can show that ⊢ and ⊨ do match-up as in the propositional logic. However, to establish that a semantical sequent is correct we have in general to show that the corresponding syntactical sequent is correct.

The derivation of the above sequent is:

Prem	(1)	Pn	
Prem	(2)	$(\forall x)\,(Px \to Mx)$	
2	(3)	$Pn \to Mn$	2 ∀E
1,2	*(4)*	*Mn*	1,3 →E

In fact we need a stronger rule of universal elimination than so far given. For we frequently have to talk of an object in carrying out arguments even where it would be inappropriate to use a proper name. For instance, in elementary geometry one begins with some general truths about, say, all triangles and with the aim of establishing Pythagoras' theorem that the square on the hypotenuse of a right-angled triangle is equal to the sum of the squares on the other two sides, One says: Let R be a right-angled triangle. One then concludes that R has whatever properties the general truths ascribe to any such triangle. Reasoning about triangle R leads to the conclusion that the square on the hypotenuse of R equals the sum of the square on the other two sides. One then concludes that Pythagoras' theorem holds for any right-angled triangle.

In the above sort of argument, 'R' names an arbitrary right-angled triangle. It is not a proper name. There is no particular triangle the name of which is 'R'. 'R' is used to refer to any arbitrary triangle fitting the description and nothing more is assumed about R over and above its fitting the description. This style of reasoning is essential for displaying the validity of many arguments in our quantificational language and we use lower-case letters from the beginning of the alphabet 'a', 'b', 'c', . . . as what will be called *arbitrary names*.. The rule of ∀E licenses us to infer from any formula of the form $(\forall x)Ax$ any formula of the form At in which t, either an arbitrary or a proper name, replaces all occurrences of 'x' in Ax. The conclusion At rests on $(\forall x)Ax$ if that formula is itself a premise, otherwise it rests on whatever premises $(\forall x)Ax$ rests on. In citing the rule of $\forall$E we give the line at which $(\forall x)Ax$ occurs.

In the discussion of the propositional logic we used letters from the beginning of the alphabet, 'A', 'B', 'C' as formula variables. Unlike 'P', 'Q', 'R', etc. which represent particular propositions, the formula variables indicate only the form of a proposition. A proposition is obtained if the formula variable is replaced by any particular formula of the language. In a similar way we use 'A', 'B', 'C' in displaying the form of propositions in the predicate language. In the above paragraph 'A' can be replaced by any predicate from our language. In addition we use 't' as a term variable. It indicates that the formula contains a proper name or an arbitrary name.

In the sort of mathematical argument given above it is shown that a certain result holds with regard to the right-angled triangle R and it is then concluded that this result holds for any right-angled triangle. This latter conclusion is an instance of what will be called *universal introduction*. This rule licenses us to infer a universally quantified formula of the form $(\forall x)Ax$ from a formula of the form Aa where 'a' is an arbitrary name and x has replaced all occurrences of 'a' in A *subject to certain restrictions*. The restrictions are that Aa is not itself a premise and does not rest on any premise in which 'a' occurs. These restrictions mean that one is not entitled to infer that everything has the property Ax from Aa unless Aa was dervied from purely general premises. That is, if one is to derive a conclusion about everything one has to start with premises about everything. If one inferred $(\forall x)Ax$ from Aa where Aa was a premise or rested on premises containing 'a', it might be a peculiarity of a that it had the property expressed by Ax in which case some things would not have that property. To infer $(\forall x)Ax$ would give a false conclusion from true premises. The force and point of these restrictions will become clearer through a consideration of the following simple argument:

> All persons are mortal.
> All mortals have Angst.
> Therefore all persons have Angst.

Letting the domain be all persons and mortals and using 'Px' for 'x is a person', 'Mx' for 'x is mortal' and 'Cx' for 'x has Angst' the formalization is:

$$(\forall x)\,(Px \to Mx),\ (\forall x)\,(Mx \to Cx) \vdash (\forall x)\,(Px \to Cx)$$

The derivation is:

Prem	(1)	$(\forall x)\,(Px \to Mx)$	
Prem	(2)	$(\forall x)\,(Mx \to Cx)$	
Prem	(3)	Pa	
1	(4)	$Pa \to Ma$	1 $\forall$E
1,3	(5)	Ma	3,4 $\to$ E
2	(6)	$Ma \to Ca$	2 $\forall$E
1,2,3	(7)	Ca	5,6 $\to$ $\forall$E
1,2	(8)	$Pa \to Ca$	3,7 $\to$ 1
1,2	(9)	$(\forall x)\,(Px \to Cx)$	8 $\forall$I

We assume at line (3) that 'a' is an arbitrary P; 'a' does not occur in the purely general premises (1) and (2) which are used with Pa to derive Ca. We cannot apply $\forall$I until we reach a conclusion which does not depend on any premise in which the arbitrary name a occurs. We obtain such a line by a step of $\to$ I. In citing $\forall$I we give the line to which it is applied. A fully precise characterization of the rules for the universal quantifiers are given in the following clauses:

Universal Elimination ($\forall E$)

> From a formula of the form $(\forall x)Ax$, one can infer At where t is an arbitrary name or a proper name which replaces all occurrences of 'x' in Ax. At rests on whatever premises $(\forall x)Ax$ rests on and will rest on $(\forall x)Ax$ if that is itself a premise. In citing the rule the number of the line of $(\forall x)Ax$ is given.

Universal Introduction (∀I)

> From a formula of the form Aa one can infer $(\forall x)Ax$ provided that Aa is not itself a premise and does not depend on any premises in which 'a' occurs. In $(\forall x)Ax$, 'x' replaces all occurrences of 'a' in Aa. $(\forall x)Ax$ rests on whatever premises Aa rests on. In citing ∀I the number of the line containing Aa is given.

A number of examples are given below to illustrate the rules for the universal quantifier.

Example 5.3.1

Argument

> Everyone is happy or rich. Icabod isn't happy so he must be rich.

Interpretation

> Domain: the set of living persons
> n: Icabod
> Hx : x is happy
> Rx : x is rich

Formalization

> $(\forall x)(Hx \lor Rx), \; \neg Hn \vdash Rn$

Derivation

Prem	(1)	$(\forall x)(Hx \lor Rx)$	
Prem	(2)	$\neg Hn$	
1	(3)	$Hn \lor Rn$	1∀E
1,2	(4)	Rn	2,3 SIS ($\neg P, P \lor Q \vdash Q$)

Note that we have used a propositional logic sequent. QL is to be regarded as an extension of PL and thus contains the theorems and sequents of PL. These may be appealed to in carrying our derivations in QL. Any formula of QL may be substituted for the propositional letters of PL. This means that we have to modify our definition of a *wff* of PL which will be done in the next chapter.

Example 5.3.2

Argument

> Nobody is happy. Those who aren't rich are happy. Therefore everybody is rich.

Interpretation

> Domain: set of living persons
> Hx: x is happy
> Rx: x is rich

Formalization

> $(\forall x)\ \neg Hx, (\forall x)\ (\ \neg Rx \rightarrow Hx) \vdash (\forall x)Rx$

Derivation

Prem	(1)	$(\forall x)\ \neg Hx$	
Prem	(2)	$(\forall x)\ (\ \neg Rx \rightarrow Hx)$	
1	(3)	$\neg Ha$	1∀E
2	(4)	$\neg Ra \rightarrow Ha$	2∀E
1,2	(5)	$\neg\ \neg Ra$	3,4 SIS ($\neg Q, P \rightarrow Q \vdash \neg P$)
1,2	(6)	Ra	5 ¬E
1,2	(7)	$(\forall x)Rx$	6 ∀I

The result at line (6), Ra, rests on no premises in which a occurs hence we can apply the rule ∀I to obtain $(\forall x)Rx$.

Example 5.3.3

Argument

> If it rains, everyone will be unhappy. So if it rains, Icabod will not be happy.

Interpretation

> Domain: the set of living persons
> P: it rains
> Hx: x is happy
> n: Icabod

Formalization

$$P \rightarrow (\forall x) \ \neg Hx \vdash P \rightarrow \neg Hn$$

Derivation

Prem	(1)	$P \rightarrow (\forall x) \ \neg Hx$	
Prem	(2)	P	
1,2	(3)	$(\forall x) \ \neg Hx$	$1,2, \rightarrow E$
1,2	(4)	$\neg Hn$	$3\forall E$
1	(5)	$P \rightarrow \neg Hn$	$2,4 \rightarrow I$

Notice that the validity of this argument does not depend on the internal of the premise 'It rains' and consequently we formalize it with the propositional letter P.

EXERCISES

1 Derive the following sequents:

(a) $(\forall x) \ (Fx \ v \ Gx) \dashv \vdash (\forall x) \ (Gx \ v \ Fx)$

(b) $(\forall x) \ (Fx \ \& \ Gx) \vdash (\forall x)Fx$

(c) $(\forall x) \ (Fx \ \& \ Gx) \dashv \vdash (\forall x)Fx \ \& \ (\forall x)Gx$

(d) $(\forall x) \ (Fx \rightarrow Gx), \ (\forall x)Fx \vdash (\forall x)Gx$

(e) $(\forall x) \ (Fx \ v \ Gx), \ (\forall x) \ \neg Fx \vdash (\forall x)Gx$

2 Formalize the following arguments and derive the resulting sequent:

(a) All students are poor. Blessed are the poor. So students are blessed.

(b) All students are poor. Therefore no one rich is a student.

(c) All Balliol student are sympatico. Reagan is not sympatico. Therefore he isn't a Balliol student.

(d) You aren't a doctor. For no doctor is enthusiastic and you are enthusiastic.

(e) Philosophers are wise but mad. So no one who is sane is a philosopher.

(f) Any philosopher is wiser than any politician. Heidegger is a philosopher and Thatcher is a politician. That means that Heidegger is wiser than Thatcher.

(g) Any Autralian is taller than any Norwegian. Bruce is an Australian. Therefore all Norwegians are smaller than Bruce.

(h) All persons are mortal. So no immortal is a person.

(i) Some politicians are fools. No fool is a philosopher. Therefore some politicians are not philosophers.

(j) Politicians are foolish or unintelligent. Some politicians are intelligent. So some must be foolish.

(k) I think. Any thinking thing exists. Therefore I exist.

(l) The meek shall inherit the earth. Balliol students are definitely not meek. Therefore none of them will inherit the earth.

4 NATURAL DEDUCTION RULES FOR THE EXISTENTIAL QUANTIFIER

If 'n' is the name of an object and if it is true that n has the property expressed by 'Fx', i.e. if Fn, it is true that something has the property expressed by 'Fx', i.e. $(\exists x)Fx$. Further, if it is true for an arbitrary name 'a' that Fa, it is true that $(\exists x)Fx$. These inferences are licensed by the rule of *existential introduction*, $\exists$I. It permits the derivation of $(\exists x)Ax$ from At where 't' is a proper name or an arbitrary name and x replaces *some or all* occurrences of 't' in At. $(\exists x)Ax$ will rest on whatever premises At rests on and rests on At if At is itself a premise. In citing the rule of $\exists$I the number of the line to which it is applied is given as illustrated below.

Example 5.4.1

Argument

Icabod is flippant. Those who are flippant are dispensable. Therefore, someone is dispensable.

Interpretation

> Domain: set of living persons
> n: Icabod
> Fx: x is flippant
> Dx: x is dispensable

Formalization

> $Fn, (\forall x)(Fx \rightarrow Dx) \vdash (\exists x)Dx$

Derivation

Prem	(1)	Fn	
Prem	(2)	$(\forall x)(Fx \rightarrow Dx)$	
2	(3)	$Fn \rightarrow Dn$	2 $\forall$E
1,2	(4)	Dn	1,3 $\rightarrow$ E
1,2	(5)	$(\exists x)Dx$	4 $\exists$I

Example 5.4.2

Argument

> Everyone is happy and loveable. So someone is loveable.

Interpretation

> Domain: set of living persons
> Hx: x is happy
> Lx: x is loveable

Formalization

> $(\forall x)(Hx \ \& \ Lx) \vdash (\exists x)Lx$

Derivation

Prem	(1)	$(\forall x)(Hx \ \& \ Lx)$	
1	(2)	$Ha \ \& \ La$	1$\forall$E
1	(3)	La	2 &E
1	(4)	$(\exists x)Lx$	3 $\exists$I

Note that the rule of $\exists$I allows the replacement of either some or all occurrences of a name (proper or arbitrary). This contrasts with rule of $\forall$I which requires that *all* occurrences of a name 't' be replaced in *At* in obtaining $(\forall x)Ax$. Using $\exists I$, given a premise that Icabod loves himself, formalized as '*Lnn*' we can infer any of the following:

$(\exists x)Lxx$: Someone loves himself

$(\exists x)Lnx$: Icabod loves someone

$(\exists x)Lxn$: Someone loves Icabod

$(\exists x)\,(\exists y)Lxy$: Someone loves someone

If it was permitted to replace only some occurrences of a name in using $\forall I$ it would be possible to derive the formalization of the following invalid argument:

Argument

Everyone loves themselves. Therefore everyone loves everyone.

Interpretation

Domain: a set of narcissistic egoists

Lxy: *x* loves *y*

Formalization

$(\forall x)Lxx \vdash (\forall x)\,(\forall y)Lxy$

Derivation

Prem	(1)	$(\forall x)Lxx$	
1	(2)	Laa	$1\forall E$
1	(3)	$(\forall y)Lay$	$2\forall I$
1	(4)	$(\forall x)\,(\forall y)Lxy$	$3\forall I$

The requirement that all occurrences of a name be replaced by a variable in appending a universal quantifier was violated in the above 'proof' at line (3) allowing the derivation of an invalid sequent.

The final rule for quantifiers is *Existential Elimination*, $\exists E$. In presenting the mechanics of this rule which are not particularly easy to grasp we will consider the following example.

Example 5.4.3.

Argument

> Someone is happy. The happy are lucky. Therefore some-one is lucky.

Interpretation

> Domain: a set of living persons
> Hx: x is happy
> Lx: x is lucky

Formalization

> $(\exists x)Hx, (\forall x)(Hx \to Lx) \vdash (\exists x)Lx$

Suppose that the domain contains only two persons named 'n' and 'm'. Knowing that, suppose we decided to use instead of the premise '$(\exists x)Hx$' the premise: $Hn \vee Hm$. In this case the formalization would be: $Hn \vee Hm, (\forall x)(Hx \to Lx) \vdash (\exists x)Lx$.

(see opposite page)

If we are dealing with a domain with a finite number of objects having the names 'n'_1' 'n'_2', . . . 'n'_n' we could use as a premise '$Fn_1 \vee Fn_2 \vee . . . Fn_n$' instead of '$(\exists x)Fx$'. However, while there is this analogy between disjunction and existential quantification, we cannot always use the former in preference to the latter. For we need to be able to deal with a situation in which there are an infinite number of objects in the domain. This cannot be dealt with as above for we would never be finished writing down the disjunction! We need a strategy for dealing with all cases uniformly, which can be developed if we notice that there is no significant difference in the sub-derivations in the two branches of the derivation given above. The only difference is in the name that occurs. If we had used a disjunction ascribing the property to a larger number of object, say, $Hm \vee Hn \vee Ho$, nothing would have been changed save the names in each sub-derivation. If we can carry out such a derivation with a name, 'n', we can carry it out with any other name. With this in mind we return to the sequent $(\exists x)Hx, (\forall x)(Hx \to Lx) \vdash (\exists x)Lx$. Under the assump-

Derivation

Prem	(1)	$Hm \lor Hn$	
Prem	(2)	$(\forall x)(Hx \to Lx)$	
Prem	(3)	Hm	
2	(4)	$Hm \to Lm$	2$\forall$E
2,3	(5)	Lm	3,4 $\to$ E
2,3	(6)	$(\exists x)Lx$	5$\exists$I
Prem	(7)	Hn	
2	(8)	$Hn \to Ln$	2$\forall$E
2,7	(9)	Ln	7,8 $\to$ E
2,7	(10)	$(\exists x)Lx$	9$\exists$I
1,2	(11)	$(\exists x)Lx$	2,3,6,7,10 $\lor$E

tion that $(\exists x)Hx$ we know that there is at least one object which satisfies the predicate 'Hx'. That is, there is some object which could be named and which has the property expressed by 'Hx'. Let us suppose that Ha where 'a' is an arbitrary name. Obviously we can use the derivation on one of the sub-branches to derive $(\exists x)Lx$ from Ha. If, as is the case, the derivation of that conclusion does not rest on any premise containing an occurrence of 'a', say, La we have arrived at the conclusion without assuming anything about a save that it satisfies Hx. We have in effect let 'a' be a temporary name of a typical satisfier of Hx. If it follows from the assumption that Ha that $(\exists x)Lx$, then it follows from $(\exists x)Hx$ that $(\exists x)Lx$ given that the derivation of $(\exists x)Lx$ from Ha does not depend on any premises containing an occurrence of 'a' save the premise Ha. This is the rule of *Existential Elimination* $\exists$E which states:

> Given that the formula Aa is obtained by replacing all occurrences of 'x' in Ax by 'a', if a conclusion C which does not contain an occurrence of a can be derived from Aa not resting on any premises containing an occurrence of 'a' (save Aa itself), the rule of Existential Elimination licenses the inference of C resting on the premise $(\exists x)Ax$ and any other premises on which C rests in the derivation of C from Aa excepting Aa. In citing the rule, we give the line at which $(\exists x)Ax$ occurs, the line at which Aa is assumed and the line at which C is derived.

Using the rule the derivation of the sequent given above is:

Prem	(1)	$(\exists x)\,Hx$	
Prem	(2)	$(\forall x)\,(Hx \rightarrow Lx)$	
Prem	(3)	Ha	
2	(4)	$Ha \rightarrow La$	2$\forall$E
2,3	(5)	La	3,4 $\rightarrow$ E
2,3	(6)	$(\exists x)Lx$	5$\exists$1
1,2	(7)	$(\exists x)Lx$	1,3,6$\exists$E

In assuming Ha we are taking a to be a typical satisfier of 'Hx', and to ensure that it is typical and not special we are not allowed to make any further assumptions concerning a on which the conclusion '$(\exists x)Lx$' would depend. We can see that the derivation of '$(\exists x)Lx$' from 'Ha' is structurally similar to each sub-derivation that would be obtained if we had used as a premise a disjunction of the form: $Hn_1 \ v \ Hn_2 \ v \ . \ . \ . \ v \ Hn_n$. Even if we did admit (as we do not) infinite disjunctions, any sub-derivation from any one of the infinite number of disjuncts would be structurally the same. This analogy between existential quantification and disjunction can thus be seen as a partial rationale for the rule of Existential Elimination. The derivation of '$(\exists x)Lx$' from 'Ha' is typical of what would have happened if we went through each disjunct of the possibly infinite disjunction. Seeing this we see that there would be no point in this possibly infinite repetition and we encapsulate this fact in the rule of Existential Elimination.

It remains to be illustrated what would go wrong if we did not require that the conclusion derived from a formula of the form Aa did not contain any occurrence of a. Without it we could derive the following invalid sequent:

$(\exists x)Fx \vdash (\forall x)Fx.$

Prem	(1)	$(\exists x)Fx$	
Prem	(2)	Fa	
1	(3)	Fa	1,2,2 $\exists$E
1	(4)	$(\forall x)Fx$	3$\forall$I

Example 5.4.4

Argument

Somebody is happy. Everybody is unhappy or busy. Therefore someone is busy.

Interpretation

Domain: set of living persons
Hx: x is happy
Bx: x is busy

Formalization

$(\exists x)Hx, (\forall x)(\neg Hx \ v \ Bx) \vdash (\exists x)Bx$

Derivation

Prem	(1)	$(\exists x)Hx$	
Prem	(2)	$(\forall x)(\neg Hx \lor Bx)$	
Prem	(3)	Ha	
2	(4)	$\neg Ha \lor Ba$	2∀E
2,3	(5)	Ba	3,4 SIS (P, $\neg P \lor Q \vdash Q$)
2,3	(6)	$(\exists x)Bx$	5∃I
1,2	(7)	$(\exists x)Bx$	1,3,6∃E

Example 5.4.5

Argument

All lions are fierce. Some lions do not drink Pernod.
Therefore some fierce creatures don't drink Pernod.

Interpretation

Domain: animals
Lx: x is a lion
Fx: x is fierce

Formalization

$(x)(Lx \to Fx), (\exists x)(Lx \,\&\, \neg Px) \vdash (\exists x)(Fx \,\&\, \neg Px)$

Derivation

Prem	(1)	$(\forall x)(Lx \to Fx)$	
Prem	(2)	$(\exists x)(Lx \,\&\, \neg Px)$	
Prem	(3)	$La \,\&\, \neg Pa$	
1	(4)	$La \to Fa$	1∀E
3	(5)	La	3 &E
1,3	(6)	Fa	4,5 → E
3	(7)	$\neg Pa$	3 &E
1,3	(8)	$Fa \,\&\, \neg Pa$	6,7 &I
1,3	(9)	$(\exists x)(Fx \,\&\, \neg Px)$	8∃I
1,3	(10)	$(\exists x)(Fx \,\&\, \neg Px)$	2,3,9∃E

Example 5.4.6

Argument

Somebody is happy. So it is false that everybody is unhappy.

Interpretation

Domain: set of living persons
Hx: *x* is happy

Formalization

$(\exists x)Hx \vdash \neg(\forall x) \neg Hx$

Derivation

Prem	(1)	$(\exists x)Hx$	
Prem	(2)	$(\forall x) \neg Hx$	
Prem	*(3)*	*Ha*	
2	(4)	$\neg Ha$	2∀E
2,3	(5)	$Ha \,\&\, \neg Ha$	3,4 &I
3	(6)	$\neg(\forall x) \neg Hx$	2,5 ¬I
1,3	(7)	$\neg(\forall x) \neg Hx$	1,3,6∃E

EXERCISES

1 Formalize the following arguments and derive the resulting sequent:

(a) If someone is happy, Reagan is happy. Therefore everyone is happy.

(b) No fossil can be crossed in love. An oyster can be crossed in love. Therefore no oyster is a fossil.

(c) Every eagle flies. Some pigs do not fly. Therefore some pigs are not eagles.

(d) Any politician is a rogue. Unfortunately there are some politicians so there are some rogues.

(e) All politicians are dispensable. Therefore nothing is a politician and indispensable.

(f) Zemindars are powerful. Therefore anything that is not powerful is not a zemindar.

(g) If it rains, the apples are happy. If it snows the children are happy. It rains or it snows. Hence something or somebody is happy.

(h) Nobody likes a fool. Icabod is a fool. Therefore nobody likes Icabod.

(i) All Canadians are boring. Someone is not boring. Therefore not everyone is Canadian.

(j) It is false that some are neither boring nor rich. Hence someone is not rich because someone is not boring.

(k) Someone loves everyone. Therefore someone loves Icabod.

(l) Someone is despicable or falsely maligned. No one is despicable. Therefore someone is falsely maligned.

(m) If someone is taller than someone then the latter is not taller than the former. Someone is taller than someone. So it is false that everyone is taller than everyone.

(n) There are children. Any child has a parent. So obviously no one lacks a parent.

2 Derive the following sequents:

(a) $(\forall x)Fx \dashv \vdash (\forall y)Fy$

(b) $(\exists x)Fx \dashv \vdash (\exists y)Fy$

(c) $(\forall x)(\forall y)Fxy \dashv \vdash (\forall y)(\forall x)Fxy$

(d) $(\exists x)(\exists y)Fxy \dashv \vdash (\exists y)(\exists x)Fxy$

(e) $(\exists x)(\forall y)Fxy \vdash (\forall y)(\exists x)Fxy$

(f) $(\forall x)(Fx \rightarrow Gx) \vdash (\forall x)\neg Gx \rightarrow (\forall x)\neg Fx$

(g) $(\forall x)(Fx \rightarrow Gx) \vdash (\exists x)\neg Gx \rightarrow (\exists x)\neg Fx$

3 Derive the following sequents:

(a) $(\forall x)Fx \dashv \vdash \neg(\exists x)\neg Fx$

(b) $(\exists x)Fx \dashv \vdash \neg(\forall x)\neg Fx$

(c) $(\forall x)(P \rightarrow Fx) \dashv \vdash P \rightarrow (\forall x)Fx$

(d) $(\forall x)(P \,\&\, Fx) \dashv \vdash P \,\&\, (\forall x)Fx$

(e) $(\forall x)(P \lor Fx) \dashv \vdash P \lor (\forall x)Fx$

(f) $(\exists x)(P \lor Fx) \dashv \vdash P \lor (\exists x)Fx$

(g) $(\exists x)(P \& Fx) \dashv \vdash P \& (\exists x)Fx$

(h) $(\exists x)(Fx \to P) \dashv \vdash (\forall x)Fx \to P$

(i) $(\forall x)(Fx \to P) \dashv \vdash (\exists x)Fx \to P$

4 Formalize the following arguments. If the argument is not valid as it stands consider whether some premise might reasonably be taken to be implicit. If the resulting argument is valid derive the sequent.

(a) All events have some event as their cause. Causes come before their effects in time. Therefore there was no first event.

(b) My hand exists. My hand is physical. Hence not everything which exists is mental.

(c) I see mountains and streams. Everything I see is an idea. Therefore mountains and streams are but ideas.

(d) Fresh strawberries are better than oranges. Oranges are better than radishes. Therefore, fresh strawberries are better than radishes.

(e) Nothing is better than God. God is better than Icabod. So, obviously, nothing is better than Icabod.

(f) Only an idea is like an idea. I have an idea which is like Icabod. So Icabod is an idea.

(g) There is no legitimate idea without a corresponding impression. There is no impression corresponding to the idea of necessary connexion. So the idea of necessary connexion is not legitimate.

(h) No moment is before itself. There is a moment before any moment. Some event happens every moment. Consequently, there was no first event.

(i) Every person has a soul. No animal has a soul. Therefore no animal is a person.

(j) If a table is red then any part of its surface is red. Atoms are part of the surface of any table. Thus some atoms are red.

(k) All conscious beings are in time. Anything in time is subject to change. So if God is conscious he is not immutable.

CHAPTER 6
Logical analysis

1 IDENTITY

Consider the following sentences:

> Jekyll is Hyde.
> Cicero is Tully.
> Everest is Chomolongolinga.

Each of these expresses an identity. Each asserts that the object denoted by one name is the same object as the one denoted by the other name. We obtained predicates by replacing names in indicative sentences by variables. Replacing 'Jekyll' by 'x' and 'Hyde' by 'y' we obtain the predicate expression 'x is y'. The 'is' here is what we will call the 'is' of *identity*. It expresses the property of *being identical to* and is to be contrasted with the occurrence of 'is' in sentences such as 'Icabod is happy' where the 'is' is the 'is' of *predication* and expresses the fact that Icabod possesses the property of happiness. It does not say that Icabod is identical to happiness. We can greatly increase the expressive power of our language if we include this predicate. We might introduce, say, 'Ixy' to express the property of identity. However, in view of the special role that this predicate will play we use the symbol '$=$', writing the predicate as '$x = y$'. Replacing the variables by names will give sentences which may or may not be true. For instance, replacing 'x' by 'Reagan' and 'y' by 'Mrs Thatcher' we would obtain the false identity statement: Reagan is Mrs Thatcher. Making the appropriate substitutions we can obtain the true identity statements with which we began.

Many interesting identity statements involve *definite descriptions*. A definite description is an expression formed by concatenating a predicate with the word 'the' as in 'the happiest man' or 'the clever student'. Examples of identity statements involving definite descriptions are:

> Icabod is the strangest student in Balliol.
> The President is Reagan, alas.
> The square root of 25 is 5.

One might introduce into our language a special symbol for the word 'the' as it functions in definite descriptions. However, it turns out that using a device of Russell's we can express definite descriptions using the quantifiers and the symbol for identity. To see how this works we reflect on what has to be true for a sentence containing a definite description to be true. For this purpose consider the sentence 'The professor is mad' uttered at a party. First, there has to be a professor present. If there is no professor it cannot be true that the professor is mad. Further, there cannot be more than one professor present. The word 'the' carries the implication of uniqueness. Definite descriptions are used to pick out unique objects to talk about. We cannot success-fully pick out an object using such a phrase if there are several objects satisfying the description following 'the'. For instance, in the context we are imagining the phrase 'the student' would fail to pick out a particular person to talk about if there were several students present. For a sentence such as 'The professor is mad' to be true, then, there has to be one and only one professor and he has to be mad.

One qualification has to be made. When someone uses a definite description he or she will have in mind some particular domain. In the above example the domain consists of the persons at the party. When we speak of one and only one professor we mean not that there is only one professor in the entire world (happy thought) but that there is only one professor in the domain. Let 'Px' express the property of being a professor and let 'Mx' express the property of being mad. The sentence '$(\exists x)Px$' says that there is a professor. The sentence '$(\forall x)(\forall y)(Px \, \& \, Py \to x = y)$' says that there is at most one professor. For using our pedantic reading we render it as: Take anything you like, x, take anything you like, y, if x and y are professors then x is y. If you have found a professor and seek to find another professor, anything that turns out to be a professor will turn out to be the one you already have. Consider the sentence '$(\forall x)(Px \rightarrow Mx)$'. This says that anything that is a professor is mad. Taking the conjunction of these three sentences gives '$(\exists x)(Px)$ & $(\forall x)(Px$ & $Py \rightarrow x = y)$ & $(\forall x)(Px \rightarrow Mx)$'. The conjunction says that there is at least one professor and that there is at most one professor and that any professor is mad. In view of the first two conjuncts, the third has the force of saying that the one and only one professor is mad. Having given this formulation we can see that it can be replaced by the terser formalization: $(\exists x)(Px$ & $(\forall y)(Py \rightarrow x = y)$ & $Mx)$. Reading this pedantically we have: you can find a professor and take anything you like, if it is a professor it is the one you already have and it is mad. In any domain in which the sentence 'The professor is mad' is true, the formalization under the given interpretation will be true for that domain. Hence we will use this technique (known as Russell's theory of descriptions) in formalizing sentences containing the definite description.

In the identity sentence 'Icabod is the mad Balliol student' the one and only one mad Balliol student is said to have the property of being identical to Icabod. We can use Russell's technique for handling definite descriptions to formulate this as follows where 'Mx' is used for 'x is mad', 'Bx' is used for 'x is a Balliol student' and the domain is students: $(\exists x)((Mx$ & $Bx)$ & $(\forall y)$ $(My$ & $By \rightarrow x = y)$ & $(x = n))$. This says that you can find a mad Balliol student and only one such and that he is Icabod where Icabod is denoted by 'n'. The above procedure enables us to express definite descriptions within our predicate language without having to introduce a special symbol for the word 'the'. However, care must be taken in applying Russell's theory of descriptions in effecting translations from English. For not all occurrences of the word 'the' indicate a definite description. For instance, if someone says that the whale is a mammal it is unlikely that he wishes to say that there is one and only one whale and that it is a mammal. In which case applying Russell's theory would be inappropriate. It is much more likely that he means that *all* whales are mammals in which case the 'the' is functioning as a disguised universal quantifier.

Example 6.1.1

Icabod's father is unhappy.

Interpretation

Domain: living persons
n: Icabod
Fxy: *x* is a father of *y*
Hx: *x* is happy

Formalization

$(\exists x)(Fxn \mathbin{\&} (\forall y)(Fyn \rightarrow x = y) \mathbin{\&} \neg Hx)$

The phrase 'Icabod's father' is idiomatic for 'the father of Icabod'. The formalization says that Icabod has a unique father and that he, the father, has the property of not being happy.

Example 6.1.2

The Prime Minister is Margaret Thatcher.

Interpretation

Domain: inhabitants of the British Isles excluding Eire
n: Margaret Thatcher
Px: *x* is a Prime Minister

Formalization

$(\exists x)(Px \mathbin{\&} (\forall y)(Py \rightarrow x = y) \mathbin{\&} (x = n))$

In this example the definite description, The Prime Minister, picks out a person who is said to be identical to Margaret Thatcher. That is, the sentence asserts that the unique thing which is Prime Minister has the property of being identical to Margaret Thatcher.

Example 6.1.3

The winner is the professor.

Interpretation

Domain: group of students and a professor
Wx: *x* is a winner
Px: *x* is a professor

Formalization

$$(\exists x)\,(Wx\ \&\ (\forall y)(Wy \to x = y)\ \&$$
$$(\exists z)(Pz\ \&\ (\forall y)(Py \to x = y)\ \&\ (x = z)))$$

In this case we formalize the thought that there is a unique winner and the thought that there is a unique professor. The unique professor is then said to be identical to the unique winner. Notice that we can re-use the 'y' in the second uniqueness clause because the scope of the first universal quantifier in 'y' is terminated by a bracket. Of course we could have used a different variable for the second uniqueness clause had we wished.

The first of our two rules of identity, *identity introduction*, says that for any proper name, say, 'n' in our language that $n = n$ or that for any arbitrary name in our language, say 'a' that $a = a$. This seems unobjectionable. How could n fail to be identical to itself? However, some qualification is required. The rule as stated would license us to write for any proper name 'a', '$n = n$' as a line of a proof not resting on any premise and not being itself a premise. Similarly for any arbitrary names, 'a', we could write '$a = a$' as a line not resting on any premise and not being itself a premise. This rule enables us to prove as a theorem that $n = n$ or that $a = a$ for any proper name 'n' or any arbitrary name 'a'. Since theorems are intended to be logical truths, if our logic is well-designed the sentence '$n = n$' will have to come out true no matter what domain we select and no matter what object in that domain we take 'n' to designate. Given the rule of identity introduction, hereafter cited as =I, we can construct the following proof:

(1) $n = n$ =I
(2) $(\exists x)(x = n)$ 1 $\exists$I

Line 2 rests on no premises. It is a theorem which states that there is something which is identical to n. Suppose that we allowed into our language a name which was not a name for anything. In which case we could use the argument above to prove that the name was a name for something after all and, indeed, that it was a name for something as a matter of logic! This reveals the restriction required. In our rule of identity introduction we have to restrict attention to names that are names for things. No interpretation will be allowed to be legitimate unless it gives the names being used a denotation within the domain being considered. Of course in English not all names are required to have a designation in all domains. For instance, in the domain of living animals 'Cerberus' has no designation. And in the domain of living persons 'Napoleon' has no designation. We will consider below how to handle in our formal language, names in English which do not have a designation.

The second rule of identity, called *identity elimination* ($=$E), states with qualifications that if $n = m$ ($a = b$), then whatever is true of n is true of m (is true of a is true of b). This principle is plausible for it amounts to saying that if an object has a property it does not matter which name for the object one uses in saying that it has the property. It is one of a pair of principles of identity associated with Leibniz (1646–1716). However, it might well have been associated with Shakespeare (1564–1616) who said, truly, that a rose by any other name smells as sweet. If you call your rose 'Henry' and if it is true that Henry smells sweet, and if you were to introduce a new name 'George' for that same rose, 'George smells sweet' will be true.

Some qualifications are required in the rule as the following example illustrates. Suppose that Cicero and Tully are names for the same person. Icabod believes that Cicero was a philosopher. Icabod does not believe that Cicero was Tully. He thinks that Tully is the name of some man of action who despised philosophy. It is then true that Icabod believes that Cicero was a philosopher and false that Icabod believes that Tully was a philosopher. But the latter can be obtained from the former by applying the principle of identity elimination. To see this we note that by removing the name, 'Cicero', in 'Icabod believes that Cicero was a philosopher' gives us a predicate 'Icabod believes that x was a philosopher', a predicate expressing a property which applies to Cicero. But since Cicero = Tully, the principle of identity elimination, if used without qualification, would license us to infer that that property applied to Tully. But it does not. Icabod, we imagine, militantly denies that he believes that Tully was a philosopher.

Philosophers and logicians do not see this sort of counter-example as providing a reason for simply rejecting the rule of $=$E outright. For there is something systematic about the counter-examples and there is general agreement on which types of case do generate exceptions. There is, however, considerable disagreement when one tries to characterize the special cases and to explain what it is about those cases that make them exceptions.

One important class of exceptions is generated by what have been called 'propositional attitude' expressions. These include: _ believes that _, _ fears that _, _ hopes that _, _ wishes that _, _ sees that _, _ thinks that _, _ imagines that _. The term 'propositional attitude' is used because many philosophers regard these expressions as conveying an attitude a person can have to a proposition. For instance, Icabod hopes that Isabel will win the lottery. One might describe Icabod as having the attitude to the proposition that Isabel will win the lottery of hoping it to be true. Whether this is the best way to regard such expressions is a controversial matter and we use the expression without implying acceptance of this construal. To further illustrate the failure of $=$E in the case of propositional attitudes consider the following situations.

Icabod knows of Dr Jekyll as a kindly and skilful doctor. Many times he has expressed the sincere hope that Dr Jekyll would agree to be his doctor. In fact Dr Jekyll is Mr Hyde. Icabod knows of Mr Hyde as a cruel and deranged incompetent. He has said he would hope never to have anything to do with such a person as Mr Hyde. If we applied $=$E to the truth that Icabod hopes that Dr Jekyll will become his doctor we obtain the falsehood: Icabod hopes that Mr Hyde will become his doctor.

Suppose Icabod is learning geometry at which he is particularly inept. In a class 'a' is introduced as the name for the hypotenuse of a right-angled triangle. Icabod realizes that $a = a$ (he has mastered the rule of $=$I if not much geometry). In fact $a = \sqrt{b_2 + c_2}$ by Pythagoras' theorem. But if we substituted $\sqrt{b_2 + c_2}$ for a in the truth 'Icabod realizes that $a = a$' we would generate a false conclusion; namely, 'Icabod realizes that $a = \sqrt{b_2 + c_2}$'. In this example we have considered substituting for a name 'a' an expression '$\sqrt{b_2 + c_2}$' which is in fact a definite description. It means: the square root of the sum of the squares of *b* and *c*. Any two expressions (names and/or definite descriptions) that refer to the same thing are said to be 'co-referring'. The basic principle of =E in English would license the substitution for a referring term by a co-referring expression. However, we will restrict the formulation to one in terms of names only. For we will be using Russell's theory of definite descriptions to dispense with phrases of the form: The F. See below for illustrations.

In addition to propositional attitude expressions, expressions for modalities also generate counter-examples to =*E*. The primary examples of modal expressions are: It is possible that _, it is impossible that _, it is necessary that _. The failure of =E in the case of modalities is illustrated in the following examples:

> It is necessarily true that 9 = 9.
> 9 = the number of planets.
> Therefore, it is necessarily true that 9 = the number of planets.

The premises are true but the conclusion false. For it might well have been that there were more than 9 or less than 9 planets.

> It could have been that Harold Wilson is the Prime Minister of England.
> The Prime Minister is Margaret Thatcher.
> Therefore, it could have been that Harold Wilson is Margaret Thatcher.

In this example the phrase 'could have been' expresses a kind of possibility, a possibility which we can easily imagined having been realized (politics being the fickle business that it is). The idea that Harold Wilson might be Margaret Thatcher is certainly false. The substitution of the co-referring expression 'Margaret Thatcher' for 'The Prime Minister' is thus seen to take us from a truth to a falsehood.

Sentences involving time may also generate failures of =E. Consider the sentence 'The Master of Balliol was in love with Florence Nightingale'. Benjamin Jowett, the famous nineteenth-century Master of Balliol, was a close friend of Florence

Nightingale and with perhaps a little bit of licence we can imagine that it was true that he was in love with her. At the present time the Master is Anthony Kenny. Thus we have a true identity: The Master of Balliol is Anthony Kenny. Substituting 'Anthony Kenny' for 'The Master of Balliol' in the true sentence above gives: Anthony Kenny was in love with Florence Nightingale. This has to be false. For Florence Nightingale was deceased long before Anthony Kenny was even born.

We have illustrated some of the types of case which produce a failure of =E. To attempt to give a systematic characterization of all types of counter-example to =E would take us beyond the scope of this work. Instead we will simply define a proposition to be *extensional* just in case it does not provide a counter-example to =E. We restrict the application of our logic to extensional propositions. No sentence which could give rise to a failure of extensionality (that is, a failure of =E) is to be represented in our logic.

Non-extensional propositions also generate problems with the existential quantifier. The rule of ∃I allows the inference of $(\exists x)(Fx)$ from the premise *Fn*, resting on whatever *Fn* rests on. Consider the non-extensional sentence: I believe Icabod is a spy. Perhaps there is some real person, Icabod, whom I believe to be a spy. Or perhaps I am even more deluded and believe in the existence of Icabod when in fact he is a product of my imagination. Applying ∃I in replacing 'Icabod' gives an ambiguity of scope which reflects these two possibilities. 'I believe someone is a spy' might mean either:

1 There is someone whom I believe to be a spy.
2 I believe there is someone who is a spy.

The former is true only if there is some real person and I believe that real person to be a spy. The latter could be true because I believe some imaginary character to be a spy. The difference between these two propositions is a matter of scope. In 1 the existential quantifier has larger scope than the sentence-forming operator 'I believe'. In 2 the existential quantifier, on the other hand, is within the scope of the belief operator.

If we were to allow non-extensional propositions to be

expressed in our language, the rule of ∃I would need restricting to prevent the derivation of a falsehood 'There is someone whom I believe to be a spy' from the truth 'I believe Icabod is a spy'. Interesting and important as the question of how to deal with quantification in the case of non-extensional propositions is, it takes us beyond the scope of this introductory work. By restricting attention to non-extensional propositions we can use =E and ∃I without restriction. In calling the proposition that I believe someone to be a spy non-extensional, we have implicitly extended the definition of that notion to include any proposition with an existential quantifier which gives a non-extensional proposition on the replacement of the quantifier by a name, i.e. as in the use of ∃E.

The rules for identity extend the range of arguments the validity of which can be established in our logic as is illustrated below.

Example 6.2.1

Bacon is Shakespeare. Shakespeare is bi-sexual. Therefore Bacon is bi-sexual.

Interpretation

Domain: all persons, who are alive or who have been alive.
n: Shakespeare
m: Bacon
Bx: x is bi-sexual

Formalization

$n = m, Bn \vdash Bm$

Derivation

Prem	(1)	$n = m$	
Prem	(2)	Bn	
1,2	(3)	Bm	1,2 =E

Notice that in citing the rule of =E we give the two lines to which it is applied. One line will be of the form $t = s$ where 't' and 's' are proper or arbitrary names. The other line will contain at least one of these names. The conclusion is obtained by replacing at least one occurrence of the one name by the other name. Notice that we have taken the domain to be persons who are alive or who have been alive. There is nothing in our logic which requires that the domain be restricted to presently existing persons or things.

Example 6.2.2

Argument

> The only monetarists are Reagan and Thatcher. Both Reagan and Thatcher are silly. So all monetarists are silly.

Interpretation

> Domain: the set of all living persons
> n: Reagan
> m: Thatcher
> Mx: x is a monetarist
> Sx: x is silly

Formalization

> $(\forall x)(Mx \rightarrow x = n \lor x = m), Sn \ \& \ Sm, \ \vdash (\forall x)(Mx \rightarrow Sx)$

(see next page)

Example 6.2.3

Argument

> Hesperus is Phosphorus. Hesperus is a planet. No planet is a star. Therefore Phosphorus is not a star.

Interpretation

> Domain: the set of heavenly bodies
> m: Hesperus
> n: Phosphorus
> Px: x is a planet
> Sx: x is a star

Formalization

> $m = n, Pm, (\forall x)(Px \rightarrow \ \neg Sx) \vdash \ \neg Sn$

Derivation

Prem	(1)	$(\forall x)(Mx \rightarrow x = n \vee x = m)$				
Prem	(2)	$Sn \ \& \ Sm$				
Prem	(3)	$(\forall x)(Mx \rightarrow Sx)$				
Prem	(4)	Ma				
1	(5)	$Ma \rightarrow a = n \vee a = m$	1 $\forall$E			
1,4	(6)	$a = n \vee a = m$	4,5, $\rightarrow$E			
Prem	(7)	$a = n$	Prem	(10)	$a = m$	Prem
2	(8)	Sn	2 &E	(11)	Sm	2 &E
2,7	(9)	Sa	7,8 =E	(12)	Sa	10,11 =E
1,2,4	(13)	Sa	6,7,9,10,12 $\vee$E			
1,2	(14)	$Ma \rightarrow Sa$	4,10 $\rightarrow$I			
1,2	(15)	$(\forall x)(Mx \rightarrow Sx)$	14 $\forall$I			

Derivation

Prem	(1)	$m = n$	
Prem	(2)	Pm	
Prem	(3)	$(\forall x)(Px \rightarrow \neg Sx)$	
3	(4)	$Pm \rightarrow \neg Sm$	3 $\forall$E
2,3	(5)	$\neg Sm$	2,4 $\rightarrow$E
1,2,3	(6)	$\neg Sn$	1,5 =E

Example 6.2.4

Argument

> Ronald Reagan is the President. The President is an actor. Therefore Ronald Reagan is an actor.

Interpretation

> Domain: the set of living American citizens
> n: Ronald Reagan
> Px: x is president
> Ax: x is an actor

Formalization

> $(\exists x)(Px \,\&\, (\forall y)(Py \rightarrow x = y) \,\&\, (x = n))$
> $(\exists x)(Px \,\&\, (\forall y)(Py \rightarrow x = y) \,\&\, Ax)$
> $\vdash An$

(see next page)

EXERCISES

1 Formalize the following sentences. Specify your interpretation and if the English sentence is ambiguous give alternative formalizations.

  (a) The zemindar is bald.

  (b) The zemindar is not bald.

  (c) The horse is a carnivore.

  (d) The horse is old.

  (e) Icabod is taller than anyone else.

  (f) The smartest student is Ronald.

Derivation

Prem	(1)	$(\exists x)(Px \ \& \ (\forall y)(Py \to x = y) \ \& \ (x = n))$	
Prem	(2)	$(\exists x)(Px \ \& \ (\forall y)(Py \to x = y) \ \& \ Ax)$	
Prem	(3)	$Pa \ \& \ (\forall y)(Py \to a = y) \ \& \ (a = n)$	
Prem	(4)	$Pb \ \& \ (\forall y)(Py \to b = y) \ \& \ Ab$	
3	(5)	$(\forall y)(Py \to a = y) \ \& \ (a = n)$	3 &E
4	(6)	$(\forall y)(Py \to b = y) \ \& \ Ab$	4 &E
3	(7)	$(\forall y)(Py \to a = y)$	5 &E
4	(8)	Ab	6 &E
3	(9)	$Pb \to a = b$	7 $\forall$E
4	(10)	Pb	4 &E
3,4	(11)	$a = b$	9,10 $\to$E
3	(12)	$a = n$	5 &E
3,4	(13)	Aa	8,11 =E
3,4	(14)	An	12,13 =E
3,2	(15)	An	2,4,14 $\exists$E
1,2	(16)	An	1,3,15 $\exists$E

(g) A man's house is his castle.

(h) The train is slow.

(i) Isabel's cousin is happier than Icabod's mother.

(j) The workers despise the boss.

(k) The first event was a big bang.

(l) The largest city in Canada is the most boring city in the world.

(m) This novel is pretentious.

(n) The devil does not exist.

(o) Nothing is more evil than the devil.

2 Formalize the following arguments and derive the resulting sequent:

(a) Icabod sings better than Robert Zimmerman. But Robert Zimmerman is Bob Dylan. So Icabod sings better than Bob Dylan.

(b) Nobody is wiser than Cicero. Therefore no one is wiser than Tully for Tully is Cicero.

(c) Icabod loves anyone who does not love her or himself. So Icabod loves himself.

(d) Icabod kissed all the girls in Grade 4. Francis Gumm was in Grade 4. Therefore Icabod kissed Judy Garland because she is really Francis Gumm.

(e) Ringo Starr is richer than anyone who lives in Builth Wells. Ringo Starr is actually Richard Starky. So Richard Starky is richer than anyone in Builth Wells.

(f) The king is bald. Henry is the king. So Henry is bald.

(g) The king is happy. Therefore there is a king.

(h) The brightest heavenly body that appears in the evening is in fact a planet. The brightest heavenly body that disappears in the morning is the brightest heavenly body that appears in the evening. Therefore the brightest heavenly body that disappears in the morning is a planet.

(i) Icabod is not the devil. The devil is the most evil creature. Therefore something is more evil than Icabod.

(j) The father of his father was unscrupulous. His grandfather was J. D. Rockefeller. Therefore J. D. Rockefeller was unscrupulous.

3 Derive the following theorems:

(a) $\vdash (\forall x)(x = x)$

(b) $\vdash (\forall x)(\forall y)((x = y) \rightarrow (y = x))$

(c) $\vdash (\forall x)(\forall y)(\forall z)(((x = y) \,\&\, (y = z)) \rightarrow (x = z))$

4 Analyse the following arguments. Consider whether any implicit premises might legitimately be assumed. Derive the resulting sequent if the argument is valid.

(a) Any thought of mine is identical to some state of my brain. All my brain states are located in space. Consequently, any thought of mine is located in space.

(b) I can think. My body cannot think. Therefore, I am not my body.

(c) For any number there is a greater number. Therefore there is no greatest number.

(d) There is no period of time without events. Therefore there is no period of time before the first event.

(e) Everything has a creator. Therefore the creator exists.

2 NUMERICAL QUANTIFIERS

The existential quantifier is used in our formal language to express the idea that at least one object satisfies the predicate to which the quantifier is applied. Having at our disposal a symbol for identity we can express the idea that at least two objects have a given property. For instance, suppose we wish to express the proposition that there are at least two students. Taking the domain to be living persons and 'Sx' as 'x is a student', we write:

$$(\exists x)(\exists y)(Sx \,\&\, Sy \,\&\, \lnot(x = y)).$$

This says that '*Sx*' is satisfied by a pair of distinct objects. To express the proposition that there are at least three students we write:

$$(\exists x)(\exists y)(\exists z)(Sx \mathbin{\&} Sy \mathbin{\&} Sz \mathbin{\&} \neg(x = y) \mathbin{\&} \neg(x = z) \mathbin{\&} \neg(z = y)$$

For any number, *n*, we can express the claim that *n* objects satisfy a given predication by using this style of formalization with *n* existential quantifiers. We can also use identity to express the idea that there is at most one object satisfying a given predicate. For instance, the proposition that there is at most one student would be represented using the above interpretation as follows:

$$(\forall x)(\forall y)(Sx \mathbin{\&} Sy \to x = y).$$

Using the pedantic reading this says that if you find objects, *x* and *y*, such that both are students it will turn out that *x* and *y* are the same object. To express the proposition that there are at most two students we write:

$$(\forall x)(\forall y)(\forall z)(Sx \mathbin{\&} Sy \mathbin{\&} Sz \to z = y \lor z = x).$$

Continuing in this fashion we can formulate the proposition that there are at most *n* objects satisfying a given predicate. The formalization in this case will require *n* universal quantifiers.

Putting these two styles of formalization together we can express the proposition that there is exactly one student, writing:

$$(\exists x)(Sx) \mathbin{\&} (\forall x)(\forall y)(Sx \mathbin{\&} Sy \to x = y).$$

We can give a terser formalization by writing:

$$(\exists x)((Sx) \mathbin{\&} (\forall y)(Sy \to x = y)).$$

This says that we can find a student and that if one finds a student that one will turn out to be the same as has already been found. Similarly we can write for 'There are two students':

$$(\exists x)(\exists y)(Sx \mathbin{\&} Sy) \mathbin{\&} (\neg(x = y) \mathbin{\&} (\forall z)(Sz \to x = z \lor y = z)).$$

Or, on the terser style of formalization we have:

$$(\exists x)(\exists y)\,((Sx\ \&\ Sy)\ \neg(x = y)\ \&\ (\forall z)(Sz \rightarrow z = x\ v\ z = y)).$$

We are able in this way to express the numerically definite quantifier: there are exactly n . . ., for any number n.

We have referred to this expression as a quantifier. For like the universal and existential quantifiers, it attaches to predicates to give a sentence saying something, in this case something definite, about the number of things in the domain that satisfy the predicate. Similarly the expressions 'there are at least n . . .' and 'there are at most n . . .' are called respectively, the *weak* and *strong inexact numerical quantifiers*. By adding the identity sign to our language we are able to express this infinite range of additional quantifiers without having to add a pair of new specific expressions for each number n. To say that, for example, there are exactly 100 Fs, we would require a very long expression. However, while the expression is complex we have a perfectly mechanical way of generating it.

What we have been able to do is of great philosophical interest. For instance, philosophers have been interested in the question of the nature of numbers. We talk about numbers as if they were objects. For instance, compare the proposition that Icabod is odd with the proposition that 5 is odd. For the former to be true there has to be something, Icabod, possessing the property of oddness. If we think of the latter proposition in this way we will conclude that there has to be something called '5', which has the property of being odd (in the mathematical sense of this term). A subject–predicate sentence with a name in the subject position is true only if there is an object named by the name. Grammatically '5' looks like a name and one might be inclined to assume that there is some object called '5'. But that object is apt to seem problematic. For one cannot perceive it. And in view of the strangeness of hypothetical numerical objects one way want to consider an alternative approach.

The sentence 'Nobody is odd' looks at the level of surface grammar to be a subject–predicate sentence. However, if we treat 'nobody' as a name and imagine a context in which that sentence is true, say that there are just you and I in the intended domain and that we are not odd, we would be led to suppose that there was some mysterious invisible and intangible person, nobody, having the property of being odd. Given the discussion in Chapter 5 we know that 'nobody' is in fact a quantifier. We remove the temptation to treat it as a name by noting that the sentence is equivalent to: Take anyone you like, he or she is not strange. Perhaps '5' could be treated more like 'nobody' than like 'Icabod'. We can see that the above procedure for formalizing the numerical quantifiers gives us a way of parsing any sentence of the form 'There are 5 *F*s' so that '5' disappears in favour of a complex of quantifiers. It is for this reason that philosophers have been particularly interested in the device given, notwith-standing the fact that it can be cumbersome. For it allows us to get rid of the use of number words in many contexts. And if it could be used to get rid of expressions for numbers in every context we could conclude that there are no objects, called the numbers, but rather that it is at most a convenient accident that we talk as if there were objects having names. Unfortunately, while this procedure works for contexts in which a number is used of a property as in 'There are *n* *F*s', it has not proved possible to apply the procedure to cases where properties such as oddness are applied to numbers. This controversy has been introduced to illustrate how results in formal logic are applied or might be applied in the study of philosophical problems which on the surface appear to have nothing to do with logic. In this case the problem is one arising in the philosophy of mathematics with regard to the nature of numbers.

EXERCISES

1 Formalize the following sentences:

   (a) Icabod loves two women.

   (b) More than one cook spoils the broth.

   (c) Nobody has two fathers.

   (d) If two or three are present the meeting will take place.

   (e) There are exactly two things.

2 Analyse the following arguments. Make explicit any implicit premises and derive the resulting sequent:

(a) There are two proctors. Therefore there is at least one proctor.

(b) I am a solipsist and so are you. That makes at least two of us.

(c) Icabod is an arrogant student. So is Isabel. They are the only ones. Thus there are exactly two arrogant students.

3 NAMES AND DESCRIPTIONS

Russell's device for handling definite descriptions is not universally accepted by philosophers. In this section we look at this controversy and consider possible further applications of the theory. If we have a vacuous definite description, that is, a definite description which does not apply to anything, on Russell's treatment of definite descriptions the sentence formed using such a description comes out false. For instance, consider the sentence 'The king of France is bald'. Given a domain of all living persons the definite description 'The king of France' is vacuous. Russell would represent the sentence as stating that there is one and only one king of France and he is bald. Using 'Kx' for 'x is a king of France' and 'Bx' for 'x is bald' the formalization of the sentence is:

$$(\exists x)(Kx \ \& \ (\forall y)(Ky \rightarrow x = y) \ \& \ Bx).$$

Clearly this is false as there is no king. However, one might argue that for the original sentence of English to be true there has to be one and only one king who is lacking in hair and for it to be false there has to be this unique existing king who has hair. If there is no king at all, the sentence fails to express something false and equally it fails to express anything true. In fact it fails to express any proposition for it fails to talk about anything. On this view a sentence with a vacuous subject term (a subject term that has no referent) fails to express a proposition on the grounds that we are not provided with any subject matter for the proposition to be about. Taking this view would complicate our logic. In our logic any sentence of the language is either true or false. On this alternative to Russell's approach sentences containing vacuous definite descriptions constitute an exception to the claim that any sentence is either true or false. This means that we would have to re-structure our logic dropping such theorems as $P \lor \neg P$. And we would have to find some other device for representing definite descriptions. In fact we will continue to use Russell's theory noting that even if one is inclined to say that 'The king of France is bald' is neither true nor false, no harm will come in counting it as false. That will enable us to use a simpler logic. One who objects to this procedure can regard it as a simplifying assumption to be relaxed at a later stage.

We noted in our earlier discussion of identity that no vacuous names are permitted in our language. However, we may well wish to say, using a name, that that name has no bearer. For instance, one may say that Cerberus did not exist. How could we express that idea? First, note how we might say that Icabod exists by writing $(\exists x)(x = n)$ where 'n' is Icabod's name. On our pedantic reading this says that you can find an object such that it is Icabod. However, if one tried to say that Icabod did not exist by denying this and writing $\neg(\exists x)(x = n)$ we have a problem. For we can prove in our logic that $(\exists x)(x = n)$ which means that the sentence which attempts to say that Icabod does not exist is inconsistent. One possible way around this difficulty is to use a definite description in place of the name. For instance, if asked who Cerberus was supposed to be, I might say that Cerberus was supposed to be the dog who guarded the gates of hell. Let us use 'Dx' for the predicate 'x is a dog who guards the gates of hell'. To say that such a dog exists we write:

$$(\exists x)(Dx \ \& \ (\forall y)(Dy \rightarrow x = y)).$$

To say that this dog does not exist we can write:

$$\neg(\exists x)(Dx \ \& \ (\forall y)(Dy \rightarrow x = y)).$$

This sentence will be false for the domain of all actual objects given that Cerberus is just an imaginary dog. And thus we can express the idea that Cerberus does not exist by using in place of a name a definite description which would pick out Cerberus if he existed. Some philosophers, notably Russell, thought that what we mean by any name used in English can be conveyed by some definite description. Given a name used in some context one finds some description which comes to mind when one thinks of the named thing.

There are many problems with this theory. How do we ascertain which description is appropriate to us? Russell's own procedure of asking us to use the description that comes to mind when we think of the named thing means that different persons may well have different descriptions associated with the same name. In which case we would have to say that they all meant something different by the same name and that is counter-intuitive. We all think that we mean the same thing by 'Ronald Reagan' even though we may differ greatly in the sort of description that comes to mind when we think of Ronald Reagan! However, replacing names by definite descriptions provides a device which enables us to express in our formal language negative existentials (e.g. Cerberus does not exist) even if the translation does not match exactly the meaning of the sentence in English.

This device for dealing with names will be referred to as the replacement of a name by its associated definite description. As long as we specify what description we are associating with a name we can say that the name has no bearer by asserting that there is no object satisfying the definite description. This device can be used in the case of all names and not only for vacuous names. We could then dispense with proper names in our formal language, always using an associated description when translating a sentence from English into our language. Even this device will not enable us to say everything we want to express. For I might want to say that Cerberus did not exist but that Cerberus had three heads. If we use the device we can say that Cerberus did not exist. However, applying that device to the sentence 'Cerberus has a head' gives the following where we write '*Hx*' for '*x* has a head' and taking *Dx* as above:

$$(\exists x)(Dx \ \& \ (\forall y)(Dy \rightarrow x = y) \ \& \ Hx).$$

But that sentence is false for there is no object satisfying the description 'is a dog who guards the gates of hell'. There is no simple way around this problem. We might take as our domain all real and fictional animals. Using the associated description given for Cerberus we can say that in that domain there is one and only one thing which guards the gates of hell and has a head using the formalization given. However, we have Cerberus as existing (in that domain) and if we want to mark the difference between him and Trout, my real and existing dog, we will have to introduce some further predicates writing, say, '*Bx*' for '*x* is real' and '*Fx*' for '*x* is fictional'.

Notice that we cannot use the existential quantifier in differentiating between Cerberus and Trout. For the quantifier is used to assert the existence in the domain of something having a given property. If the domain covers both fictional and real animals, to say there is a dog is to say that one can find in the domain something that is a dog which may be a real dog or a fictional dog. Some philosophers do not favour the introduction of such domains. It may seem to give equal status to very different things – real dogs and fictional dogs. However, there is nothing in the mechanics of our logic that precludes the introduction of such domains and they provide one way of expressing the idea that while Cerberus is fictional and does not exist, Cerberus had properties. We will not pursue this controversy further. My point is simply to illustrate some of the things that can be done by selection of the domain of discourse.

FURTHER READING

On Russell's theory of description:
B. Russell, 'On Denoting' in *Philosophical Logic*, ed. P. F. Strawson (Oxford University Press, 1967).
P. F. Strawson, 'On Referring' in ibid.

On names:
W. V. O. Quine, *Methods of Logic* (Cambridge, Mass.: Harvard University Press, 1982).

On numbers and numerical quantifiers:
D. Bostock, *Logic and Arithmetic* (Oxford University Press, 1974).

CHAPTER 7
The theory of relations

1 WHAT ARE RELATIONSHIPS?

One-place predicates such as 'x is happy', 'x is green', 'x is square' express properties which can be possessed by single objects. Two-place predicates such as 'x loves y', 'x is the brother of y', 'x is taller than y' express two-term relations which can be possessed by pairs of objects. Three-place predicates such as 'x is between y and z' express three-term relations which can hold between triples of objects. In this chapter we study the properties of two-term relations, a subject of great philosophical and mathematical interest.

The relation of loving which is expressed by the predicate 'x loves y' holds between certain pairs of objects and not between others. It was supposed to hold between Romeo and Juliet but not (apparently) between Carter and Reagan. Notoriously this relation may hold one way between a pair of objects but not the other way. This means that we need to introduce the notion of an *ordered pair* of objects. We will use the notation $\langle O_1, O_2 \rangle$ to indicate a pair of objects to be taken in the order first O_1 and then O_2. If Icabod loves Isabel but Isabel does not love Icabod, we say that the relation of loving holds between the pair $\langle$Icabod, Isabel$\rangle$ but not between the pair $\langle$Isabel, Icabod$\rangle$. Using the notion of satisfaction introduced in Chapter 5 we can say that in this particular case the ordered pair $\langle$Icabod, Isabel$\rangle$ satisfies the predicate 'x loves y' and the ordered pair $\langle$Isabel, Icabod$\rangle$ does not satisfy 'x loves y'. Given a domain of objects and a two-place predicate in English we can seek to ascertain the set of ordered pairs that satisfy the predicate. If our domain is Romeo, Juliet, Carter, Reagan, Icabod and Isabel and the relation holds as above and if in addition the only person who loves himself is Icabod the ordered pairs which satisfy the predicate loving 'x

loves *y*' are:

> {⟨Romeo, Juliet⟩ ⟨Juliet, Romeo⟩
> ⟨Icabod, Isabel⟩ ⟨Icabod, Icabod⟩}.

Given a two-place predicate we will say that it expresses a relation and that the set of ordered pairs which satisfy the relation for a given domain is the *extension* of the relation for that domain. If Reagan and Carter neither love nor like anyone and if Juliet and Romeo love and like only one another and if Icabod likes Isabel and himself and she likes nobody, the relations of loving and liking on the domain given above have the same extension. Different relations thus can have the same extension. We will see that the properties of a relation on a given domain are determined by the extension of the relation on that domain. Thus from the point of view of the properties of relations, the difference between loving and liking is not relevant for domains in which the extension is the same. This fact leads mathematicians to talk of what I have called the extension of a relation as the relation itself. They define a relation to be a set of ordered pairs of objects. We will, however, stick more closely to ordinary language and talk of a relation as what is expressed by a two-place predicate and refer to the set of ordered pairs of objects which satisfy the relation as being the extension of that relation or predicate. While our focus will be on two-place predicates and the relations they express, one can generalize and say of any *n*-place predicate that it expresses an *n*-term relation the extension of which will be a set of ordered *n*-tuples of objects. For instance, the predicate '*x* is between *y* and *z*' applied to the spatial array given below has as its extension the set of ordered 3-tuples:

$$\{\langle b,a,c\rangle,\ \langle c,b,d\rangle,\ \langle b,a,d\rangle,\ \langle c,a,d\rangle\}$$
$$a \text{——} b \text{——} c \text{——} d$$

It will sometimes be convenient to give spatial representations of the extension of relations using what are called Hasse diagrams. We represent each object in the domain by a labelled dot and draw an arrow from object *a* to *b* just in case ⟨*a*,*b*⟩ satisfies the predicate. If ⟨*b*,*a*⟩ also satisfies the predicate we put a head on both ends of the line. If an object bears the relation to itself we put an arrow from the object which snakes back to the object. In the case of the relation of loving on the domain given above the Hasse diagram is:

As a further illustration of the use of Hasse diagrams, we represent four possible situations with a domain of four persons a, b, c, d with regard to the relation of love:

Unrequited and uncomplicated love   *Unrequited but complicated love*

Requited but boring love   *Requited and exciting love*

EXERCISES

1 Give the extension of the following relations:

(a) x is greater than y. Domain is the set {1,2,3,4}.

(b) x is the next largest number to y. Domain is the set {1,2,3,4,5}.

2 Represent the following relations by a Hasse diagram:

(a) x is equal to or less than y. Domain is the set {1,2,3,4}.

(b) x is equal to 2 times y. Domain is the set {2,4,6,8,10}.

2 THE PROPERTIES OF RELATIONS

It may be that a relation on a domain is such that each object bears the relation to itself. Such a relation is said to be *reflexive* on the domain. Formally we define a relation expressed by the predicate 'Rxy' to be reflexive if and only if $(\forall x)Rxx$ where the domain of interpretation is the domain of the relation. In a Hasse diagram for a reflexive relation each object will have a little arrow snaking back on itself. The relation expressed by the predicate 'x is the same age as y' is reflexive on the domain of persons. For any person is the same age as him or herself. The relation expressed by 'x is the mother of y' is not reflexive on that domain for no one is his or her own mother.

Some relations are such that on a given domain, no object bears the relation to itself. Such relations are said to be *irreflexive* on the domain. Formally we define a relation expressed by the predicate 'Rxy' to be irreflexive on a given domain if and only if $(\forall x) \neg Rxx$. The relation expressed by 'x is larger than y' defined on the infinite set of counting numbers $\{1,2,3,4, \ldots\}$ is irreflexive for no number can be larger than itself.

It may be that a relation on a domain is neither reflexive nor irreflexive. That is, there may be some objects which bear the relation to themselves and other objects which do not bear the relation to themselves. Some people are said to hate themselves. Others obviously do not. That being so the relation of hating on the domain of persons is said to be *non-reflexive*. Formally the relation expressed by 'Rxy' is non-reflexive if and only if $\neg(\forall x)Rxx$ & $\neg(\forall x) \neg Rxx$. It is easy to show that this is equivalent to: $(\exists x) \neg Rxx$ & $(\exists x)Rxx$. In a Hasse diagram for such a relation some dots will have arrows snaking back on themselves and others will not.

A relation may be such that on a given domain whenever object a bears the relation to object b, object b bears the relation to object a. Such relations are *symmetrical*. Formally, the relation expressed by the predicate 'Rxy' is symmetrical if and only if $(\forall x)(\forall y)(Rxy \rightarrow Ryx)$. In the Hasse diagram for a symmetrical relation, any arrow between a pair of objects will have two heads. And in the set of ordered pairs giving the extension of the relation, we will have for each pair $\langle a,b \rangle$ the pair $\langle b,a \rangle$. Examples of symmetrical relations include: being the same age as, being a sibling of, being equal to.

If a relation is such that whenever object a bears it to object b, b does not bear the relation to a, it is *asymmetrical*. Formally, the relation expressed by the predicate 'Rxy' is asymmetrical if and only if $(\forall x)(\forall y)(Rxy \rightarrow \lnot Ryx)$. In a Hasse diagram, there will be no double-headed arrows. Asymmetrical relations include: being greater than, being taller than, being the mother of.

A relation may be neither asymmetrical or symmetrical. That is, it may be the case that $\lnot(\forall x)(\forall y)(Rxy \rightarrow Ryx)$ & $\lnot(\forall x)(\forall y)(Rxy \rightarrow \lnot Ryx)$. This is equivalent to: $(\exists x)(\exists y)(Rxy$ & $\lnot Ryx)$ & $(\exists x)(\exists y)(Rxy$ & $Ryx)$. In the extension of such a relation which is called *non-symmetrical*, there is at least one pair of objects such that the relation holds both ways and at least one pair where the relation holds one way but not the other. Loving, liking, hating are examples of non-symmetrical relations.

Transitive relations are ones such that if object a bears the relation to b, and b bears it to c, a bears the relation to c. Formally, the relation expressed by the predicate 'Rxy' is transitive if and only if $(\forall x)(\forall y)(\forall z)(Rxy$ & $Ryz \rightarrow Rxz)$. Transitive relations include: being the same age, being taller than, being greater than. If a relation is such that whenever a bears it to b and b to c, a does not bear it to c, it is *intransitive*. Formally the definition is: the relation expressed by the predicate 'Rxy' is intransitive if and only if $(\forall x)(\forall y)(\forall z)(Rxy$ & $Ryz \rightarrow \lnot Rxz)$. Intransitive relations include those of being the next biggest number to (in the domain of the counting numbers) and being the father of. Non-transitive relations are those which are neither transitive nor intransitive. Formally the relation expressed by 'Rxy' is non-transitive just in case $\lnot(\forall x)(\forall y)(\forall z)(Rxy$ & $Ryz \rightarrow Rxz)$ & $\lnot(\forall x)(\forall y)(\forall z)(Rxy$ & $Ryz \rightarrow \lnot Rxz)$ which is equivalent to: $(\exists x)(\exists y)(\exists z)(Rxy$ & Ryz & $Rxz)$ & $(\exists x)(\exists y)(\exists z)(Rxy$ & Ryz & $\lnot Rxz)$. Examples of non-transitive relations are loving, liking, disliking.

To conclude the list of basic properties of relations that will concern us we define a *strongly connected* relation to be one which holds one way or the other of any pair of objects from the domain in question. That is, '*Rxy*' expresses a strongly connected relation if and only if $(\forall x)(\forall y)(Rxy \vee Ryx)$. The relation of being equal to or less than is strongly connected on the domain of the counting numbers. If for every *distinct* pair of objects a relation holds one way or the other it is *connected*. Formally, '*Rxy*' expresses a connected relation if and only if $(\forall x)(\forall y)$ $(\neg(x = y) \rightarrow Rxy \vee Ryx)$. The relation of being less than on the domain of the counting numbers is connected.

Not all the properties of relations given above are independent of one another. That is, if a relation has one particular property it may be that it has to have another particular property or that it cannot have another particular property. For instance, if a relation is asymmetric it must be irreflexive. This can be established by deriving the sequent: $(\forall x)(\forall y)(Rxy \rightarrow \neg Ryz) \vdash (\forall x)$ $\neg Rxx$.

Prem	(1)	$(\forall x)(\forall y)(Rxy \rightarrow \neg Ryx)$	
1	(2)	$(\forall y)(Ray \rightarrow \neg Rya)$	1 $\forall$E
1	(3)	$Raa \rightarrow \neg Raa$	2 $\forall$E
1	(4)	$\neg Raa$	3 SIS $(P \rightarrow \neg P \vdash \neg P)$
1	(5)	$(\forall x) \neg Rxx$	4 $\forall$I

No relation can be both intransitive and reflective. To establish this it suffices to derive a contradiction from the formula for intransitivity and reflexibility.

To show that both these properties cannot be realized by the same relation we need only show that the assumption that they can leads to a contradiction as below:

Prem	(1)	$(\forall x)(\forall y)(\forall z)(Rxy \& Ryz \rightarrow \neg Rxz)$	
Prem	(2)	$(\forall x)Rxx$	
1	(3)	$(\forall y)(\forall z)(Ray \& Ryz \rightarrow \neg Raz)$	1 $\forall$E
1	(4)	$(\forall z)(Raa \& Raz \rightarrow \neg Raz)$	3 $\forall$E
1	(5)	$Raa \& Raa \rightarrow \neg Raa$	4 $\forall$E
2	(6)	Raa	2 $\forall$E
2	(7)	$Raa \& Raa$	6,6 &I
1,2	(8)	$\neg Raa$	5,7 $\rightarrow$E
1,2	(9)	$Raa \& \neg Raa$	6,8 &I

Clearly no relation can be both reflexive $(\forall x)Rxx$ and irreflexive

$(\forall x)\ \neg Rxx$. For applying $\forall$E would give us directly Raa and $\neg Raa$. If a relation is reflexive on a domain there must be some objects in that domain and it must hold on that domain. For from $(\forall x)Rxx$ we can derive $(\exists x)Rxx$; that is, something bears the relation to itself. There can be relations and domains which are such that nothing in the domain bears the relation to anything else in the domain. For instance, on the domain of living persons, the relation of being a female brother does not hold. Suppose we take as our domain an empty set, say, the set of married bachelors. No relation could be irreflexive on that domain. For from $(\forall x)\ \neg Rxx$, we can derive $(\exists x)\ \neg Rxx$; that is, there is some object which does not bear the relation to itself.

It might seem that on such funny domains, no relation would have any property. However, that is not so because of the conditional form of the definitions of symmetry, asymmetry, transitivity and intransitivity. Any relation on an empty domain has *all* these properties. For example, the definition of symmetry says that *if* a relation holds between a pair of objects $\{a,b\}$ it holds between $\{b,a\}$. It does not say that the relation actually holds for any pair of objects. That a relation does not hold is expressed by the sentence $\neg(\exists x)(\exists y)Rxy$ or by the equivalent sentence $(\forall x)(\forall y)\ \neg Rxy$. Assuming $(\forall x)(\forall y)\ \neg Rxy$ we can establish that 'Rxy' expresses a symmetrical relation by deriving $(\forall x)(\forall y)(Rxy \rightarrow Ryx)$ as follows (similar arguments show that 'Rxy' expresses a relation which is asymmetric, transitive and intransitive).

Prem	(1)	$(\forall x)(\forall y)\ \neg Rxy$	
Prem	(2)	Rab	
1	(3)	$(\forall y)\ \neg Ray$	1 $\forall$E
1	(4)	$\neg Rab$	3 $\forall$E
1,2	(5)	Rba	2,4 SIS $(P,\ \neg P \vdash Q)$
1	(6)	$Rab \rightarrow Rba$	2,5 $\rightarrow$I
1	(7)	$(\forall y)(Ray \rightarrow Rya)$	6 $\forall$I
1	(8)	$(\forall x)(\forall y)(Rxy \rightarrow Ryx)$	7$\forall$I

Notice that while we considered an empty domain, if the domain is not empty but the relation does not hold, it is trivially symmetrical, asymmetrical, transitive and intransitive. However, in neither case can it be non-symmetrical or non-transitive for only a relation which holds on a domain can have these properties.

EXERCISES

1 What are the properties of the following relations? State what domain you are assuming.

  (a) x is fatter than y
  (b) x is as fat as y
  (c) x is no fatter than y
  (d) x is indistinguishable in size from y
  (e) x loves y
  (f) x is the sister of y
  (g) x is the father of y
  (h) x is the comrade of y
  (i) x uses the same wine merchant as y
  (j) x is as valuable as y
  (k) x is more valuable than y
  (l) x killed y

2 Show that any intransitive relation is irreflexive.

3 Show that any irreflexive and transitive relation is asymmetric.

4 Show that no relation can be asymmetric and non-reflexive.

5 Show that no relation can be transitive, non-symmetrical and irreflexive.

6 Using as a domain the set of *wff*s of the propositional logic define a relation R to hold between *wff*s A and B just in case $A \dashv \vdash B$. What are the properties of R? Would it make any difference if we changed the definition so that R holds just in case $A \dashv \vDash B$?

7 Define a relation to be *serial* just in case everything bears the relation to something. Show that identity is a serial relation.

Show that any serial, transitive and symmetric relation is reflexive.

3 EQUIVALENCE AND ORDERING RELATIONS

The relation of being the same age as is reflexive. For any person has the same age as himself. It is symmetric because if I have the same age as you, you have the same age as me. And it is transitive. If I have the same age as you, and you have the same age as Icabod, I have the same age as Icabod. Any relation which is reflexive, symmetric and transitive is called an *equivalence relation*. The relation of identity is an equivalence relation as are those of being the same weight as, being the same height as, being the same size as. In general, while there are some exceptions, relations expressed by a predicate of the form 'x is the same ___ as y' are equivalence relations. The blank is filled so as to indicate in which respect equality is asserted, i.e., age, height, weight.

An equivalence relation has an interesting effect on its domain. If one asks a group of persons to so arrange themselves that all those of the same age are standing together, one finds the original set divided into other sets (sub-sets) such that everyone is in at least one set and no one is in two of the sub-sets. Whenever there is a person who is not the same age as anyone else, he will form a set all by himself. Any equivalence relation operates in this way to generate what is called a *partition*. A partition is defined to be a division of a set into sub-sets such that each member of the original set is in one of the sub-sets and no member is in two sub-sets. In the case of an equivalence relation, each member of any sub-set generated in this way bears the equivalence relation to each other member in the sub-set and does not bear the relation to any member of any other sub-sets. If we have represented our domain by a set of points in a circle, we can represent the partition generated by the equivalence relation by a division of the circle into non-overlapping regions such that everything gets into one of these regions. This is illustrated below with the set of fractions: $\{\frac{1}{2}, \frac{2}{4}, \frac{3}{6}, \frac{6}{12}, \frac{1}{3}, \frac{3}{9}, \frac{2}{3}, \frac{4}{6}, \frac{8}{12}\}$ and the equivalence relation of being the same number as.

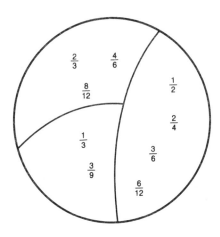

If S is a set and R is an equivalence relation the domain of which is S we define the *equivalence set* of any member of S to be the set of all objects in S that bear R to that object. Thus the equivalence set of $\frac{1}{2}$ in the above example is $\{\frac{1}{2}, \frac{2}{4}, \frac{3}{6}, \frac{6}{12}\}$. For the relation of being the same age as, the equivalence set of a person in the domain is the set consisting of himself and all other persons who have the same age as him. The procedure outlined can be regarded as one for the construction of new objects from a given set of objects with the help of an equivalence relation. We start with a set of objects, apply an equivalence relation to it and generate a new set of objects, objects which are themselves sets of objects from the original set. Philosophers have often sought to make use of this technique of construction in giving philosophical analyses. To illustrate this we consider two examples, a relatively uncontroversial mathematical one and a highly controversial non-mathematical one.

The controversial illustration concerns time, about which Augustine remarked that he knew what it was so long as no one asked him. If anyone asked, he did not know. This is a common situation in philosophy. Like Augustine we often know how to use a concept like time. We regulate our daily life with it and our conversation is permeated with explicit and implicit use of it. However, we are likely to be at a loss to say what we understand by 'time'. For instance, what, after all, is a moment or period of time? We talk about such items all the time as when, for instance, we say such things as '*The moment* Icabod started to lecture, Isabel yawned'. What is it that this definite description 'The moment he started to lecture' denotes? Such items seem problematic because they are abstract and not given in experience. Events such as Icabod's lecturing or Isabel's yawning seem less problematic for we can observe them. No one has ever seen and no one ever will see a moment of time. Clearly moments, as short periods of time, are closely related to events. For we standardly pick out moments by reference to events either directly as in the case given above or more indirectly when we say: 'The first five minutes of Monday 13 November 1981'. This identifies a period of time by reference to the event of the earth's carrying out a certain partial rotation with respect to the sun.

It will not do to equate a moment to the event which we cite in identifying it. For we want to be able to say, for example, that the moment Isabel yawned is the moment Icabod started lecturing. In this case the events cited are different but the moment is the same. Hence the moment cannot simply be a particular event. Setting aside complications due to relativistic physics, the relation of being simultaneous is an equivalence relation. By simultaneous events I mean events that start together and end together. This relation produces a partition on the set of events. What is the equivalence class of the event of Icabod's starting to lecture? It is the set of all events simultaneous with that event. One suggestion is that that set is the moment. That is, 'the moment Icabod started to lecture' designates the set of all events simultaneous with his starting to lecture. The moment Isabel yawned, on this construal, is the set of events simultaneous with her yawning. Since *ex hypothesi* her yawning and his beginning to lecture were simultaneous, the two equivalence sets are identical. And this gives us the result we want: the moments are the same even though the events cited in identifying them are different.

Within the confines of this work we cannot evaluate this definition of a moment of time. If the definition can be defended, it will be a first step in the vindication of what is called the *relational* theory of time. The relationalist thinks that time can be defined entirely by reference to events. The relationalist rejects the picture of time (sometimes attributed to Newton) as some sort of container in which events occur and which exists independently of events. For him all talk of time and the parts of time (i.e. moments, intervals, instants) can be reduced to talk about events in a way that makes time no more mysterious than the events in terms of which it is defined.

Krönecker once said that the counting numbers 1,2,3, . . . were made by God and all the other numbers were man's work. Among the other numbers are the rational numbers or fractions, i.e. $\frac{1}{2}$, $\frac{17}{19}$, $\frac{14}{211}$. We can use the theory of equivalence relations to show how to define the rational numbers in terms of the counting numbers. So that if one day God did create the counting numbers he did not need on another occasion to create anew the rationals. For they can be constructed out of counting numbers. To see this we first note that we identify a rational number by giving a pair of counting numbers writing e.g. $\frac{3}{7}$. We cannot define a rational number just as a pair of counting numbers. For in writing $\frac{3}{7}$ and $\frac{6}{14}$ we use different pairs of counting numbers but we say that they represent the same rational number. Let us assume we have the set of all pairs of counting numbers. We will define a relation R on this set as follows: $\langle a, b \rangle$ bears R to $\langle m, n \rangle$ just in case $an = bm$. It is easily shown that R is an equivalence relation on the set of all pairs of counting numbers. As in the case of simultaneity we ask what are the equivalence sets. Note that the equivalence set of $\frac{1}{2}$ contains among other pairs the following $\frac{2}{4}$, $\frac{3}{6}$, $\frac{6}{12}$ . . . . Mathematicians treat these equivalence sets as being the rational numbers. This gives the result that $\frac{1}{2}$ and $\frac{2}{4}$ are the same rational number for they are the same set of pairs of rational counting numbers. For $\frac{1}{2}$ is the equivalence set containing all pairs $\langle x, y \rangle$ such that $2x = y$ and $\frac{2}{4}$ is the equivalence set containing all pairs $\langle x, y \rangle$ such that $4x = 2y$. Clearly these two sets are identical.

Much more needs to be done to vindicate the suggestion that rational numbers are nothing more than equivalence sets of pairs of counting numbers. References are given at the end of this chapter to works where this suggestion is fully developed.

However, enough has been said about this case and about the case of moments of time to suggest that whenever we are faced with an equivalence relation on a given domain one should ask how the equivalence sets can be construed. It may be that answering this question will enable one to construe something relatively abstract and/or complex in terms of something more concrete and/or simple. In the case of moments of time, it was suggested that one might explore construing them as equivalence sets of events and in the case of the rational numbers it was suggested that they may be just sets of pairs of counting numbers.

Another important type of relation are those which are asymmetric, transitive and irreflexive. Such relations are one type of *ordering relation* and include as examples being older than, being taller than, being greater than. In general, the predicates for such relation are of the form: 'x is ——er than y'. These relations have the effect of inducing an order on at least some pairs of objects from the domain (given that the relation holds on at least one pair from the domain). In the case of the relation of being older than, it tells us which of a pair to take first, unless the pair selected are of the same age, in which case no order is induced on that pair. If there are pairs that the relation does not distinguish between as in this case it is called a *partial order*. If on the other hand it is the case that for all distinct objects, either one bears the relation to the other or *vice versa* the order is said to be *total* or *linear*. The relation of being greater than on the set of counting numbers is a total or linear order, for it holds one way or the other between any pair of distinct objects. A Hasse diagram for such a relation will be a number of dots along a line as illustrated below for the relation of being greater than on the set of numbers $\{1,2,3,4,5,6,7,8,9\}$.

```
·→·→·→·→·→·→·→·→·
1  2  3  4  5  6  7  8  9
```

Since we are dealing with transitive relations we adopt the convention that any pair of points in the diagram that can be linked by following the arrows on a path through the diagram are related. This enables us to have less cluttered Hasse diagrams.

The relation defined on the set of numbers {1,2,3,5,6,10,15,30} of *being an integral multiple of* is a partial order. This relation, *R*, holds between numbers *a* and *b* if and only if there is some counting number *n* such that *n* times *a* is *b*. Thus 1 bears *R* to 3 but not vice versa; 2 bears *R* to 6 but not vice versa. 6 does not bear *R* to 10 nor does 10 bear *R* to 6. The partial order is represented in the Hasse diagram below.

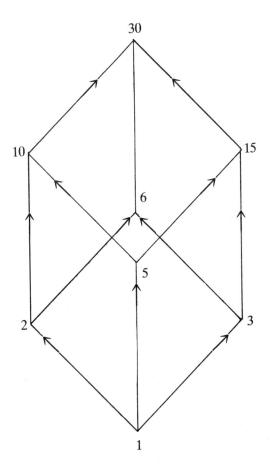

EXERCISES

1 Given a partition of a set show how to define an equivalence relation on the set.

2 Define a relation, R, on the set of all pairs of counting numbers to hold between pair $\langle a,b \rangle$ and the pair $\langle c,d \rangle$ just in case $a+d = b+c$. Show that R is an equivalence relation. Can you suggest a construal of the equivalence sets generated by R?

3 Let R be the equivalence relation defined on page 172, i.e. A bears R to B just in case $A \dashv \vdash B$. We will use the notation $[A]$ to represent the equivalence sets generated by R. We define the following operations on the equivalence sets:

$$[A] \cap [B] = [A \,\&\, B]$$
$$[A] \cup [B] = [A \lor B]$$
$$-[A] = [\neg A]$$

Show the following:

(a) $[A] \cap [B] = [B] \cap [A]$
(b) $[A] \cap ([B] \cap [C]) = ([A] \cap [B]) \cap [B]$
(c) $[A] \cup [B] = [B] \cup [A]$
(d) $[A] \cup ([B] \cup [C]) = ([A] \cup [B]) \cup [C]$
(e) $[A] \cap ([B] \cup [C]) = ([A] \cap [B]) \cup ([A] \cap [C])$
(f) $[A] \cup ([B] \cap [C]) = ([A] \cup [B]) \cap ([A] \cup [C])$
(g) $[A] \cup -[A] = [P \lor \neg P]$
(h) $[A] \cap -[A] = [P \,\&\, \neg P]$

What do the equivalence sets $[P \lor \neg P]$ and $[P \,\&\, \neg P]$ represent?

Proving the above equivalences shows that this system of equivalence sets of *wff*s of the propositional calculus forms what mathematicians call a Boolean algebra. This means that mathematical theorems proved about Boolean algebras can be used to establish results about the propositional calculus. For illustrations of this see the books by Stoll cited below.

FURTHER READING

On the theory of relations in general:
R. Stoll, *Sets, Logic and Axiomatic Theories* (San Francisco: W. H. Freeman, 1961).

On the relational theory of time:
H. G. Alexander (ed.), *The Leibniz–Clarke Correspondence* (Manchester University Press, 1956).
W. H. Newton-Smith, *The Structure of time* (London: Routledge & Kegan Paul, 1980).
B. van Fraassen, *An Introduction to the Philosophy of Time and Space* (New York: Random House, 1970).

On the construction of the numbers:
B. Russell, *An Introduction to Mathematical Philosophy* (New York: Touchstone, 1971).
R. Stoll, *Set Theory and Logic* (New York: Cover, 1979).

CHAPTER 8
Predicate logic semantics

1 THE PREDICATE LANGUAGE

Logic is the study of valid arguments. In the early chapters of this work we developed a propositional language and provided a definition of validity for arguments expressible in that language. We saw that there were valid arguments not expressible in the propositional language. Hence we enriched it to obtain a predicate language. We have yet to develop a definition of validity appropriate to this enriched language. This is a considerably more complex business than was the case for the propositional language. A valid argument is one which is such that if the premises are true the conclusion must be true. Thus a detailed definition of validity for the arguments expressible in a given language depends on a definition of truth for the sentences of that language. In the case of a propositional language it is relatively simple to explicate the notion of truth of an arbitrary sentence of that language by reference to the notion of the truth of a simple sentence taken together with the notion of a truth-table. That is, we arrive at the truth-value of a complex sentence from an assignment of truth-values to the simple sentences which are parts of the sentence with the aid of truth-tables. However, in the case of the predicate language, the parts of our complex sentences are not necessarily sentences. To see this compare the propositional language sentence '$P \rightarrow Q$' with the predicate language sentence '$(\forall x)(Fx \rightarrow Gx)$'. In the former case some parts, i.e. 'P', 'Q' are themselves sentences. In the latter case neither '$(\forall x)$', 'Fx', nor 'Gx' are sentences. The complexities that this produces will take us some time to explore and in this introductory work we will not be able to do more than indicate the direction to be followed in developing a rigorous definition of truth. The first step is to give a characterization of the predicate language analogous to that given in Chapter 4 for the propositional language.

181

In our quantificational language we use the following symbols in addition to the symbols of our propositional language: $\exists$, $\forall$, n, x, a, $F =$ and the numerals 1, 2, 3, . . . which are used as subscripts for 'n', 'x' and 'a' and as subscripts and superscripts for 'F'. Subscripts are always used with 'n', 'x' and 'a'. Both superscripts and subscripts are always used with 'F'. Expressions of the form 'n_i' where i is a numeral are called *proper names*. Those of the form 'a_i' are called *arbitrary names*. And those of the form 'x_i' are called *variables*. Expressions of the form 'F_i^j' are called *atomic predicate letters*. In all these cases the subscripts give us an unlimited number of expressions of each type. In the case of the predicate letters the superscript indicates the number of places in the predicate. Thus a predicate of the form 'F_i^1' is an expression for a property holding of a single object. 'F_i^2' indicates an expression for a two-term relation such as loving and 'F_i^3' indicates an expression for a three-term relation such as being between. It is very cumbersome to write predicate letters with subscripts and superscripts and consequently we will revert in due course to our practice of using different letters of the alphabet —F,G,H— for predicates without subscripts or superscripts. And we will on many occasions follow our past practice in regard to proper names, variables and arbitrary names. The point of having introduced this device is to illustrate the possibilities of having a language with unlimited expressive capacities and in which the number of places in a predicate would be explicitly expressed. For the purposes that follow we count the expression for equality, '$=$', as being a two-term atomic predicate letter.

A formula of the propositional language was defined to be any sequence of symbols from the vocabulary. Similarly we define a formula of the predicate language to be any sequence of symbols from the above vocabulary. Our aim is to define the notion of a sentence or *well-formed formula* (*wff*). To this end we define an *atomic predicate sentence* to be either a propositional letter or an atomic predicate letter followed by n (not necessarily distinct) terms. A term is a proper name, a variable or an arbitrary name. n is the superscript of the predicate letter. A *wff* is any formula which meets the following condition:

    1 Any atomic predicate sentence is a *wff*.

2 If A is a *wff*, $\neg A$ is a *wff*.

3 If A and B are *wff*s, $(A \,\&\, B)$ is a *wff*.

4 If A and B are *wff*s, $(A \lor B)$ is a *wff*.

5 If A and B are *wff*s, $(A \to B)$ is a *wff*.

6 If A and B are *wff*s, $(A \leftrightarrow B)$ is a *wff*.

7 If A is a *wff*, then $(\forall x_i)A$ is a *wff*.

8 If A is a *wff*, then $(\exists x_i)A$ is a *wff*.

In setting up a definition of the notion of a well-formed formula there is scope for a certain amount of stylistic variation. On the above definition, for instance, extra quantifiers can be affixed to a *wff* and still give a *wff*. '$(\forall x_1)Fx_1$' is a *wff* and so too is '$(\forall x_2)(\forall x_1)Fx_1$'. Allowing such expressions to count as *wff*s simplifies our definitions and is quite harmless. For as can be seen from the semantics given below such redundant quantifiers have no effect on the truth or falsity of a *wff*. It does mean that we depart somewhat from English style. The expression 'There is there is a tree' would not be counted as a sentence of English. For this reason other authors prefer a more complicated definition of a *wff* which would exclude redundant quantifiers.

The definition of a *wff* involves a more substantial departure from English in that expressions such as 'Fx_1,x_2' count as *wff*s. Such expressions correspond to English predicates and will be called *predicate expressions*. That is, predicate expressions are *wff*s containing variables that are not in the scope of any quantifier (see below for the precise definition of scope). A predicate expression in English such as 'is taller than' does not say anything and so is not capable of being assessed as true or false. The semantics to be provided gives a definition of what it is for a *wff* of the language to be true. Since predicate expressions count as *wff*s there will be contexts in which such expressions count as true. This only arises, however, when the corresponding universal closure of the *wff* in question is true. The *universal closure* of a *wff* is obtained by prefixing a universal quantifier $(\forall x_i)$ to the front of the *wff* for each variable 'x_i' in the *wff* which is not within the scope of a quantifier. This means, for example, that the predicate expression 'Fx_1,x_2' only counts as true in the case where everything in the domain bears the relation F to everything in the domain. While this departure from English style should be noted, it is a harmless simplification which enables us to use a terser definition of the notions of a *wff* and of the truth of a *wff*.

The *scope* of a quantifier is defined as follows:

Given a *wff* $(\forall x_i)A$, if A is a *wff* then the scope of $(\forall x_i)$ is A. And given a *wff* $(\exists x_i)A$, if A is a *wff* then the scope of $(\exists x_i)$ is A.

For instance, the scope of $(\exists x_1)$ in '$((\exists x_1)FX_1 \rightarrow (\forall x_2)Gx_2)$' is '$Fx_1$'. '$Fx_1$' is a *wff* whereas '$Fx_1 \rightarrow (\forall x_2)Gx_2$' is not a *wff*. For while 'Fx_1' and '$(\forall x_2)Gx_2$' are *wff*s, '$Fx_1 \rightarrow (\forall x_2)Gx_2$' is not a *wff*. By clause 5 above it fails to be a *wff* as it lacks the requisite bracket. If we add this to obtain the *wff* '$(Fx_1 \rightarrow (\forall x_2)Gx_2)$' and attach the quantifier '$(\exists x_1)$' the resulting *wff* '$(\exists x_1)(Fx_1 \rightarrow (\forall x_2)Gx_2)$' is one in which the scope of '$(\exists x_1)$' is '$(Fx_1 \rightarrow (\forall x_2)Gx_2)$'. As in the case of the propositional calculus, brackets are often suppressed where the scope is clear in any event. In addition brackets may be omitted if the resulting ambiguity of scope makes no difference to the truth or falsity of the *wff* in question. However, when in doubt it is better to use more rather than fewer brackets. The notion of scope is further reviewed in the examples below.

Example 8.1.1

The king of France isn't bald.

This sentence might be used by one who thought that there was a king who had lots of hair on his head. On this reading the sentence is construed as: There is one and only one king of France and he is not bald. Using 'Kx' for 'x is a king of France' and 'Bx' for 'x is bald' the formalization would be:

$$(\exists x)((Kx \ \& \ (\forall y)(Ky \rightarrow x = v)) \ \& \ \neg Bx)$$

In this formalization the negation operator has small scope, governing only 'Bx' whereas the existential quantifier has large scope. The English sentence could also be used by one who wished to deny that there is one and only king of France who is bald. On this construal the formalization would be:

$$\neg(\exists x)((Kx \ \& \ (\forall y)(Ky \to x = y)) \ \& \ Bx)$$

In this case the negation operator has greater scope than the existential quantifier. It does not make any difference to an assessment of the truth of either of these *wff*s whether we take the first occurrence of '&' as having greater scope than the second occurrence. That is, it would not have made any difference if in the case of the first formalization we had written:

$$(\exists x)(Kx \ \& \ ((\forall y)(Ky \to x = y) \ \& \ \neg Bx))$$

In view of this we can suppress the brackets without any harm and write instead:

$$(\exists x)(Kx \ \& \ (\forall y)(Ky \to x = y) \ \& \ \neg Bx)$$

Example 8.1.2

Someone wins the lottery every time.

This sentence might be used to express the idea that there are no lotteries without winners. It might also be used to express the envious thought that some particular person has been winning some particular lottery each time it is held. Presumably if used in this sense the speaker would have in mind a restricted domain. That is, there is an ambiguity of domain. The domain on the first construal being all lotteries and on the second construal being some particular group of lotteries. Using 'Wxy' for 'x is a winner of y' and 'Lx' for 'x is a lottery the formalizations are respectively:

$$(\forall x)(\exists y)(Lx \to Wyx)$$
$$(\exists y)(\forall x)(Lx \to Wyx).$$

On the former construal the universal quantifier has the larger scope; on the latter construal the existential quantifier has the larger scope.

EXERCISES

Determine whether each of the following is a *wff*:

(a) Q

(b) $x = n$

(c) $(\forall x)(Fx \rightarrow Gx)$

(d) $(\forall x)(\forall y)Hx$

(e) $(\forall x)(Fx \rightarrow Hx) \leftrightarrow (\forall x)(Gx)$

(f) $(\exists x)(Hxy \rightarrow (\forall x)Gx)$

(g) $m = \forall n \rightarrow (\forall x)(Fnx) \leftrightarrow (\forall y)(Fmy)$

(h) $(\exists x)(Rx \rightarrow (x = n \text{ v } Tnx))$

(i) $Fxyz \rightarrow Q$

(j) $(\forall x)(\forall y)(\forall z)(Bxyz \ \& \ Bzxy \rightarrow Byxz)$

2 Give the scope of each quantifier and each truth-functional operator in the sequents in Exercise 2 on p. 138.

3 Give three sentences of English which display ambiguities of quantifier scope. Give formalizations which resolve the ambiguities.

2 THE SEMANTICS OF THE LANGUAGE

In giving interpretations we have specified a domain of objects and assigned expressions of English to the predicate letters as when, for example, we let 'Hx' be 'x is happy'. Knowing how a predicate letter is to be understood is only the first step in determining the truth-value of a *wff*. To do that we have to ascertain which objects in the domain have the property expressed by the English phrase. For instance, to know whether or not it is true for a given interpretation that '$(\exists x)Hx$' we have to ascertain whether there is at least one object in the domain having the property of being happy. Thus from the point of truth it matters not that 'Hx' expresses the property of happiness but only which objects have the property expressed by 'Hx'. In future, then, as we move to a more rigorous and abstract approach to the notion of truth we will think of an interpretation in terms of the objects having the property expressed by the predicate letter. This is what was called the extension of a predicate (cf. p. 166). An interpretation of a one-place predicate will be a set of objects (possibly an empty set for it may be that no object in the domain has the property in question) from the domain. The interpretation of a two-place predicate will be a set of ordered pairs (again, possibly empty) drawn from the domain which are to be thought of as the objects which satisfy the predicate under the interpretation. In general, an interpretation assigns to an *n*-place predicate a set of ordered *n*-tuples (possibly an empty set) which by definition of the interpretation are the set of *n*-tuples of objects which satisfy that predicate. In addition an interpretation of a language or fragment of a language will assign one object from the domain to be the referent of any proper name. Note that empty domains are excluded. Finally, since our quantificational language is an extension of the propositional language our interpretation has to deal with propositional letters to which it assigns either the value *T* or the value *F*.

Our aim is to explicate what it is for a *wff* to be true for a given interpretation. The crucial notion in this explication is what was called *satisfaction* (cf. p. 112). If for the moment we restrict attention to atomic predicate letters written with variables, an object satisfies a predicate if that object is in the set of objects assigned to the predicate by the interpretation. A pair of objects satisfies a two-place predicate if that pair of objects is in the extension (the set of ordered pairs) assigned to the predicate by the interpretation. To see where we are going consider the *wff* '$(\forall x)Fx$' under some interpretation. Intuitively we see that that *wff* is true if and only if every object in the domain satisfies the predicate 'Fx'. For if every object satisfies that predicate everything is in the extension assigned to 'Fx' by the interpretation and it is true that '$(\forall x)Fx$'. Similarly, we can see that '$(\exists x)Fx$' is true just in case some object in the domain satisfies the predicate 'Fx'. In this fashion we reduce the question of the truth or falsity of these quantified *wff*s to questions about which objects satisfy which predicates. An interpretation, then, determines the truth-value of these simple *wff*s via the notion of satisfaction.

Unfortunately truth is rarely simple and in developing this

intuition into a satisfactory definition of truth things becomes more than a little complex. The student is urged to work through this section doing the relevant exercises at the points indicated in the text. The first complication arises from the fact that it will not be adequate to talk simply of objects satisfying predicates. For we have to deal with two-place predicates which require pairs of objects, three-place predicates which require triples of objects, . . ., *n*-place predicates which require *n*-tuples of objects. We do not want to set down in advance any limit on the complexity of predicates to which the definition of truth can be applied. For that reason we will use infinite sequences of objects drawn from the domain. Since we need to deal with relations an object can have to itself we allow repetition of objects in the sequence. Given, for example, a domain with three objects O_1, O_2, and O_3 the following would represent the *beginnings* of some sequences to be taken into account:

$O_1, O_2, O_3, O_1, \ldots$

$O_1, O_3, O_3, O_1, \ldots$

$O_3, O_3, O_3, O_2, \ldots$

$O_2, O_1, O_2, O_1, \ldots$

We are going to define a *wff* to be true for an interpretation just in case every sequence satisfies the *wff*. Using a list of recursive clauses (given below) we reduce the question of whether a given sequence satisfies a given *wff* to a question about which sequences satisfy which propositional letters and atomic predicate letters. Given that the sequences have an infinite number of members we have to have some rule which determines which objects from the sequence are to be considered. We consider first atomic predicate sentences. If the sentence is a propositional sentence, the sequence satisfies it just in case the interpretation assigns the sentence the value *T*. If it is an atomic predicate letter, the sequence assigns to any proper name the object assigned to the name by the interpretation. If the predicate letter, contains, say, the arbitrary name 'a_n' or variable 'x_n', the sequence assigns to 'a_n' or 'x_n' its *n*-th member. In this way an *m*-place predicate letter is assigned by any given sequence, a sequence of m-objects (not necessarily distinct). The infinite sequence satisfies the predicate just in case that sequence of m objects is in the extension assigned to the predicate by the interpretation.

To illustrate, consider an interpretation with a domain consisting of the counting numbers 1,2,3, . . . which assigns to the predicate 'F_1' the set of all ordered pairs from the domain such that the first is less than the second. That is, 'F_1' is can be thought of as expressing the property of being less than. Consider a sequence which beings $\langle 2,3,4,1,11, \ldots \rangle$. This sequence satisfies the *wff* 'F_1a_2,a_3' because 3 is assigned to 'a_2' and 4 is assigned to 'a_3' and $\langle 3,4 \rangle$ is in the extension assigned to 'F_1' by the interpretation. If we suppose that the interpretation assigned to the proper name 'n', 1, then the sequence does not satisfy 'F_1x_5n' since the pair $\langle 11,1 \rangle$ is not in the extension assigned to F_1. Given the above interpretation and sequence, we see it does not satisfy the predicate expression F_1x_5,x_4. For $\langle 11,1 \rangle$ is not in the extension assigned to F_1. The predicate expression 'F_1x_1,a_3' is satisfied by the sequence for 2 is less than 4 and hence is in the extension assigned to F_1. The reader is advised to do question 1 from the exercises at the end of this section at this juncture.

A *wff* is true for an interpretation if every sequence satisfies it. As noted above we reduce the question of whether a sequence satisfies a *wff* the truth of which we are considering to questions about which sequences satisfy which atomic predicate sentences by means of a list of recursive clauses. These clauses deal with each form a *wff* can have. They are called recursive because they achieve this end in a purely mechanical fashion. The clauses for the truth-functional operators are given below:

Negation

A sequence s satisfies a *wff* of the form $\neg A$ if and only if s does not satisfy A.

Conjunction

A sequence s satisfies a *wff* of the form A & B if and only if s satisfies A and s satisfies B.

Disjunction
>   A sequence *s* satisfies a *wff* of the form A v B if and only if either *s* satisfies A or *s* satisfies B.

Conditional
>   A sequence *s* satisfies a *wff* of the form $A \rightarrow B$ if and only if either *s* does not satisfy A or *s* satisfies B.

Biconditional
>   A sequence *s* satisfies a *wff* of the form $A \leftrightarrow B$ if and only if *s* satisfies both A and B or *s* satisfies neither A nor B.

In the case of the existential quantifier we define:
A sequence *s* satisfies a *wff* of the form $(\exists x_i)Ax_i$ if and only if there is a sequence differing in at most the ith place from *s* which satisfies 'Ax_1'. As a partial vindication of the definition consider how it works in the case of an existentially quantified one-place predicate '$(\exists x_i)Fx_i$'. Intuitively that *wff* is true if some object in the domain satisfies the predicate 'Fx_i'. Our definition says that a *wff* is true if every sequence satisfies it. We take an arbitrary sequence of objects $\langle O_1, O_2, O_3, \ldots \rangle$ from the domain. That sequence satisfies the *wff* if some sequence like it except possibly in the ith place satisfies 'Fx_i'. If some object is in the extension assigned to 'Fx' then there will be such a sequence and hence the given sequence satisfies '$(\exists x_i)Fx_i$'. If there is such an object then any other sequence will satisfy '$(\exists x_i)Fx_i$'. For we look to a sequence differing in the ith place, to see if there is one which satisfies Fx_i and, *ex hypothesi*, there is one. Thus if one sequence satisfies '$(\exists x_i)Fx_i$' every sequence does. In the case of this simple *wff* the result of applying the definition matches up with our intuitive account of truth.

Suppose we have a *wff* with four variables only one of which is quantified, i.e. '$(\exists x_2)Gx_3x_2x_1x_4$'. A sequence *s* will assign its third member to 'x_3', its first member to 'x_1' and its fourth member to 'x_4'. The sequence *s* satisfies that just in case there is another sequence making the same assignments to 'x_1', 'x_3' and 'x_4' and which assigns its second member to 'x_2' where this ordered four-tuple satisfies the predicate '$Gx_3x_2x_1x_4$'. We can see from this that our formal definition does what we would expect if it matched up with our more intuitive grasp of the existential quantifier. For it requires us to search through the domain to see if we can find an object which when taken with those assigned to the variables not quantified in '$(\exists x_2)Gx_3x_2x_1x_4$' satisfies '$Gx_3x_2x_1x_4$'.

The clause for the universal quantifier is as follows:

> A sequence s satisfies a *wff* of the form $(\forall x_i)Ax_i$ if and only if every sequence differing from s in at most the ith place satisfies 'Ax_i'.

This means that a one-place universally quantified predicate '$(\forall x)Fx$' is true just in case every sequence satisfies it. A sequence s will satisfy '$(\forall x)Fx$' just in case every object is in the extension assigned by the interpretation to 'Fx'. If one such sequence satisfies '$(\forall x)Fx$' every sequence satisfies '$(\forall x)Fx$' and hence if one satisfies '$(\forall x)Fx$' for a given interpretation, '$(\forall x)Fx$' is true for that interpretation.

Finally we need a clause for the identity symbol which is as follows:

> A sequence s satisfies a *wff* of the form $t_i = t_j$ if and only if s assigns the same object to 't_i' that it assigns to 't_j'.

In the above clause 't_i' and 't_j' may be proper names or arbitrary names or variables. In the case of proper names the sequence assigns to the name whatever object the interpretation assigns to the name. In the case of arbitrary names or variables, the subscript of the name or variable determines which object in the sequence is assigned. This clause is unsurprising and simply means that our special predicate '$=$' is to be interpreted as expressing the relation of identity. Do Exercise 2 at this point.

For a propositional language an interpretation for a *wff* or a set of *wff*s was an assignment of truth-values to the atomic sentence letters in the *wff* or set of *wff*s. We found that some *wff*s were true for any interpretation. These were called tautologies. We have explicated the notion of the truth of a *wff* of our quantificational language for a particular interpretation. As in the case of the propositional language, some *wff*s are true in all possible interpretations. For instance, the *wff* '$(\forall x_i)(Fx_i \vee \neg Fx_i)$' is easily shown on the basis of the above clauses to be such that it comes out true on all interpretations. We will call any *wff* of the quantificational language which is true for any interpretation a *quantology*. This name has been used to draw attention to the fact that such *wff*s are the analogues for a quantificational language of the tautologies of the propositional logic. Many authors call such *wff*s logical truths. This is unfortunate. For we have a general idea of logical truths, i.e. sentences true in virtue of their logical form, and we need specific characterizations of logical truths for each specific language. Tautologies are those logical truths expressible in a propositional language. Since it is not to be assumed that all logical truths are expressible in the quantificational language we need a specific name for those that are and we will use the term 'quantology'. Other authors call such *wff*s valid *wff*s. But this is even worse. For validity is a property of arguments not of *wff*s and to use the term in this context can engender confusion.

It can be established that a given *wff* is not a quantology by finding an interpretation and a sequence from the domain of the interpretation which does not satisfy the *wff*. To illustrate, consider the *wff* '$(\exists x_1)Fx_1 \rightarrow (\forall x_1)(Fx_1)$'. Let the domain of the interpretation be the set of all counting numbers: 1,2,3 . . . . Let the extension of 'F' be the set of all even numbers: 2,4,6 . . . . If there is a sequence which satisfies '$(\exists x_1)Fx_1$' but not '$(\forall x_1)Fx_1$', that sequence does not satisfy '$(\exists x_1)Fx_1 \rightarrow (\forall x_1)Fx_1$' and hence that *wff* is not true for the interpretation and is thereby seen not to be a quantology. Such a sequence is any one beginning: 2,2,3,3,4,5 . . . . That sequence satisfies '$(\exists x_1)Fx_1$' for there is a sequence (namely the same one) which satisfies 'Fx_1' since 2 is in the extension assigned to F. That sequence does not satisfy '$(\forall x_1)Fx_1$'. For while it does satisfy 'Fx_1' there are sequences which differ only in the first place (i.e. any one beginning: 1,2,3,4,4 . . .) which do not satisfy 'Fx_1'. Hence the original sequence does not satisfy '$(\forall x_1)Fx_1$'. Do Exercise 3 at this point.

For the sake of completeness we introduce the definition of a notion that in a sense comes between that of truth for an interpretation and that of a quantology. There are *wff*s that are true for all interpretations in a domain of a given size but not true in all interpretations in all domains. A *wff* which is true for all interpretations in a domain of size *n* will be said to be *n*-true. One result that can be established is that any *wff* which is *n*-true for some specific *n* is also *m*-true for any *m* equal to or less than *n* (but greater than zero).

The definition of semantic entailment for the propositional language, $A_1, A_2, \ldots, A_n \vDash B$ required that whenever each of the premises $A_1, A_2, \ldots, A_n$ is true the conclusion B is true. In the case of the predicate logic the definition is framed in terms of satisfaction not truth:

$A_1, A_2, \ldots, A_n \vDash B$ if and only if for any interpretation any sequence that satisfies each of $A_1, A_2, \ldots, A_n$ satisfies B.

This condition is stronger than that required in the case of the propositional logic. To see this consider the sequent $Fa_1 \vDash (\forall x_1)Fx_1$. Let I be an interpretation which makes 'Fa_1' true. In this case every sequence from the domain satisfies 'Fa_1'. That is, the first member of every sequence is in the extension assigned to 'F' in I. And that means that the first member of every sequence satisfies 'Fx_1' and hence '$(\forall x_1)Fx_1$' is true for I. But we cannot derive $Fa_1 \vdash (\forall x_1)Fx_1$ and nor do we want to be able to. For that would be tantamount to concluding that because an arbitrary thing had the property expressed by F everything had that property. It is, however, easily shown that the sequent in question is not semantically valid on the definition given in terms of satisfaction. If we were to use the definition in terms of truth this sequent would count as semantically valid as we have illustrated. Consider an interpretation J in which some members of the domain are in the extension of 'F' and some are not. Since some members are in the extension of 'F', sequences beginning with one of those members will satisfy 'Fa_1'. But those sequences will not satisfy '$(\forall x_1)Fx_1$' for that would require that every sequence satisfy 'Fx_1'. *Ex hypothesi* some sequences do not. Therefore on the definition of $\vDash$ in terms of satisfaction, the sequence which we do not want to be semantically valid is not in fact semantically valid.

In a well-designed logic the syntactical notion of a derivable sequent matches up with the semantical notion of a semantically valid sequent. In the case of the propositional logic this was proved. In the case of the predicate logic any syntactically derivable sequent is semantically valid and any semantically valid sequent is syntactically derivable. The structure of the proof of the former result (the consistency of the logic) is indicated below. The latter result (the completeness of the logic) is a more sophisticated matter that falls outside the scope of the present work. The interested student is referred at the end of this chapter to various sources for this proof. A consequence of this result is that a *wff* is derivable as a theorem just in case it is a quantology.

In the case of the propositional calculus circumstance surveyors can be used to determine in a mechanical fashion whether a sequent is semantically correct. No mechanical determination is possible for the predicate logic. In the predicate logic we have to deal with an infinite number of different domains including domains having an infinite number of members. This means that there can be no mechanical procedure which must terminate in finite time giving us the answer to the question whether any sequence in any interpretation that satisfied $A_1, \ldots, A_n$ would also satisfy B in order to answer the question whether the sequent $A_1, \ldots, A_n \vDash B$ was semantically correct. It is for this reason that we investigated arguments through the syntactical approach, considering whether we could derive the corresponding syntactical sequent, $A_1, \ldots, A_n \vdash B$. Since the completeness result can be established we have the assurance that if any sequent is semantically correct, it can be shown to be so by deriving the corresponding syntactical sequent. However, while we can check mechanically any proffered derivation for correctness, there is no mechanical means of generating a proof of a given derivable sequent.

A proof that any derivable sequence is semantically valid can be given which parallels the proof given of this result for the propositional calculus. One first considers the shortest possible syntactical derivation; namely, that which would establish $A \vdash A$. Trivially, for any interpretation, any sequence that satisfies A, satisfies A. Hence, $A \vDash A$. Next we assume the result holds for derivation n lines in length. That is, if $A_1, \ldots, A_n \vdash B$ is established in n lines then $A_1, \ldots, A_n \vDash B$. Taking each rule in turn we find that extending the derivation by a single line preserves the result. It is concluded by mathematical induction that the result holds generally. Thus any syntactically derivable sequent is semantically valid.

As a special case of the above result we conclude that if $\vdash A$ then $\vDash A$. That is, any theorem is a quantology. This shows that the logic is syntactically consistent. That is, there is no A such that $\vdash A$ and $\vdash \neg A$. Suppose that were so. Then it follows that $\vDash A$ and $\vDash \neg A$. But it is contradictory to suppose that every sequence both satisfies and does not satisfy A. Hence by *reductio ad absurdum* we reject the supposition of syntactical inconsistency.

EXERCISES

1 Consider the following interpretation:

Domain: 1,2,3,4,5

F: $\langle 1,1 \rangle, \langle 2,2 \rangle, \langle 3,3 \rangle, \langle 4,4 \rangle, \langle 5,5 \rangle$

G: $\langle 1,2 \rangle, \langle 2,3 \rangle, \langle 3,4 \rangle, \langle 4,3 \rangle$

n: 3

Consider sequences which begin as follows:

s_1: $\langle 1,1,1,1,1, \ldots$

s_2: $\langle 2,2,2,2,2, \ldots$

s_3: $\langle 3,4,3,4,3, \ldots$

s_4: $\langle 1,4,3,5,2, \ldots$

s_5: $\langle 4,3,1,2,5, \ldots$

Which sequences satisfy the following:

Fx_2, x_3

Gx_1, x_2

Fn, x_2

2 Consider a domain consisting of Icabod, Isabel and Henry. Icabod loves Isabel and Isabel loves Henry. No one else in the domain loves anyone else in the domain. Icabod hates Henry but no one else hates anyone. Using '*Lxy*' for '*x* loves *y*' and '*Hxy*' for '*x* hates *y*' find the first three places of sequences which will show that the following sentences are false:

(a) $(\exists x_1)(\forall x_2)Lx_1,x_2$.

(b) $(\forall x_1)(\forall x_2)Hx_1,x_2$.

(c) $(\forall x_1)(\exists x_2)Lx_1,x_2$.

(d) $(\exists x_1)(\forall x_2)Hx_1,x_2$.

(e) $(\forall x_1)(\exists x_2)Hx_1,x_2$.

3 Show that the following *wff*s are not quantologies by giving an interpretation and the first three places of an infinite sequence which does not satisfy the *wff* for the interpretation:

(a) $(\exists x_1)Fx_1$

(b) $(\exists x_1)(\forall x_2)Fx_1,x_2 \ v \ (\forall x_2)(\exists x_1)Fx_1,x_2$

(c) $(\exists x_1)(\exists x_2)((x_1 = x_2) \ \& \ (\forall x_3)(x_3 = x_1 \ v \ x_3 = x_2))$

(d) $(\forall x_1)(Fx_1 \rightarrow Gx_1) \rightarrow (\exists x_1)Fx_1$

(e) $(\exists x_1)Fx_1 \ \& \ ((\exists x_2)Fx_2 \rightarrow (\exists x_3)(Fx_3 \ \& \ Gx_3))$

(f) $(\forall x_1)(Fx_1 \ v \ Gx_1) \rightarrow ((\forall x_2)Fx_2 \ v \ (\forall x_3)Gx_3)$

(g) $((\forall x_1)Fx_1 \rightarrow P) \rightarrow (\forall x_1)(Fx_1 \rightarrow P)$

FURTHER READING

On the meta-theory of the predicate logic (including completeness):
G. Hunter, *Metalogic* (Berkeley: University of California Press, 2nd edn, 1971)
R. H. Thomason, *Symbolic Logic* (London: Macmillan, 1970).

On philosophical applications of predicate logic semantics:
M. Platts, *Ways of Meaning* (London: Routledge & Kegan Paul, 1979).

CHAPTER 9
Challenges and limitations

In this chapter we look at arguments which present a challenge to our logic as so far developed. In some cases these arguments can be dealt with more or less satisfactorily by deploying the logic with ingenuity. In other cases some enrichment is required. Further lines of development are indicated through the readings at the end of the chapter.

1 COMPARATIVE ADJECTIVES

Consider the following arguments:

> Ronald Reagan is a bald actor. Therefore, Ronald Reagan is an actor.

> Ronald Reagan is a bald actor. Therefore, Ronald Reagan is bald.

These are obviously valid and it is trivial to derive the formalization. Using 'n' for Ronald Reagan and 'Bx' for 'x is bald' and 'Ax' for 'x is an actor' these are, respectively:

$Bn \ \& \ An \vdash An$
$Bn \ \& \ An \vdash Bn$

Consider the following pair of arguments which appear to have the same form:

> Ronald Reagan is a good actor. Therefore Ronald Reagan is an actor.

> Ronald Reagan is a good actor. Therefore, Ronald Reagan is good.

The first is entirely acceptable, the latter not at all. Reagan is not good in general. He is merely a good actor. Good actors can be far from good. Suppose we were to formalize these arguments using '*Gx*' for '*x* is good'. We have:

> *Gn* & *An* ⊢ *An*
> *Gn* & *An* ⊢ *Gn*

Since these sequents are derivable something is wrong with our formalization. The problem is that such words as 'good' cannot be represented as simple predicates. If we treat them in that fashion we will be committed to representing as valid arguments which patently are not valid. This problem is common to all comparative adjectives; that is, adjectives which are used to say something about an object in a certain respect in comparison with other objects. To take another example consider the arguments:

> Bruce is a small Australian. Therefore, Bruce is an Australian.

> Bruce is a small Australian. Therefore, Bruce is small.

The former is obviously valid but the latter not. Australians being in general very large it does not follow that small Australian is small without qualification. Bruce could be a small Australian but still be much taller than the average person in the world. But using '*m*' for Bruce, '*Sx*' for '*s* is small' and '*Dx*' for '*x* is an Australian' the following formalizations represent derivable sequents:

> *Sm* & *Dm* ⊢ *Dm*
> *Sm* & *Dm* ⊢ *Sm*

As in the case of 'good' we cannot formulate the arguments by treating smallness as a simple property of objects.

The problem is that Reagan is not good. He is good as an actor. Bruce is not small. He is small for an Australian. One might try formalizing the arguments by representing 'good actor' and 'small Australian' by a single predicate letter, say, '*Fx*' and '*Hx*' respectively. In which case the four arguments would be formalized as:

Fn ⊢ *An*
Fn ⊢ *Gn*
Hm ⊢ *Dm*
Hm ⊢ *Sm*

Certainly we can no longer derive the sequents corresponding on this formalization to the invalid pair of arguments. But unfortunately neither can we derive the sequents corresponding to the valid pair of arguments.

In the face of such problems it is always worth considering how one might paraphrase in English the problematic premises. For instance, one might treat being small as a matter of being smaller than some particular class of thing or things. Perhaps one could construe 'Bruce is a small Australian' as meaning that Bruce is smaller than the standard Australian who we shall suppose is called 'George'. Using '*o*' for George and '*Sxy*' for '*x* is smaller than *y*' the formalization of the arguments would be:

Dm & *Smo* ⊢ *Dm*
Dm & *Smo* ⊢ *Smo*

Both of these are derivable sequents and correspond to the following valid arguments:

> Bruce is an Australian and is smaller than George.
> Therefore Bruce is an Australian.

> Bruce is an Australian and is smaller than George.
> Therefore Bruce is smaller than George.

Using this style of formalization we cannot derive something corresponding to the invalid argument: Bruce is a small Australian. Therefore Bruce is small. We can only derive something which is intended to represent the thought that he is small for an Australian, i.e. smaller than George, the standard Australian.

But the paraphrase considered above is not a plausible construal of the problematic premise. For in asserting that Bruce is a small Australian we do not have in mind some particular Australian, George, who has the standard height. It would be more plausible to suppose that we meant that Bruce is smaller than most Australians. However, on this construal we cannot represent the validity of the argument at all. For we cannot express the inexact quantifier 'most' in our language. And, furthermore, this construal is not appropriate for all comparative adjectives. We would not necessarily accept that Ronald Reagan's being a good actor meant that he was a better actor than most actors. For we might face a situation in which we have been inflicted with a host of bad actors so that while Reagan was not a good actor he was better than most. In this case we have in mind some standard which is not necessarily embodied by any actors in relation to which we judge Reagan to be a good actor. But in our predicate language we can only compare Reagan to other objects and not to some abstract standard. Consequently we have to conclude that comparative adjectives cannot be adequately represented in our language. Unfortunately there is no simple modification which would allow them to be represented.

2 ADVERBS

Icabod is a languid, slow-moving dim-witted fellow who once, on answering the telephone, uncharacteristically spoke quickly. Reflecting on that situation someone advances the following pair of arguments:

> Icabod spoke quickly. Therefore, Icabod spoke.
> Icabod spoke quickly. Therefore, Icabod is quick.

The former is valid but the latter is not. It also looks as though the validity and invalidity arises from a matter of form not content. For if we use other verbs and adverbs we can construct a corresponding pair of arguments, one valid and one invalid. For example, let us suppose that Icabod uncharacteristically and briefly runs fast:

> Icabod ran fast. Therefore, Icabod ran.
> Icabod ran fast. Therefore, Icabod is fast.

If using 'Sx' for 'x spoke' and 'Qx' for 'x is quick' and 'n' for

Icabod we formalize the arguments both correspond to derivable sequents:

$$Sn \ \& \ Qn \vdash Sn$$
$$Sn \ \& \ Qn \vdash Qn$$

Clearly this style of formalization will not do. For while it represents the valid argument as valid it represents the invalid argument as valid. The problem is that the adverb 'quickly' does not qualify Icabod, it qualifies the action of Icabod's speaking. It is his speaking and not he himself which is quick. The formalization given errs in representing the quickness as a property of Icabod. We want to apply the term 'quick' to the state of affairs: Icabod spoke. That state of affairs can be represented by: Sn. The problem is that in our language we do not have a way of applying a property to a state of affairs instead of objects. Some logicians are exploring extensions of the quantificational language which would permit the attachment of properties to Icabod's speaking as well as to Icabod. A consideration of this would take us beyond the confines of the present work. However, there is something which we might do in order to cope with such arguments within our existing language. Indeed some philosophers hold that the solution given below is entirely adequate and that no extension is needed to deal with adverbs.

Icabod's speaking is an event. It is something that happens and it is something we can discourse about. Let us take as our domain the set of all *events* as well as the set of all living persons. The quickness which cannot be attributed to Icabod can be attributed to the event in question. A possible paraphrase of the English sentence 'Icabod spoke quickly' is: There was an event, produced by Icabod (it is *his* speaking with which we are concerned), which was a speaking (that is the kind of event produced) and it was a quick event. To formalize this we use the interpretation below:

Domain: the set of all events and the set of living persons.

Ex : x is an event
Pxy : x was produced by person y
Sx : x was an act of speaking

Qx : x was a quick event
n : Icabod
Qx : x is a quick person

The formalization of the pair of arguments is then:

$(\exists x)\,(Ex \ \& \ Pxn \ \& \ Sx \ \& \ Qx) \vdash (\exists x)\,(Ex \ \& \ Pxn \ \& \ Sx)$
$(\exists x)\,(Ex \ \& \ Pxn \ \& \ Sx \ \& \ Qx) \vdash Qn$

The former sequent corresponding to the valid argument is derivable. The latter sequent corresponding to the invalid argument is not derivable. Thus this device enables us to represent adverbs in our language by including events in our domain.

This approach involves an ontological commitment to events. That is, we have to say that there are events as well as persons and objects. Some philosophers think it is strange to lump Icabod and his speaking together. They would prefer to give some construal to our talk about events that prevents events becoming some sort of object. However, it is unlikely that any other approach to this problem will enable us to stick to a parsimonious ontology.

3 TIMES

To this juncture we have ignored a pervasive and important feature of ordinary discourse. This is its temporal aspect. Consider the following three sentences:

It is raining.
It will rain.
It has rained.

The second and third are the future and past tense versions of the first. More perspicuously we can write:

It is raining.
It will be that (it is raining).
It was that (it is raining).

This representation suggests that if we wish to replicate the functioning of tenses in our logic we would have to add new sentence-forming operators using, say, '$\bar{P}$' as the past tense operator and '$\bar{F}$' as the future tense operator. If 'it is raining' is symbolized by 'R' the three sentences above would be represented as:

R
$\bar{F}R$
$\bar{P}R$

One reason for wishing to extend the logic is that there are arguments involving tenses which are valid in virtue of an aspect of form which relates to tenses and which we cannot represent in our logic as it stands. For instance, the following argument is valid and any argument obtained by replacing 'it is raining' by any other present tense sentence would be valid:

It is raining
Therefore, it will be that it has rained

The formalization of this would be: $R \vdash \bar{F}\bar{P}R$.
We might develop an extension of our propositional logic with rules for the tense operators which would enable us to derive this formalization.

We will not explore further the possibilities of developing what is called a tense logic. For we are restricting ourselves in this work to truth-functional propositional logic and clearly the sentence-forming operators 'It will be that _' and 'It was that _' are not truth-functional. If I know that it is now raining I cannot on the basis of that information alone decide whether it is true or false that it will rain or that it has rained. That is a matter of meteorology or history.

In our logic we have treated propositions as being true or false. Some logicians reflecting on tensed discourse have concluded that this is too simplistic a view. For the sentence 'It rains' expresses a truth at some times and expresses a falsehood at other times. They hold that 'It rains' thus expresses a proposition the truth-value of which changes with time. Other logicians prefer to treat propositions as always being either true or false. They regard the sentence 'It rains' as expressing a different proposition each time it is used. If it is used at 4 o'clock on Monday, 15 December 1981 (call that time, time *t*) it expresses the proposition expressed by the sentence 'It rains at time t'. This latter sentence is treated tenselessly. That is, it has a truth-value which depends on the weather at that time and does not change. The proposition expressed at time t by the sentence 'It will rain' is taken on this approach to be more perspicuously represented by the sentence: There is a time t' later than time t and it rains at t'. Analogously the proposition expressed by the past tense sentence 'It rained' said at time t is rendered as: There is a time t' earlier than t and it rains at t'.

This latter way of thinking of what is expressed by tensed sentences gives an approximation to tensed English discourse in the predicate logic by including in our domain, times. Consider the present tense sentence 'Icabod is running' said at time t. Instead of treating that as ascribing a one-place property expressed by 'x runs' to Icabod we treat that as ascribing a two-term relation expressed by 'x runs at y' between Icabod and time t. Using 'Rxy' to express the predicate the formalization with 'n' for Icabod is: Rnt. The sentence, said at time t, 'Icabod will run' is then expressed by '$(\exists x)(Tx \mathrel{\&} Lxt \mathrel{\&} Rnx)$' where the domain contains both persons and times and 'Tx' is 'x is a time' and 'Lxy' is 'x is later than y'. The sentence, said at time t, 'Icabod has run' is represented by: '$(\exists x)(Tx \mathrel{\&} Ltx \mathrel{\&} Rnx)$'.

As a further illustration of how we can use the predicate logic to approximate some aspects of temporal discourse consider the sentence: 'Dodos are extinct'. Letting 'Dx' be 'x is a dodo' and 'Ex' be 'x is extinct' we might try representing this as '$(\forall x)(Dx \rightarrow Ex)$'. This is not in fact a successful rendition of the English for it amounts to saying that if you found a dodo you would find that it did not exist. And, furthermore, given that there are no dodos, if we use this representation, we would have to count it as true that dodos are not extinct. For that would be represented as: '$(\forall x)(Dx \rightarrow \neg Ex)$'. What we mean by saying that dodos are extinct is that at one time there were dodos but at the present time there are no dodos. If we let our domain be past and present animals plus times and letting 'Dxy' be 'x is a live dodo at time y' and 'Ax' be 'x is an animal' we can formalize the problematic sentence as follows with 't' for the present time:

$$(\exists x)(\exists y)(Tx \mathrel{\&} Ltx \mathrel{\&} Ay \mathrel{\&} Dyx) \mathrel{\&} \neg (\exists x)(Ax \mathrel{\&} Dxt).$$

4 MODALITIES

There are valid arguments the validity of which depends on the functioning of the words 'necessary' and 'possible'. Examples are:

> It is necessary that bachelors are unmarried.
> Therefore, bachelors are unmarried.

> Concorde is flying.
> Therefore, it is possible that Concorde is flying.

> It is necessarily the case that $2+2 = 4$.

Following standard convention we write '□' for the sentence-forming operator 'It is necessarily the case that _'and ' ◊ ' for the sentence-forming operator 'It is possibly the case that _'. Clearly these operators are not truth-functional. For from the truth of the proposition that grass is green I cannot ascertain whether or not it is true that it is necessarily true that grass is green. And from the fact that it is false that grass is red I cannot decide whether or not it is possible for grass to be red. The branch of logic that studies these operators is called *modal logic*. In English these modalities are more often expressed by such colloquial expressions as given below:

> Sugar *must* dissolve in boiling water
> The square on the hypotenuse *has to be* the sum of the squares on the other two sides.
> A monk *could be* sexually experienced.
> Grass *might be* red.

A consideration of these and other examples that there are several kinds of necessity and possibly. For instance consider the following:

> It is not possible to fly from Peterborough to Ottawa. (There are no scheduled flights.)

> It is possible to fly from Peterborough to Ottawa. (It is technically feasible to do this.)

> It is not possible to fly to the moon. (It is not technically feasible to do this.)

It is possible to fly to the moon. (There is nothing in the laws of nature to rule this out even if technology is not sufficiently advanced at present to allow this.)

It is not possible to fly faster than the speed of light (The laws of nature rule this out.)

While you cannot imagine round squares, it is possible to imagine flying faster than light. (Possible in the sense of not involving a contradiction.)

As our purpose is only to illustrate the very beginnings of modal logic, attention will be restricted in what follows to the notions of *logical necessity* and *logical possibility*. A proposition S is logically necessary if and only if the denial of S is inconsistent. This means that any proposition which is logically true is necessarily true. And any analytic proposition will be necessarily true as will the truths of mathematics. For S to be logically possible means that S is consistent. In point of fact we can define logical possibility in terms of logical necessity. For if S is possible it must be false that not-S is necessarily true. For if not-S is necessarily true then not-not-S, i.e. S, is inconsistent. And if it is false that not-S is necessarily true there is no contradiction in the proposition not-not-S i.e. S. Thus we will define logical possibility by the schema: $\Diamond S$ if and only $\neg \Box \neg S$.

To develop a propositional logic for logical necessity we add the symbols '$\Box$' and '$\Diamond$' to our vocabulary and alter our rules of well-formedness by adding the clauses:

if A is a *wff* then $\Box A$ is a *wff*
if A is a *wff* then $\Diamond A$ is a *wff*.

As before we have an introduction and elimination rule for '$\Box$'. The elimination rule (to be cited as $\Box$ E) licenses the inference of A from $\Box A$. In citing this rule one gives the line to which it is applied. The resulting *wff* rests on whatever premises the line to which it applied rests or rests on that line itself if it was a premise.

The rule is intuitively acceptable. For it is safe to infer that A is true, if A is necessarily true. The rule of □-introduction, to be cited as □I, allows us to infer a *wff* of the form □A from any line A given that A is not a premise and does not rest on any premises. In citing the rule one gives the line to which it is applied. The result of applying the rule will not rest on any premises. The restriction on this rule means in effect that we can only introduce '□' in front of a *wff* which is a theorem. Seperate rules for ' ◊' are not given as we are treating ' ◊' as an abbreviation for ' ⌐□ ⌐'. In addition we need rules which determine how '□' interacts with the other propositional symbols. Below are two of these rules. The characterization of the remaining rules is left as an exercise:

R_1: Given a line of the form □$(A \rightarrow B)$ rule R_1 licenses the inference of □$A \rightarrow$ □B resting on whatever premises □$(A \rightarrow B)$ rests on or on □$(A \rightarrow B)$ if it is itself a premises. In citing this rule the number of the line of □$(A \rightarrow B)$ is given.

R_2: Given a line of the form □ ⌐A the rule R_2 licenses the inference of ⌐□A resting on whatever premises □ ⌐A rests on or on □ ⌐A if it is itself a premise. In citing this rule the number on the line of □ ⌐A is given.

As noted above the modal operators '□' and ' ◊' are not truth-functional. This means that we cannot use truth-tables in evaluating formulae containing them. Logicians have found it useful in this context to introduce the notion of a *possible world*. A possible world is a way things could have been, the actual world being one among the possible worlds. A world in which the assassination attempt on Archduke Ferdinand was not successful and in which history evolved differently thereafter is another possible world. In another possible world the conditions necessary for life to appear on the earth never developed.

In what follows we will make some highly simplifying assumptions. Let us suppose that we have a list of sentences '$P_1, \ldots, P_n$' which are all independent of one another. That is, fixing the truth-value of each sentence has to be done independently of the others. If we think of each sentence as expressing a proposition, we can think of an assignment of truth-values to each sentence as expressing a way things could be, i.e. as describing a possible world. One distribution makes each 'P_i' true, another makes each 'P_i' false, others make some 'P_i' true and some false. Given a particular assignment of truth-values which describes the possible world we can work out for that world the truth-values of sentences formed using only the truth-functional operators of the propositional logic. For example, if in world W_a 'P_i' and 'P_j' are true and 'P_m', 'P_n' false then 'P_i & P_j' is true, '$P_i \rightarrow P_m$' is false, '$P_j \rightarrow P_n$' is false and so on. We will say that $\Box A$ is true in a world if and only if A is true in *every* world. The only *wff*s which will come out true in every world are the tautologies. Given the definition of ' $\Diamond$ ' in terms of '$\Box$' we can see that a *wff* of the form $\Diamond A$ will be true in a world if and only if $\Box \neg A$ is false in that world. That is, there must be some world in which not-A is false, i.e. some world in which A is true. On these definitions if $\Box A$ is true in a world, A is true in every world and so in any world $\Diamond A$ is true. This means that our definition of truth for sentences of the form $\Box$ A corresponds to Leibniz's definition of necessary truths as truths which are true in all possible worlds. This is but the barest of beginnings of a complex and controversial area of logic.

5 PROPOSITIONAL ATTITUDES

Propositional attitude expressions are such expressions as hopes, believes, fears, wishes, imagines, etc. These have been called propositional attitudes on the grounds that they express the holding of an attitude to a proposition, e.g. an attitude of hoping that Santa Claus will come tonight, or of believing that Santa Claus does not exist. We saw in our discussion of identity that these expressions can occur in contexts in which the rule of identity elimination fails. For instance, it may be true that Everest is Chomolongolinga, that Icabod believes that Everest is a nice mountain and yet false that Icabod believes that Chomolongolinga is a nice mountain. This means that we cannot represent such locutions in our quantificational logic since it was developed on the assumption that the identity elimination rule holds. In any event we do not even have a category of expression of the type which would be needed to represent propositional attitudes. For such expressions as '. . . believes that . . .' require for completion a name of a person or a quantifier over persons for the first blank and a proposition or quantifier over propositions for the second blank. The propositional attitude expression is in some ways like a predicate (with respect to the first blank) and in other ways like a sentence forming operator (with respect to the second blank). To express propositional attitudes requires the introduction of such hybrid expressions and restrictions to preclude the application of identity elimination within propositional attitude contexts.

It might seem that this particular problem would not arise in the case of propositional attitude expressions used without completion by a proposition. For instance, consider the sentence 'Icabod wants Dr Jekyll' which we can compare with 'Icabod hit Dr Jekyll'. Let 'n' stand for Icabod and let 'm' for Dr Jekyll and 'o' for Mr Hyde. Using 'Hxy' for 'x hit y' and 'Wxy' for 'x wants y', the formalization of the second sentence would be 'Hnm' and of the first sentence 'Wnm'. There is no problem in substituting 'o' for 'm' in the latter sentence. If Icabod hit Dr Jekyll he hit Mr Hyde and that is true regardless of whether or not Icabod realizes that Dr Jekyll is Mr Hyde. However, the substitution of o for m in the former sentence may well not preserve truth. Icabod may detest Mr Hyde, but failing to realize that Mr Hyde is Dr Jekyll he has formed an intense desire to have Dr Jekyll as his doctor having heard laudable things about him. In this case it may be true that Icabod wants Dr Jekyll but false that he wants Mr Hyde. Thus even if a propositional attitude occurs as a predicate and not as a hybrid predicate/operator we cannot formalize it in our quantificational language if it occurs in a context which is a counter-example to unrestricted identity elimination. However, whenever a propositional attitude word is used in relation to a referring expression or quantifier and not a proposition and in such a way that the identity elimination rule holds, we can formulate the sentence using a predicate for the propositional attitude expression.

The failure of identity elimination in propositional attitude contexts also gives rise to problems with quantification as was indicated in Chapter 6. Consider the sentence 'Icabod wants to see a dragon'. If we construe the scope of the quantifier as being the entire sentence we have: There is a dragon and Icabod wants to see it. This latter sentence commits its user to the existence of a dragon. That may be what is wanted. It may be that in making this report about Icabod one wishes to align oneself with those who believe in dragons. If I (as a dragon believer) report on Icabod this may be the correct representation of what I meant by the original sentence. However, I might be a sceptic where dragons are concerned. In this case my sentence should be construed as follows so as to give the existential quantifier small scope. Icabod wants it to be the case that there is a dragon and that he sees it. By taking the existential quantifier inside the scope of the propositional attitude we can use it without committing ourselves to the existence of a dragon.

As was seen in Chapter 6 care must be taken in introducing quantifiers into propositional attitude contexts. Suppose for instance that Icabod believes in dragons. In fact he believes that Henry is a dragon. Applying existential introduction to the sentence 'Icabod believes Henry is a dragon' to obtain 'There is something which Icabod believes is a dragon' would in certain contexts generate a falsehood from a truth. For if there are no dragons there is nothing in the domain which Icabod believes to be a dragon (we suppose that this is so rather than that there is something, say a snake, called 'Henry' which Icabod falsely believes to be a dragon). Thus one cannot always apply the rule of existential introduction to propositional attitude contexts. The same point applies in the case of modal contexts. Logicians express this point by saying that one cannot quantify into non-extensional contexts, i.e. contexts in which the identity elimination rule fails.

6 INTUITIONISM

Perhaps the most central challenge to the logic presented in this book is not that it is too weak (i.e. that there are many types of argument which cannot be analysed by it) but that it is in one way too strong. The logic is built on the assumption that any proposition is true or is false. That is, that there are two truth-values and any proposition has at least one of them and at most one of them. This is revealed in the fact that within the logic we can prove the Law of the Excluded Middle (hereafter cited as *LEM*), $P \vee \neg P$, and the Law of Non-Contradiction, $\neg(P \& \neg P)$ to be tautologies. Ever since Aristotle there have been logicians who doubted that *LEM* was a genuine law of logic. And in recent years a group of logicians called *intuitionists* working on the foundation of mathematics have developed a critique of *LEM*. Other philosophers have sought to support this critique by arguments drawn more from the study of language and meaning.

One starting point for a version of this critique is to note that one should not assume without argument that any indicative sentence is capable of being true or false. For instance, some philosophers hold that sentences such as 'His action was wrong' are not in fact capable of being true or false on the grounds that they are disguised imperatives having something like the following force: Let neither me nor anyone else do that kind of thing. Given that some apparent indicatives have been regarded as lacking a truth-value, how does one establish that a sentence really is true or false? If one could outline a procedure which if followed would give as an answer to the question 'Is it true or false?' we might feel entitled to hold it was one or the other prior to our having carried our the procedure. That is, if we can outline a technique which could in principle be followed and which would terminate if followed in a 'yes-no' verdict in finite time to the question 'Is P true?' then we are entitled to think that P is true or false even if we have not carried out the procedure and hence do not actually know which of the two possibilities obtain.

If there are indicative sentences for which we do not have such a procedure we cannot justify in this way the claim that they are true or false. And we cannot simply say that they are true or false by appeal to the *LEM* for that would beg the question. *LEM* is law of logic only if there are no propositions with non-vacuous referring terms that lack a truth value. The intuitionist does not see why he should assume that any sentence for which we lack such a procedure has a definite truth-value. Of course his position would not be very interesting if it turned out that there were no such sentences. However, there are reasons to think that there are such sentences both in mathematics and in everyday discourse. To take an example which has been much discussed. Suppose that Jones lived and died without ever having been put in those testing circumstances in which behaviour of one kind gives evidence of bravery and behaviour of another kind gives evidence of a lack of bravery. We do not know whether to say that Jones was brave or that Jones was not brave. Indeed, there does not seem to be any procedure which we could follow to settle this issue. Even if we were to know everything that Jones did, we would not, in the circumstances we are imagining, know whether he was or was not brave. The intuitionist does not assert that either Jones was brave or Jones was not brave. That is, if the interpretation of '*P*' is 'Jones is brave' he does not assert *P* v ¬*P* and hence does not regard *LEM* as a genuine law of logic.

To arrive at a formal logic which reflects this line of argument we take our propositional logic and drop the law of negation elimination. Having dropped this it is not possible to derive *P* v ¬*P*. The nearest one comes to this is a derivation of ¬¬(*P* v ¬*P*). Without ¬-elimination one cannot get from ¬¬(*P* v ¬*P*) to (*P* v ¬*P*). The intuitionist does not assert ¬(*P* v ¬*P*). For since he admits ¬¬(P v ¬*P*) as a theorem, asserting ¬(*P* v ¬*P*) would render his logic inconsistent. Thus he simply refrains from asserting (*P* v ¬*P*) without asserting ¬(*P* v ¬*P*).

The only other change the intuitionist makes is to add a rule which in effect says that anything follows from a contradiction. That is, he adds a rule which licenses one to conclude *B* from a line of the form *A* & ¬*A*. A further discussion of the intuitionist's motivations lies outside the scope of this work. It is to be noted that the intuitionist does not use truth-tables to explain the functioning of the connectives of his propositional logic. For it is clear that if we use our truth-tables then '*P* v ¬*P*' is a tautology. Instead the intuitionist uses what we might call *assertability tables*. Instead of saying that '*P* v *Q*' is true just in case '*P*' is true or '*Q*' is true he says: '*P* v *Q*' can be asserted just in case '*P*' can be asserted or 'Q' can be asserted. If we consider '$P \vee \neg P$' we see that there will be cases such as that discussed above in which the intuitionist thinks that 'P' cannot be asserted and that '$\neg P$' cannot be asserted and hence that '$P \vee \neg P$' is not assertable. For him something is assertable just in case we have a procedure which would in principle determine whether we should assert that 'P' is true or that 'P' is false.

7 THE SCOPE OF LOGIC

We began by defining logic as the study of valid arguments where a valid argument was defined as one in which if the premises are true the conclusion must be true. We also said that logic concerned form and not content. Initially we investigated those arguments the validity of which depended on the occurrence in them of truth-functional sentence-forming operators. There were arguments the validity of which could not be displayed in our propositional logic. Consequently we enriched it so as to be able to study arguments the validity of which depended on the occurrence of the exact quantifiers 'all' and 'some'. In this chapter we have looked at some arguments which are valid but beyond the scope of even our enriched logic. The study of yet more enriched logics designed to cope with these and other arguments is less developed and more controversial than the quantificational and propositional logics. One reason for this underdevelopment stems from the fact that the interest in logic in the first half of this century stemmed from the desire of Russell, Frege and others to put mathematics on a firm foundation. And it turns out that the quantificational logic which we have been using is adequate to analyse all the arguments of mathematics. Hence given the original motivation there was reason to rest content with the development of that logic.

The development of further extensions of logic has arisen in large measure from a shift of interest on the part of logicians from mathematics to language in general. And that has brought with it an interest in the validity of arguments which simply have no place in mathematics. This in turn raises the question of the scope of logic. We remarked that logic is concerned with form and not content. That being so there are valid arguments whose validity is not a matter of logic. For instance consider the following argument:

> Object *a* is red.
> Therefore *a* is not green.

This, given our definition, is valid. For if the premise is true the conclusion must be true. But logicians are unlikely to seek to develop a logic of colour to cope with it. Their feeling is that the validity arises from content and not form. It depends on the meaning of the words 'red' and 'green' and if we were to produce another argument by substituting other predicates we would not preserve validity. For instance, if we put 'square' for 'red' and 'heavy' for 'green' the argument is patently invalid. But how do we distinguish between form and content? Might not someone hold that the following argument which is valid is not so in virtue of logic:

> It is necessarily true that $2 + 2 = 4$.
> Therefore, it is true that $2 + 2 = 4$.

For if we substitute for 'it is necesarily true that' the phrase 'it is believed true that' the resulting argument is invalid. That is, one might say that the validity of the original argument stems from the content, the meaning of 'necessity' and not from the logical form.

We can put the problem succinctly as follows: Logic is the study of arguments the validity of which arises from the form and not the content of the argument. Such an argument remains valid if we carry out substitutions which preserve the form. Which expressions are those on which substitutions are not carried out? That is, which expressions must be held *constant* to preserve form? Logicians are agreed up to a point on the answer to this question. For virtually all would agree that 'and', 'or', 'if . . . then', 'not', 'if and only if', 'all', 'some' and 'is' (of identity) are to be counted as *logical constants*. Many would go further and agree to count 'necessary' and 'possible' as well. Some count the propositional attitude words such as 'believes' and 'knows' as logical constants and seek to develop logics of belief and knowledge. Unfortunately there is not even general agreement on the principle that should be invoked in settling disputes about which expressions are to count as logical constants. In the end this is perhaps not a very important issue. We have an interest in all types of arguments and it does not matter greatly how widely we construe the class of arguments the validity of which is to be regarded as arising from logical form. If construing logic in a wider sense has the effect of generating a careful study of a wider class of arguments than would otherwise be the case, let us construe it widely. However, in construing it widely we must not assume that we will have the same degree of rigour and precision in a logic of, say, inexact quantifiers or of belief that we have in the logic of exact quantifiers or the propositional logic.

Hopefully the reader has obtained some sense of the point of logic, of its successes and of its problems. It was noted at the beginning of the book that many writers take the point of logic to be the improvement of our reasoning. That logic will help in this way is so difficult to establish at the level of elementary logic (the propositional calculus) that it was suggested we look for another rationale. This was found in the fact that articulating the rules of logic gives in part an explanation of how it is we are able to recognize intuitively the difference between good and bad arguments. While this remains as good a reason as any to study logic, my exaggeration in playing down the importance of logic as a tool in reasoning should now be qualified. For it is highly likely that in the last five chapters the reader has encountered arguments the validity or invalidity of which could not be seen at a glance. In such cases the explicit deployment of the rules of logic would have been an aid to reasoning.

Other reasons for studying logic have emerged. For instance, we have illustrated how equivalence relations have been deployed in giving philosophical analyses (e.g. of time and of numbers). And the attempts to extend our basic logic brings into sharp focus interesting and important philosophical questions. For instance, the consideration of adverbs leads to the metaphysical question as to whether events should be thought of as existing alongside objects. Further, once alleged laws of logic are explicitly formulated we can and ought as philosophers to inquire as to their justification. Asking this in regard to the Law of the Excluded Middle (*LEM*) has generated a fruitful and far-reaching controversy touching all areas of philosophy. In a nutshell the issue is: if the truth-value of an indicative sentence '*S*' cannot be decided (even in principle) how should we think of the situation? One who has adopted *LEM* thinks that there is some fact, some inaccessible fact, which makes '*S*' true or makes '*S*' false. That '*S*' is undecidable simply shows that the human condition is one with a certain degree of utterly inescapable ignorance. For the Intuitionist, on the other hand, *LEM* is not genuine law of logic and if '*S*' is undecidable there is no reason to hold that it has a truth-value. The world is simply indeterminate in respect to '*S*'. Pleasingly, then, we have no inescapable ignorance. Any time we are in a position to hold that there is a matter of fact at stake we can in principle at least get at that fact. However, the world while knowable in principle in all its aspects becomes somewhat plastic, somewhat indeterminate, at the edges. My concern is not to develop or even to adequately characterize this controversy but merely to indicate that an apparently simply dispute about what is or is not a law of logic leads us into the deepest waters of epistemology and metaphysics.

The objects we have defined in this study, the propositional and predicate languages and logics, are precise, abstract, rigid, rigorous and clearcut. Our natural language and our ordinary thought can look the very antithesis of this. How then can the former help with the latter in any way at all? After all have we not been continually introducing such idealizations that we have lost touch with what was supposed to be our concern: arguments expressed in English? There are two ways of responding, either of which gives further point to the study of logic. Some readers will think that our ideal construction fits its natural counterpart surprisingly well. Logic shows the simple patterns behind the apparent complications and complexities of natural language. Other readers will see the idealizations as distorting (e.g. the treatment of 'if . . . then . . .' as a truth-function) and the simplification as mystifying (e.g. the treatment of all predicates as precise, as having no vagueness). However, even they can learn something about natural language through the study of logic. For the comparison between the abstract model and the intended subject matter shows (so they can urge) what a diverse unregimented motley is our natural language. One way or the other, then, there is something to be learned from the study of logic.

FURTHER READING

On adjectives and adverbs:
James D. McCawley, *Everything That Linguists Have Always Wanted to Know about Logic But Were Ashamed to Ask* (Oxford: Blackwell, 1982
M. Platts, *Ways of Meaning* (London: Routledge & Kegan Paul, 1979).

On tense logic:
A. N. Prior, *Past, Present and Future* (Oxford University Press, 1967).
N. Rescher and A. Urquart, *Temporal Logic* (New York: Springer-Verlag, 1971).

On modality:
G. H. Hughes and M. J. Cresswell, *An Introduction to Modal Logic* (London: Methuen, 1968).
R. Bradley and N. Swartz, *Possible Worlds* (Oxford: Blackwell, 1979).

On propositional attitudes:
A. N. Prior, *Objects of Thought* (Oxford University Press, 1971).

On intuitionism:
M. Dummett, *Truth and Other Enigmas* (London: Duckworth, 1978).
S. Haack, *Deviant Logic* (Cambridge University Press, 1975).

On the scope of logic:
W. C. Kneale and M. Kneale, *The Development of Logic* (Oxford University Press, 1961).

Appendix

MANUAL FOR TRUTH

TRUTH is a programme which provides practice in determining whether a formula is a *wff* and in the construction of truth-tables. This programme and its counter-part *PROVE* were written for Oxcom Ltd by A. F. Boucher. Both are available from Routledge & Kegan Paul, Broadway House, Newtown Road, Henley-on-Thames, Oxon RG9 1EN, on either disc or cassette to run on the BBC Micro Model B. Versions for other micros will be available shortly. Information on this and on up-dates in the BBC programmes can be obtained from Oxcom Ltd, 92 Lonsdale Road, Oxford, OX2 7ER (phone: (0865) 55436). In the event of any difficulties with the programme contact Oxcom Ltd. This manual follows the standard practice of using 'angle brackets', i.e. '⟨' and '⟩', to indicate what is to be typed when instructing the computer. Do not type the brackets themselves but do type exactly what is inside them with the exception of '⟨Ret⟩' which is used to indicate that the return key is to be hit. Notice that after giving any instruction to the computer you must hit ⟨Ret⟩. If this is not done the computer does not know whether you have finished giving it your instructions.

To start, insert the cassette or disc and type ⟨CHAIN *TRUTH*⟩ and hit ⟨Ret⟩, the return key. The programme will then load and run, displaying first the main menu which offers the following five alternatives:

1 ⟨WC⟩, ⟨Ret⟩   Selecting 'WC' for '*wff*-checker' enables you to check whether formulae which you input are *wff*s.

2 ⟨WT⟩, ⟨Ret⟩   Selecting 'WT' for '*wff*-tester' provides a test of your ability to determine whether a formula supplied by the computer is a *wff*.

3 ⟨TC⟩, ⟨Ret⟩   'TC', 'truth-table checker', displays the truth-table of a *wff* you have inputted and determines its logical status (i.e. tautological, contradictory or contingent).

4 ⟨TT⟩, ⟨Ret⟩   This is a truth-table test. The computer will offer you a *wff* to determine its logical status.

5 ⟨QUIT⟩, ⟨Ret⟩   Type this to exit from the programme.

WFF-CHECKER

Selecting this option leads to a menu offering the choice between typing ⟨M⟩, ⟨Ret⟩ for return to the main menu, typing ⟨1⟩, ⟨Ret⟩ for the propositional calculus or ⟨2⟩, ⟨Ret⟩ for the predicate calculus. In the case of option ⟨1⟩ and of option ⟨2⟩ you will be invited to input a formula to be tested as a *wff*. Before inputting a formula note carefully the table below. For, in some cases, there are differences between the symbols used in the text and those accepted by the computer:

English	*Text*	*Computer*
not	⌐	–
and	&	&
if . . . then . . .	→	→
if and only if	↔	← →
or	*v*	*v*

For reasons that are not entirely clear the key for '→' on the BBC Micro is labeled ']' and the key for '←' is labeled '['. To input '← →' for 'if and only if' you type first '[' and then ']'. The universal quantifier is represented by upper case '*V*', disjunction by lower case '*v*' and the existential quantifier by upper case '*E*'. In view of this '*E*' and '*V*' cannot be used as predicate variables nor can '*v*' be used as a name. That is, for example, the computer does not count the expressions '*ExVx*' or '*Ea*' or '*Fv*' as *wff*s. *Note carefully that the quantifiers are not surrounded by brackets.* That is, for example, one inputs *Ex(Fx & Gx)* and *Vy(Fy → Gy)*. If you opt for the predicate calculus either propositional or predicate formulae can be inputted. If the propositional calculus is selected predicate formulae cannot be entered. Remember in inputting propositional formulae that the variables must be in upper case rather than lower case, i.e. *P,Q,R, . . .* not *p,q,r, . . .* .

While testing your *wff* the computer breaks it down into bits which are displayed on the left of the screen. If the formula is a *wff* each bit in the list will either be an atomic *wff* (e.g. *P* or *Fn*) or a *wff* formed by an application of one of the rules from bits below it in the list. If the formula is not a *wff* the computer will stop at the first bit which is not a *wff*.

To use the *wff*-checker programme, selected by typing ⟨WT⟩, ⟨Ret⟩ at the main menu, you type a number from 1 to 20 for the propositional calculus or from 21 to 40 for the predicate calculus, followed by ⟨Ret⟩. A formula is displayed for you to determine whether it is a *wff*. Type ⟨Y⟩, ⟨Ret⟩ if you think it is, otherwise ⟨N⟩, ⟨Ret⟩.

TC, truth-checker, constructs truth-tables for *wff*s which you input. Limitations of the screen display mean that no truth-table of more than 16 lines can be displayed and hence that no *wff* having more than four propositional variables is allowed. And the *wff* cannot have more than 26 symbols in all. The double vertical bars on the right of the screen indicate the maximum possible length of a *wff*. Once the *wff* is inputted and ⟨Ret⟩ has been hit the computer will display on the screen the truth-table. The listing of all possible truth-values for the atomic variables is given in green. The truth-values under the main connective are in red and the remainder in blue. If, however, the main connective happens to be adjacent to another connective (e.g. as in the *wff P v–Q*) the values will remain displayed in blue. To avoid cluttering the display the values of the propositional variables are not repeated under the *wff* being checked. If the *wff* is contingent the last line which gives the value F is displayed in a sort of purple. When the table is completed the logical status of the *wff* (i.e. contingent, tautological, contradictory) is displayed and you are offered the opportunity to print the table. If you have a printer connected type ⟨Y⟩, ⟨Ret⟩ for a print out. Otherwise type ⟨N⟩, ⟨Ret⟩. If when no printer is connected and turned on, ⟨Y⟩, ⟨Ret⟩ is accidentally inputted it will be necessary to press the escape key, followed by ⟨Control C⟩ (i.e., press 'C' while holding down the control key) and ⟨RUN⟩, ⟨Ret⟩. This returns the programme to the main menu.

If a truth-table is printed the computer will substitute ')' for '→' and '(' for '←'. This regrettable transformation arises from the fact that on the BBC micro the keys labelled ']' and '[' send to the screen the symbols '→' and '←', repectively, while sending to the printer ']' and '['. In fact the computer cannot send the symbol '→' to the printer at all! Consequently the programme substitutes ')' for '→' and '( )' for '← →' in printing out which means, also, that while printing out the same substitution is made on the screen display. An alternative would have been to use '(' and '( )' throughout for 'if . . . then . . .' and '. . . if and only if . . .' respectively. This was ruled out for on the screen display ')' is often virtually indistinguishable from the bracket ')'

The final option on this programme, TT or truth-test, enables you to select one of fifty *wff*s by typing a number from 1 to 50 followed by ⟨Ret⟩ to be tested on your ability to establish its logical status. In doing this you may wish to construct a truth-table with pencil and paper. Once you have entered your answer the computer will display the truth-table.

MANUAL FOR PROVE

PROVE is a programme which enables you to input on the BBC model B micro-computer proofs of theorems and sequents in both the proposition and predicate calculus. It monitors your work at each stage, noting errors and prompting you to correct them. When a derivation is successfully completed it offers you congratulations. The resulting derivation can then be printed out.

To start, insert the cassette or disc and type ⟨CHAIN *PROVE*⟩ and ⟨Ret⟩. The programme is very long (25K) which means that the cassette version will take some minutes to load. Once loaded the main menu is displayed offering the choice of typing ⟨P⟩ ⟨Ret⟩ to prove a *wff* (either as a theorem or from a set of assumptions) or typing ⟨Q⟩ ⟨Ret⟩ to leave the programme. As noted in the manual for *TRUTH*, following any instruction to the computer you must hit ⟨Ret⟩. Otherwise the computer does not know when you have finished your instruction to it.

If you select to prove your own *wff* the second menu will be displayed offering the choice of typing ⟨1⟩ for the propositional calculus, ⟨2⟩ for the predicate calculus or ⟨M⟩ for return to the main menu. In each case your choice must be followed by ⟨Ret⟩. Whether you choose the proposition or predicate calculus the next menu to be displayed is the same. But note that while you can input a propositional calculus proof if you have selected the predicate calculus you cannot input a predicate calculus proof if you have selected the propositional calculus. The menu offers you the possibility of returning to the main menu by typing ⟨M⟩ and ⟨Ret⟩. Otherwise you are invited to input your premises, hitting ⟨Ret⟩ after each one up to a maximum of four. The limited memory capacity of the BBC Micro precludes derivations with more than this number of initial premises. One can introduce further premises in the course of the derivation which are to be subsequently discharged. Once you have inputted all the premises of the sequent to be derived hit ⟨2⟩ and ⟨Ret⟩. You will then be invited to input your conclusion. As before, once this is done, hit ⟨Ret⟩.

In inputting premises and conclusions the computer will refuse any formula that is not a *wff* and that applies, of course, to the formulae that are inputted in the course of a derivation. Note in particular that propositional variables must be in upper case ($P,Q,R, \ldots$) not lower case ($p,q,r, \ldots$). Since the computer uses 'E' for the existential quantifier and 'V' for the universal quantifier it is not possible to use 'E' and 'V' as predicate variables. That is, for example, the computer does not count the expressions '$ExVx$' or 'Ea' as *wff*s. And, as was noted in the *TRUTH* manual, brackets are not put around quantifiers. Insead of inputting, for example, $(Ex)Fx$ or $(Vy)(Fy \ \& \ Gy)$ you input $ExFx$ and $Vy(Fy \ \& \ Gy)$. Also, 'or' is represented by lower case 'v', 'not' by the dash '—', 'and' by '&', 'if . . . then . . .' by '→' and 'if and only if' by '← →'. Also, the key for '→' and for '←' are labelled on the BBC micro as ']' and '[' respectively. If you input a *wff* with brackets around the entire *wff* the computer will strip off these outer brackets when displaying your premises and conclusion. That is, for example, if you type ⟨⟨⟨(P & Q)]P)⟩ this will be treated by the computer as: $(P \ \& \ Q) \to P$.

The premises will be displayed at the top of the screen above the hatched line with your conclusion at the bottom of the screen. To start your derivation type ⟨Prem⟩ ⟨Ret⟩. 'Prem' may be written in either upper or lower case. On hitting ⟨Ret⟩ the computer will number the line automatically and await your inputting of the first line which is most likely to be one of the previously specified premises (if you are deriving a theorem you will have to input an appropriate premise). Note that the premises (if any) from which the conclusion is to be derived and the conclusion itself must be entered in the derivation in exactly the same form that they were initially entered (i.e. the form displayed at the top and bottom of the screen on starting the derivation). The display after hitting ⟨Ret⟩ will be:

   Prem   (1)

Input the first premise and hit ⟨Ret⟩. Supposing, for example, that you are attempting to derive in the propositional calculus the following sequent: $P \rightarrow Q, -Q \vdash -P$. You would follow the above by typing ⟨P → Q⟩⟨Ret⟩. As was noted in the manual for *TRUTH* one inputs '→' by typing ']' and one inputs '← →' by typing '[ ]'. The display then appears:

   Prem   (1) $P \rightarrow Q$

Type ⟨Prem⟩ ⟨Ret⟩ to input the second premise:

   Prem   (1) $P \rightarrow Q$
   Prem   (2)

Follow this by the second premise, ⟨–Q⟩ ⟨Ret⟩:

   Prem   (1) $P \rightarrow Q$
   Prem   (2) $-Q$

In this derivation one assumes P and establishes $-P$ by *reductio ad absurdum*. This means that the third line will start with typing ⟨Prem⟩ ⟨Ret⟩ followed by typing ⟨P⟩ ⟨Ret⟩:

   Prem   (1) $P \rightarrow Q$
   Prem   (2) $-Q$
   Prem   (3) P

The next stage is to derive Q from lines (1) and (3). First type the numbers, (1) and (3), on which Q depends. There are to be cited in numerical order and separated by a space or by a comma whichever you prefer. After inputting these numbers hit ⟨Ret⟩. The computer will add the appropriate line number automatically and await the inputting of the *wff* for that line. This extends the above display:

   1 3   (4)

inputting the *wff*, Q, and follow it by the number of the lines to which the rule is applied and the citation of the rule. Line numbers must be cited in numerical order and separated by a space or a comma. Hit ⟨Ret⟩ only after the *wff*, the line numbers and the rule have been cited. The display changes to:

   1 3   (4) Q $1,3 \rightarrow$ E

For the next line cite the premises on which it depends, then hit ⟨Ret⟩. Input the *wff*, cite the lines to which the rule is applied and then cite the rule. Hit ⟨Ret⟩ to obtain:

   1 2 3   (5) $Q \& -Q$ 2,4 & I

Continue by using –I to drop premise 3. Type ⟨1 2⟩, ⟨Ret⟩. Then type ⟨-P 3 5 –I⟩, ⟨Ret⟩ to obtain:

    1 2   (6)   –P   3,5 –I

That completes the derivation successfully. The display will offer congratulations on your success and the option of printing the derivation. Type ⟨Y⟩, ⟨Ret⟩ if you have a printer and wish a print-out. Otherwise type ⟨N⟩, ⟨Ret⟩ which will return you to the menu from which you can opt to do another propositional derivation or exit to the previous menu. If you accidentally type ⟨Y⟩ for a print-out when no printer is connected it will be necessary to press the escape key followed by ⟨Control C⟩ (i.e., press 'C' while holding down the control key) and ⟨Run⟩, ⟨Ret⟩. This will return the display to the main menu. For the reasons given in the manual for *TRUTH*, the symbolds '⟩' and '⟨ ⟩' will be substituted for '→' and '← →' repectively in the print-out and on the screen during the print-out.

The limitations of the screen display force one major difference in the way that derivations are displayed. In the textbook *vE* proofs are represented by branching proofs: given $A \, v \, B$ there is one branch which develops the consequences of assuming A and another on which one hopes to derive the same conclusion form B as illustrated below in the derivation $P \to R, Q \to R, P \, v \, Q \vdash R$:

Prem	(1)	$P \to R$				
Prem	(2)	$Q \to R$				
Prem	(3)	$P \, v \, Q$				
Prem	(4)	P				
1 4	(5)	R	$1 \, 4 \to E$	Prem	(6)	Q
1 2 3	(8)	R	$3 4 5 6 7 \, v \, E$	2 6	(7)	R $2 \, 6 \to E$

In using the computer you must input the proof in the linear fashion indicated below:

Prem	(1)	$P \to R$	
Prem	(2)	$Q \to R$	
Prem	(3)	$P \, v \, Q$	
Prem	(4)	P	
1 4	(5)	R	$1 \, 4 \to E$
Prem	(6)	Q	
2 6	(7)	R	$2 \, 6 \to E$
1 2 3	(8)	R	$3 4 5 6 7 \, vE$

However, the computer draws attention to the essentially branching nature of *vE* proofs by re-displaying a successful derivation using different colours for the parts which would have been written on separate branches if the style of the textbook were followed.

The method of inputting derivations for the predicate logic is precisely the same as that illustrated above for the propositional calculus. The limitations in the memory of the BBC micro means that derivations longer than eighteen lines will be refused. An error message 'PROOF TOO LONG. SORRY. TYPE "QUIT" ' will be displayed. In which case there is nothing to do but type ⟨Quit⟩, ⟨Ret⟩ and start again either being more ingenious in finding a shorter proof or deriving another sequent or theorem. You may, before doing this, opt to print out the derivation as far as it went to guide you in a further attempt. This problem could also arise with a shorter proof if you were using *particularly long wff*s. In this case you may get an error message 'OUT OF MEMORY'. The programme then ceases to function. To start again type ⟨RUN⟩, ⟨Ret⟩. However, in the case of the vast majority of derivations you will encounter the number of lines allowed is adequate. Versions of the programme which will be available for computers of larger memory will not have this limitation.

The programme has a number of routines to assist in inputting derivations. The routines are selected by typing the letter indicated, followed by ⟨Ret⟩, when the cursor is in the position appropriate for starting a new line. If you wish to exit to one of these procedures in the course of typing a line simply type ⟨Ret⟩ and then the letter for the procedure followed by another ⟨Ret⟩:

⟨P⟩,⟨Ret⟩   This routine generates a print-out of the derivation (this option is offered automatically once a derivation is successfully completed).

⟨D⟩,⟨Ret⟩   This routine deletes lines of the derivation. You will be asked at what line the deletion is to start. It will end always at the last line. The default (i.e. the result if you do not answer but simply hit ⟨Ret⟩) is no deletion at all.

⟨S⟩,⟨Ret⟩   This re-displays the premises. At first the premises will be on display at the top of the screen but they may be pushed out of view once a derivation reaches a certain length.

⟨C⟩,⟨Ret⟩   This enables you to enter the *change mode* which is useful if you make errors in inputting the derivation. Details of the change mode are given below.

⟨L⟩, ⟨Ret⟩   'L', for list, re-displays the derivation deleting lines containing errors which were subsequently re-typed without error. The computer will ask for the line at which to start listing and the line at which to finish listing. The default (that is, the effect of simply typing ⟨Ret⟩) is from the first to the last line. When you exit from the change mode this is done automatically. 'L' can be helpful in 'cleaning up' a proof that has been cluttered with re-typed lines.

⟨QUIT⟩,⟨Ret⟩   Typing ⟨QUIT⟩ takes you out of the derivation and back to the previous menu.

⟨H⟩, ⟨Ret⟩   A listing of the above routines is display by this input.

CHANGE MODE

If you make a mistake either in typing or in logic in inputting a line the computer will display an error message once the return key has been hit. The message will give some guidance as to what has gone wrong. The erroneous line can simply be re-typed. The computer will automatically give it the same number as the corrected line. It may well be easier to enter the change mode by typing ⟨C⟩, ⟨Ret⟩. This generates a display in yellow rather than white of the line to be changed. Holding down either the '.' key or the space-bar moves the cursor along under the line to be changed. Typing ⟨D⟩, ⟨Ret⟩ will delete only the single character directly above the cursor. Typing ⟨R⟩ followed by any number of characters and ⟨Ret⟩ leads to the replacement of the character directly above the cursor by the string of characters typed. Typing ⟨I⟩ followed by any number of characters and ⟨Ret⟩ inserts the string of characters directly above the cursor. To exit from the change mode simply hit ⟨Ret⟩ again. On exiting the derivation will automatically be re-listed suppressing the lines that have been corrected. If your corrections have not been logically accept-able it may be necessary to enter the change mode and try again. If you notice that you have made a mistake early on while inputting a line, hitting ⟨Ret⟩ and re-typing the line is the easiest way to correct the mistake. If, on the other hand, the mistake is further on, it may be preferable to complete the line and use the change mode for the neces-sary correction.

ERROR MESSAGES

In view of the limitations of memory some of the error messages are not as full as would be ideally desirable and consequently the following points should be borne in mind:

1   If, following the input of a *wff*, you give line numbers, say 4 and 6, but either fail to cite a rule or make a typing error in citing the rule, the error message will read: Rule 46 incorrect. As you have not inputted a rule the computer recognizes it cannot check to see if that rule is correct. Whenever the error message appears to cite a rule by number rather than by name you have failed to cite the rule. The number cited is simply a concatenation of the numbers you listed.

2   The computer takes seriously the rule cited at each line. It may find that for the particular rule used the premises cited are not appropriate and in such a case the error message 'PREM (n) INCORRECT' will be displayed. It may be that, given the move you intended to make, the premises cited are the appropriate ones but you made an error in giving either the wrong rule or the wrong line numbers for the application of that rule. That is, given the cited rule the cited premises are not correct.

But you may wish to stick by the premises and change the rule.

3 If you input a premise line and erroneously cite a rule in justification an error message 'FORMULA OF LINE *n* NOT A WFF' will be displayed. The computer, not expecting any justification for a premise, treats whatever is inputted after the line number as intended to be part of a *wff* as illustrated below:

Prem (1) *P* & *Q* 1 & I
NOT A WFF

Computers are in fact very bad at guessing your intentions. If, for example, you input a premise and make two further mistakes by citing a rule while failing to give any line numbers the computer will construe everything that is inputted as an attempt to produce a *wff*. For, after all, on a premise line nothing but 'Prem', the line number and a *wff* should appear. Consider, for example, the following:

Prem (1) *P* & I

To the computer, ignoring spaces as it does, this looks like an attempt to introduce the *wff P* & *I* as a premise. In effect it is giving you the benefit of the doubt. For *P* &*I* is a *wff* and could be a useful premise in some contexts. But & I on its own without any line numbers preceding it is never a correct rule citation and, in any event, no rule should be cited for a premise line. Assuming that you intend to input *P* & I as a premise rather than *P* the computer does not give an error message but proceeds on the assumption that that is indeed your intended premise. Depending on what you subsequently do, error messages may appear. Consequently care must be taken to avoid the simple-minded error of citing a rule in the case of a premise line. In spite of this tolerance the computer will not allow you to derive any arguments that are not valid.

4 The *wff*s *P* &(*Q* & *R*) and (*P* & *Q*) & *R* are logically equivalent as you can show by constructing their truth-tables (or by using *TRUTH* to construct the tables for you). Consequently it is common in logic to write *P* &*Q* & *R* to stand in place of either *wff*. Similarly *P* v *Q* v *R* is used in place of either *P* v(*Q* v *R*) or (*P* v *Q*) v *R*. If the computer is faced with the expression *P* & *Q* & *R* or the expression *P* v *Q* v *R* it has to decide which of these pairs of alternatives is intended. In such cases it is assumed that the *first* occurrence of '&' or of 'v' is the main-connective. That is, if you input *P* & *Q* & *R* the computer will treat this as *P* &(*Q* & *R*). And *P* v *Q* v *R* will be treated as *P* v (*Q* v *R*). It is best to input *wff*s with full bracketing (excepting the outer brackets). If you chose to suppress them bear in mind how the computer will construe the resulting formula. This has an impact on proofs, as is illustrated below. Suppose you wish to derive *P* & *Q* & *R* from the premises *P*,*Q* and *R*. This conclusion will be construed as *P* & (*Q* & *R*), making the following

derivation acceptable:

Prem	(1)	*P*	
Prem	(2)	*Q*	
Prem	(3)	*R*	
2 3	(4)	*Q & R*	2 3 & I
1 2 3	(5)	*P & Q & R*	1 4 & I

The derivation below, on the other hand, will be rejected by the computer:

Prem	(1)	*P*	
Prem	(2)	*Q*	
Prem	(3)	*R*	
1 2	(4)	*P & Q*	1 2 & I
1 2 3	(5)	*P & Q & R*	3 4 & I

For the *wff* on line (5), *P & Q & R*, is construed as *P &(Q & R)* whereas adding R to line (4), *P & Q*, using & I would give *(P & Q) & R*: a logically equivalent but different *wff*. Consequently, in constructing proofs, you must bear in mind exactly how *wff*s with suppressed brackets will be construed. Alternatively (and preferably for the beginner) you can put the brackets in explicitly when inputting the *wff*s.

Symbols and Abbreviations

&	18	&E	49–50	TI	69
⌐	18	&I	51	SI	69
v	19	⌐E	51	PL	117
→	26	⌐I	52	QL	117
↔	36	→I	52	LEM	211
⊨	28	→E	53		
⊢	49	vI	55		
∀	111	vE	55–6		
∃	111	↔E	56		
=	141	↔I	58		
⊢̄P	203	∀E	122		
⊢̄F	203	∀I	126		
□	205	∃I	129		
◊	205	∃E	131		
		=I	145		
		=E	146		

Index